Group Therapy with Children

Alfons Aichinger · Walter Holl

Group Therapy with Children

Psychodrama with Children

Springer

Alfons Aichinger
Ulm
Germany

Walter Holl
Ulm
Germany

ISBN 978-3-658-15812-5   ISBN 978-3-658-15813-2   (eBook)
DOI 10.1007/978-3-658-15813-2

Library of Congress Control Number: 2016959394

© Springer Fachmedien Wiesbaden GmbH 2017
Previously published in german language under the title: "Gruppentherapie mit Kindern."
Translation: Mary Dobrian, Cologne, Germany.

Printed on acid-free paper

This Springer imprint is published by Springer Nature
The registered company is Springer Fachmedien Wiesbaden GmbH
The registered company address is: Abraham-Lincoln-Str. 46, 65189 Wiesbaden, Germany

Foreword to the English-Language Edition

The smallest social unit is not an individual person, but rather, a person along with his or her social environment—with her most important family members, her friends, a few close co-workers.

An individual cannot develop all by herself. Consequently, Moreno first conceived of psychodrama as a process of group psychotherapy; he researched the structures of relationships and described the way attraction, rejection, choice, interaction, cohesion and dynamics within a group become significant and operative factors for change. Psychodrama as individual therapy emerged only later.

In psychotherapy with children and adolescents, special psychodrama settings have been developed for a variety of age groups, in which the children can use their own 'language'—the language of play—in order to express themselves, to understand, to try out new things, and to grow from within. Psychodrama has become one of the most popular and effective approaches to working with children and adolescents in the German-speaking world.

This is most particularly the achievement of Alfons Aichinger, who has trained numerous therapists and published three outstanding books as well as many articles on the subject of psychodrama psychotherapy with children. In these publications, he outlines his method of working and describes it perceptively and sensitively using case studies.

The first book that Aichinger published together with his colleague Walter Holl is now presented to you here in its English translation. As our translator, we are very grateful to have Mary Dobrian, who has translated numerous works of psychodrama literature with sensitivity, intelligence and stylistic precision. We wish to thank our colleague Dorothy Langley in London for her helpful suggestions for correction. We are grateful to the members of the Deutscher Fachverband für

Psychodrama (German Professional Association for Psychodrama—DFP), who helped finance the translation through their membership dues. We wish to extend our very special thanks to Dr. Barbara Krebs of Frankfurt am Main for her generous donation.

We hope that our book finds many enthusiastic readers in the English-speaking world.

March 2016   Dr. Ulrike Fangauf, MD
                                                         DFP, Past President

Foreword to the Second German Edition

With the First Edition and reprints now out of stock, our book appears here in a Second Edition from the VS Verlag für Sozialwissenschaften. We are gratified by this great interest in psychodrama with children, and we are particularly pleased by the Polish and Russian translations of the work.

In this Second Edition, we have not only taken more recent literature into account; we have also improved and expanded upon the work as a whole.

We are grateful to Kea Brahms of the Psychology Editing division at VS Verlag for her great support with this Second Edition.

Alfons Aichinger
Walter Holl

Foreword to the First German Edition

Among therapists, group therapy with children is considered a difficult undertaking. It repeatedly presents them with problems for which there is scarcely any help to be found in the few publications that exist. This may be one of the reasons why the number of therapists who use group therapy with children is very small. Our aim in this book is to confront some of these problems and examine the difficulties that arise in group therapy work with children in detail. Our work comprises experiences and findings which we have gained in over 30 years of work in therapy groups at the Caritas Association's Psychological Counselling Centre for Parents, Children and Youth in Ulm and in supervision groups at the Moreno Institut in Stuttgart, the Szenen-Institut in Bonn, the German Caritas Association and the *Bundeskonferenz für Erziehungsberatung* (German National Conference on Educational Counselling—BKE). We wish to make a contribution to the further development of group therapy treatment for children which is based not on dogmatic official doctrine but on what, in our experience, are the needs of children facing external, internal and internalized conflicts.

Here we describe the version of psychodrama for children which we developed. We have limited ourselves to a presentation of the therapeutic 'tool' of children's psychodrama as it is applied in therapeutic work with children in a group therapy setting. However, since psychodrama is not a collection of techniques, but rather a process which encompasses a line of therapeutic anthropology and specific blueprints for the interpretation of individual and social reality—such as role theory and the concepts of spontaneity and creativity—we refer to fundamental texts which have developed the essential contemporary features of a theory of psychodrama therapy based on Moreno's original guiding principles (Krüger 1997; Fürst et al. 2004; von Ameln et al. 2009; Schacht 2009).

Nevertheless, our book is not intended as a recipe book. Instead, through the use of detailed examples, we hope to stimulate our readers' creativity and spark their enthusiasm for experimentation. Certainly, a repertoire of techniques can reduce one's own insecurity in groups of children when spontaneous creativity is not sufficient to frame the often difficult situations. Strict adherence to these, however, can easily result in the technique taking on a central role, ahead of the immediate situation in the group and a process-oriented approach. Therefore, the methods depicted here, and their accompanying techniques, are always subject to the spontaneity of the acting therapists who tailor them to fit the therapeutic situation at hand.

The examples presented here more often deal with boys. This is because at our counselling centre, approximately two-thirds of the children enrolled are boys, and we therefore frequently work with groups consisting exclusively of boys.

This book is aimed primarily at practitioners who work with children in a therapeutic setting—no matter what school or approach they follow—who are curious about trying out these ideas in their particular context.

We wish to express our special thanks to our colleagues Barbara Geier, Helga Schultheis, Regine Reisinger and Eugen Schönle, who were willing to join us in searching for new directions in group therapy and to assist us with their advice and support. Their many suggestions and critical observations have been integrated into this book.

We are very grateful to our secretary, Karin Amann, who wrote our manuscript.

We thank Ms. Laubach from the Matthias-Grünewald-Verlag for her professional interest and trusting cooperation in the development of this book.

Alfons Aichinger
Walter Holl

Contents

Introduction

1

Alfons Aichinger

Abstract

The particular significance of peer groups in a child's development and personality formation has been an important subject in developmental psychology, social psychology and sociological work for a long time. The peer group has proven to be a factor in socialisation whose effect is comparable to that of the family. Relationships with peers are an additional developmental resource; they constitute a 'developmental support factor' (Ahnert 2005, p. 349); peers are, in fact 'developmental assistants' (Seiffge-Krenke 2004, p. 121 ff). The peer group fulfils important functions in childhood development all the way up to adolescence: it provides children with the opportunity to live out and act out conflicts in the context of shared play. It allows them to test and practice new roles which—unlike those in the family—are not determined by age or gender, and to test the degree to which norms are binding or obligatory. By socialising them in terms of communication and cooperation, the peer group prompts children to move beyond self-centredness; it strengthens egalitarian aspects within the child through acknowledgment and rejection; it presents the child with the task of defining his or her relationship to these 'others'. In a peer group situation, children have to express their needs, declare their intentions, and, in a process of mutual consent, agree upon norms, rules and sanctions— and perhaps change them once again.

This new behavioural experience leads to a profound change in the child's self-concept. Entering the peer group allows him or her to experience what it means to be a boy or a girl among many others. Community and commonalities become clear, and in the face of these, it is important to retain one's individuality; otherwise one remains either a follower or an outsider and cannot win others over

© Springer Fachmedien Wiesbaden GmbH 2017   1
A. Aichinger and W. Holl, *Group Therapy with Children*,
DOI 10.1007/978-3-658-15813-2_1

for one's own plans. Acknowledgment and popularity are largely dependent upon a person's ability to cooperate, to engage competently in disputes over norms and expectations, and to reach satisfactory agreements, reconciliations and arrangements (cf. Krappmann 1982; Grunebaum and Solomon 1982; Lott 1986). 'In terms of children's social development as well as their cognitive and emotional development, it becomes clear here that relationships with others of the same age and interactions with others in the context of groups of children present a special and independent potential for learning' (Brandes 2008, p. 179).

These functions that the peer group fulfils in the process of a child's development are simultaneously the things that constitute their therapeutic effectiveness (cf. Lutz 1981). If we take these findings seriously, it is actually incomprehensible that the healing and prophylactic power of the group in therapeutic work with children is so little used (cf. Grunebaum und Solomon 1980). In all areas of paediatric therapy, group therapy is much less widely used than individual therapy. Quite contrary to the significance that has been attributed to the group, publications on the subject of children's group therapy are rare (cf. Guldner 1991).

The fact that psychodrama in particular, with its elaborated group concept, has not gained more currency in group therapy with children is even more surprising considering that Moreno's therapeutic work was actually inspired by improvisational play with groups of children. 'Historically, psychodrama emerged from the basis of play... but a new view of play emerged when we began playing with children in the gardens and streets of Vienna during the years before the outbreak of the First World War: play as a principle of self-healing and group therapy, as a form of primal experience; ...play as a *sui generis* phenomenon, a positive factor connected to spontaneity and creativity. We shaped play ... into a methodological, systematic principle' (Moreno 1973, p. 80 f). In his early creative period, Moreno still worked intensively with children: in sociometric studies with infants and children at the children's hospital in Mitterndorf from 1917 to 1919; in kindergartens and schools in New York from 1931 to 1932; and in role and spontaneity training at the Hudson School, a reformatory school for delinquent girls. He processed these experiences in his theories of roles and development (Moreno 1934) and derived his most important psychodrama techniques from children's role development (cf. Schacht 2003).

Despite this early, intensive concentration on children, Moreno developed psychodrama as a therapy method exclusively for adults, not for children. He described psychodrama as 'that method (...) which delves into the truth of the soul through action' (Moreno 1959, p. 77). The constituting principle of psychodrama is the 'scenic realisation of the immaterial, meaningful content of the client (system) as a material, theatrical arrangement with the help of dramatic elements (e.g. a stage, properties, fellow actors). The client can then … explore and reshape the symbolic elements of the resulting experience space in an active manner—with the support of special psychodramatic techniques—in order to construct new meaningful content, develop new incentives for action and experiment with new behaviour' (von Ameln et al. 2009, p. 6).

In the period that followed, practitioners tried out varying approaches in order to apply this methodology in therapeutic work with children. In the United States, attempts were made to transpose classical psychodrama into paediatric therapy with only minimal adaptations: e.g., Drabkova 1966, Lockwood and Harr 1973, Shearon 1980, Stockvis-Warnaar and Stockvis 1962, Zacharias 1965. Dr. Ella Mae Shearon, for example, arrived at the following changes when applying the phases and techniques of classical psychodrama to work with children: 'When applying the classical psychodrama process to work with children, it is often necessary to limit the play phase, since children's capacity for concentration is short-lived. On the other hand, the warm-up phase takes on greater importance when working with children. The play itself should only last a short time. Greater emphasis is placed on the repetition phase, in which new roles are learned, rehearsed and intensified. In our work with children, we place less emphasis on abreactive catharsis, since this releases tremendous amounts of aggression, repressed emotions or trauma' (1980, p. 255 f).

In work with children in France, psychodrama developed in a completely different way: here, psychodrama was adopted by paediatric psychoanalysts at Serge Lebovici's Paris school, who oriented psychodrama toward the techniques and theories of psychoanalytic treatment and developed it further into an analytical form of psychodrama that was shaped by the work of child analysis (cf. Anzieu 1984, p. 79 ff; Petzold 1979, p. 28 ff; Basquin et al. 1981, p. 19 ff; Bettschart 1984, 1988).

More than 30 years ago, when we began working in children's psychodrama groups at the Psychological Counselling Centre for Parents, Children and Youth in Ulm, we initially attempted to apply classical psychodrama—with minimal modifications, similarly to the way it is described in the American psychodrama literature—to children's therapy. We made the same mistakes as all the other schools of therapy: just as in medieval painting, we tried to treat the children like miniature adults. The children resolutely resisted these attempts (cf. Aichinger 1993). We needed to take account of the special characteristics of group therapy with children as compared to work with adults, as described by Slavson and Schiffer (1976, p. 33 f). These include the rapid conversion of ideas and feelings into motor expression; a weak ego structure with low frustration tolerance and control; insufficient formation of the super-ego; non-verbal communication through actions and a great need for playfulness and freedom of movement. With children, we cannot assume that they will be willing or able to limit themselves to verbalising their fantasies, wishes, thoughts and feelings. The younger a child is, the more likely it is that his or her inner life will be demonstrated through play, actions and dramatization. Conversely, the older a child is, the greater her verbal contributions will become. Among older youth, the work methods will begin to approach those used for adults. If children are denied their natural forms of expression and communication through play—or if they are overwhelmed by insufficient options for communication—this can lead to resistance, which is frequently expressed in the form of restlessness, fooling around, aggression or bored withdrawal. Consideration of these special characteristics and of the developmental dynamics of children led us to make significant changes in form, style and technique. In a painstaking process which extended over 30 years, with over 130 groups of children, we allowed the children to guide us toward the creation of a method that suited their needs.

In contrast to the American tradition, which aims to represent realistic situations with children, we consider symbolic play to be the primary medium of therapy, as it is in French analytical psychodrama. The children illustrate their inner scenarios, condensed into symbolic play using changing forms, in order to find solutions for the tasks, conflicts and problems contained in the scenes. In treating neurotic behaviour in children (1922), Moreno also applied the methods of symbolic psychodrama (1973, p. 221 ff). He considered symbolic psychodrama to be an important technique which nevertheless should not preclude the use of other methods where they are indicated (1973, p. 108).

This play is not only the creatively abstracted staging of a conflict; it also constitutes the active implementation and processing of experiences—a means of coping. In play, the child experiences him or herself as an inventive builder—the co-creator of his own life environment. 'Every playing child behaves like a poet, in the sense that he creates a world of his own or—to put it more accurately—places the elements of his world in a new order which is more pleasing to him' (Freud 1907, p. 214). In symbolic play, the child discovers the creative dimension and relegates concrete existence into its true categories: one world among possible worlds. In this way, the child takes part in the creative power of God and gains the 'perspective of the active creator' (Moreno 1946, p. 28) with regard to his own life. Thus, children's psychodrama becomes a place of rebirth into a different, more satisfying life—just as Bastian, the failure, is able to achieve it in Michael Ende's novel *The Neverending Story*. 'There are people who can never come to Fantastica,' says Mr. Coreander, 'and there are people who can, but they stay there forever. And then there are a few who go to Fantastica and come back again—like you. And they make both worlds well again' (1979, p. 426).

Viewing play as a form of communication suited to children led us to change our psychodramatic techniques. We needed to focus our attention on nonverbal processes and learn to understand the actions of the games analogically, in their figurative content, and to answer them analogically. We did this—contrary to Moreno's recommendations—by participating in the dramatic play as a two-person team of therapists; we became fellow actors in the children's scenes, selecting our roles as actors at the symbolic level in such a way that they stimulated and supported the therapeutic process for the children. The transference/countertransference relationships that were triggered by the therapist pair's participation in the scene became an important element in the treatment.

The constellation of a pair of therapists and several children represents a family-like situation, which in turn fosters the emergence and playing out of corresponding scenarios. Since the group constructs a constellation similar to that of a family, in which the events of childhood can be dramatized and acted out, the group of children is particularly suitable for developing internalised atmospheres and internal scenarios through play with the therapists. The process that occurs in the group of children can be seen—as Sandner (1978) pointed out—as the re-enactment of specific phases in a child's development within his or her social context. This situates therapeutic group work within a model of development theory. In a process of development and resocialisation, which must be accomplished by the individual child together with the entire group, healing can take place.

In contrast to classical psychodrama and most systems of analytical psychodrama—which often consist of individual therapy in a group setting—we take a group-centred approach. We shift the group as a whole into central focus and the network of relationships between the children into their respective context, and are not concerned only with the development of the individual child within the group and the associated intrapersonal and interpersonal processes.

Like Petzold and Schneewind (1986), we see the group not only psychodynamically, as a place where scenes from the family, its subsystems and its environment are reproduced, but also sociodynamically—as a social reality in which social competence and performance can be developed. In this way, the group takes on important functions in fostering development and socialisation. Moreno's theory of personality (Hutter 2004), which regards the human individual as a 'social atom'—as an 'inter-actor'—consequently requires treatment in and by groups, in which healing takes place through encounters. Cooperative mutual help is seen as a significant factor in healing.

Children's psychodrama that is based on Moreno's anthropology of the human being as creator regards the fostering of an expressive, creative personality as its central goal and does not limit itself to rectifying problems. It aims to promote spontaneity and creativity in the child and, in cases where these things have been limited or restricted, to reawaken them and help them to blossom. Since psychodrama includes a differentiated system of intervention techniques designed to facilitate and activate 'free creativity' (Krüger 2002), Moreno considered psychodrama to be the most clear and complete form of play psychotherapy (Krüger 1982, p. 128). The specific features of children's creativity are particularly manifested in symbolic play. Symbolic play is therefore centrally important in children's psychodrama—as it is in all forms of children's psychotherapy. Thus, it is essential for children's psychodramatists to comprehend its nature.

Hildegard Pruckner's (2001) work in Austria dealt intensively with children's psychodrama. She adopted significant elements from us—such as the basic structure, play as a form of presentation and processing for the child, and the importance of network analysis. Nevertheless, on certain points—such as the role of the therapist in the play session and therapeutic interventions—her work developed in a different way. In Pruckner's approach, the leader never participates in the scenario; rather, as in classical adult psychodrama, he or she remains at the edge of the playing stage, in order to intervene in the action as a director or in a doubling role. One or more co-leaders may, however, participate in the play if the children so desire.

We will now present a short overview of this book's individual chapters:

In Chapter 1 we describe the preparations that are made before group work begins, and we deal with questions related to setting and indications. In Chapter 2, we are concerned with the external framework, the furnishing and equipment of the group room and the temporal framework. In Chapter 3, we describe in detail the structure of a group session and the modified intervention techniques used in children's psychodrama. Chapter 4 focuses on the phases through which the development process within a group of children takes place. In Chapter 5, we examine disorder-specific interventions, using the examples of fearful and aggressive children; Chapter 6 focuses on group-process-oriented interventions. Chapter 7 examines the specific demands that a group of children places on the therapists. Finally, Chapter 8 deals with the accompanying network analysis.

Preparing for the Group

Alfons Aichinger

2

Abstract

As group therapy is a complicated process, certain clarifications and preparations are necessary before a child is accepted into a group and work in a children's group can begin.

2.1 Indication

In addition to fostering children's potential for emotional growth and helping them to master developmental tasks, a further aim of children's psychodrama therapy is the reduction of behavioural disorders.

Group therapy is suitable for treating children between the ages of 4 and 12, or until puberty. In her study, Fried (2004) was able to show that preschool children were only capable of co-constructing a 'shared framework' during mutual play beginning at the age of approximately four years; this, therefore, is the minimum starting age for group processes. Among children under four years of age, we can observe a clear dominance of dyadic relationships (cf. also Schacht 2003, p. 121). Since children in puberty regard symbolic play as 'kid stuff' and no longer allow themselves to play in this way, they require an even greater degree of disassociation—for example, pretending that they are famous actors shooting a film. Alternatively, it is possible to work in group-centred sociodrama with pubescent children and in protagonist-centred sociodrama with adolescents (cf. Biegler-Vitek et al. 2004).

© Springer Fachmedien Wiesbaden GmbH 2017
A. Aichinger and W. Holl, *Group Therapy with Children*,
DOI 10.1007/978-3-658-15813-2_2

7

Group therapy is especially indicated in the treatment of internalising disorders such as anxiety (ICD-Diagnosis-F93), social inhibitions, depressive disorders (ICD-10-Diagnosis-F32) and diminished self-esteem, but it is also useful for externalising disorders such as oppositional, aggressive or dissocial disorders (ICD-Diagnose-F91/F92).

Children's psychodrama therapy can only be applied as a comprehensive process for treating a wide variety of psychological disorders in children if the treatment concept is oriented toward the disorders. Successful paediatric psychotherapy cannot be carried out without a differentiated concept for intervention. The earlier view held by many humanistic schools of therapy—that therapists can rely on children's ability to heal themselves—is a myth, and it ignores the fact that children also need to be given help in coping. We therefore developed a differentiated range of strategies both with regard to the work with the child as well as to that with the family and the environment, and we also tailor our interventions specifically to correspond to each child's respective disorders. For example, we make use of supportive doubles for impulsive and aggressive children; we mirror the internal working model in the case of information processing disorders; or we provide more structure when there is a lack of control.

Group therapy is also appropriate for children with attachment disorders. Like Lutz (1976, p. 15) we attribute our success in this area to the fact that the group offers the child a new experience which communicates a feeling of security and, because of its widely varied possibilities for attachment, seems less unsettling or frightening to the child than what individual therapy can offer. Thus, Kleiner (2008) was able to demonstrate that paediatric group psychodrama therapy is an effective method for working with children with insecure attachments, while Wicher (2006) had similar results with traumatised children.

Independently of the predominant symptoms, the generally recognised clinical rule is to recommend group psychotherapy for those children for whom a group presents a better possibility for expressing themselves and their problems than a one-on-one relationship would.

It is also important to keep targeted indications in mind. Through interactions and relationships with others of their own age, children learn fairness, reciprocity and cooperation. Children can only acquire these important skills—as well as the ability to deal constructively with aggression—through relationships with their peers. Consequently, meaningful changes to difficulties in these areas can only be achieved in a group therapy context.

In addition, where group therapy is generally indicated, we must pay attention to the intersubjective indication: Can I, as a therapist, with my particular personality and experience, work together with this special child in this group composition? Many therapists, when they begin working with groups of children, overtax themselves by accepting into the group the most difficult children that they allow their colleagues to refer to them. Just as no one can have any fun skiing if she sets off on a 'black' run at the very beginning instead of trying out her first curves on the practice slope, no one would want to continue leading groups of children if he or she were only longing for the session to end so that the chaos will finally be over. This is confirmed by embodiment research (Storch et al. 2006), which demonstrates that therapists can only work creatively and flexibly when they are feeling good and are not under stress.

Whether, in individual cases, children's psychodrama therapy with the systematic involvement of the parents or systemic family therapy is indicated, or whether a child will be admitted to individual or group therapy—this question of setting is always dependent on a thorough diagnostic procedure (exploration with parents, caregivers and teachers, play observation with the child, behavioural and psychological diagnosis). The child's current state, his or her resources and possibilities, as well as the context of his life with his family and networks must all be included in the diagnostic considerations. As Hutter (2008) points out, in addition to the individual/biographical and the sociometric/relationship dynamic-related dimensions, it is important in the psychodrama diagnosis process to take into account the child's physical condition and signals, the societal dimension—such as basic economic conditions, milieu affiliation or immigration-related phenomena—and the cultural-axiological dimension, such as values, norms, traditions and philosophies of life. The symbolic techniques of children's psychodrama—such as, for example, the depiction of family interactions or inner parts with animal figures are well suited for this. However, in psychodrama therapy, diagnosis is understood to be a process: in other words, it is not completed with the diagnostic workup before an individual is accepted into the group.

2.2 Size and Composition of the Group

2.2.1 The Children

In selecting children for the group, we bear in mind the criteria which Slavson and Schiffer (1976, p. 101 ff) established for group therapy with children. An important factor for accepting a child into the group is his or her ability to respond to other children and negotiate a mutual understanding of the elements of the game so that mutual play in an imaginary world that is shared with the others is possible at least to a limited degree, and to benefit from corrective experiences with the other children. If the child does not have these abilities, individual therapy is indicated.

We accept a maximum of six children into each of our groups. Since preschool children depend largely on being able to survey the group in order to register the reactions of the other group members and communicate with several members at the same time, we limit groups of this age to four children. Observations in preschools and kindergartens (Brandes 2008) have also shown that children most often spontaneously and independently form groups of this size.

In composing the group, we choose children who are at a similar stage of development so that the group is concerned with mastering the same developmental tasks and so that the scenarios that are acted out have a similar significance for all members of the group.

In order that the children can profit from one another—so that each child can be the therapeutic agent of the other and learning through modelling is possible—the particular strength of one child should correspond to the weakness of another. We select children with different symptoms and take care to find the best possible balance between inhibited and aggressive children—and whenever possible, a balanced mixture of both genders—in order to offer the children different possibilities for interpersonal learning. The differences prompt the children to seek out other models and to learn from them. At the same time, heterogeneous groups correspond more closely to everyday reality, where children are confronted with a variety of other children in kindergarten, school or in their free time.

Homogenous groups have proven to be effective in specific groups of children in separation/divorce situations (Heidegger and Lintner 2001; Betz 2006), among children of addicts (Heger 2002; Diözesan-Caritasverband 2004; Weiss 2008) or mentally ill parents, or in work on the prevention of sexual violence toward children (Kubina 2009).

Making reference to gender research, Brem (2008) argues in favour of gender-homogenous groups, since gender-homogenous groups of boys or girls allow children to better process their conflicts at a deeper level.

2.2.2 The Dual-Gender Therapist Team

The group is always led by a pair of therapists of opposite genders. This facilitates the transference and projection of internalised object relationships onto the male or female therapist and aids in the re-enactment of early childhood fantasies and conflicts. The constellation of the therapist pair and the children represents a family-like situation which fosters the emergence and playing out of family-related scenarios. In particular, children project onto the therapists any negative or traumatic experiences they may have had with adults. Likewise, the playing out of oedipal themes and problems of triangulation with attempts at the formation of 'two-against-one' coalitions is facilitated within the triad, as are themes related to sibling rivalry. Furthermore, this triangular constellation provides a good setting for processing experiences in separation and divorce situations and blended families.

2.3 The Contract

Before a child is accepted into the group, we discuss the meaning and purpose of group therapy with the child and the parents. Since children are often are afraid that the group therapy is intended to 'treat away' their 'symptomatic part'—the part of the child about which his or her parents complain—it is important to discuss the therapy contract in detail. Psychodramatic work with animal figures provides a child-friendly approach to this:

Example

Parents are seeking therapy for their 5-year-old son because he scratches and bites other children in conflict situations in his kindergarten and in play groups, and is therefore regularly excluded. During the preliminary meeting I ask him, 'If you and your parents were animals, what animals would you be?' I point to my collection of Ostheimer wooden animals. Paul chooses a tortoise to be himself. When I ask him what tortoises can do well, he says that they have a thick shell that protects them. For his father he chooses a St. Bernard dog—it is good-natured and can rescue people; for his mother he chooses a sheep—it is so soft and cuddly. I let him place the animals on the floor: he places the tortoise between the two other animals, very close to the sheep. 'I heard from your mother earlier that you want your parents and other children to like you, and that you can also behave very gently and lovingly toward them. What kind of animal would this side of you be?' He chooses a little rabbit: it is good at cuddling. However, I go on to tell him that there is also a side that constantly scratches and bites and rages: what animal would that be? For this animal, Paul chooses a little lion: it has sharp claws and teeth. 'Are the rabbit, the lion and the tortoise friends with each other?' I ask. 'No, they can't stand the lion.' I express surprise that they don't want to have such a strong animal as their friend. 'Because he is so mean.' I ask whether he can show me how the little lion acts mean and uses his claws and teeth on the other animals. He takes the St. Bernard and the sheep and uses these figures to kick the lion away. I double the lion: 'That makes me very sad when nobody likes me', and I ask him whether he then becomes fiercer or more peaceful. 'Then I get really wild.' 'What do the sheep and the St. Bernard do then?' I ask the lion. 'Then they want to lock me up in a cage, but they can't do it.' He then uses the lion to attack the sheep and the dog. 'And then the dog and the sheep are scared', I say, doubling the two animals. 'After all, farm animals don't know very much about wild animals.' 'What would have to change in order that the sheep and the St. Bernard are happy to have such a strong lion as their friend, so that he wouldn't have to be so sad?' I ask Paul and his parents, who are following the game with great interest. 'Do the sheep and the St. Bernard need to become like lion parents, or must the little lion gradually learn to control his teeth and claws?' Paul sees as a solution that the lion starts to gain better control over his claws and teeth; the parents think both things are important.

In order that the sheep and the St. Bernard can become better acquainted with the lion and make friends with him, I recommend ten family play therapy sessions for the family and briefly explain the intended goal of this mutual play and how it will work.

Then I turn my attention back to Paul: 'You said that the rabbit and the tortoise don't like the lion because he gives them so much trouble. But it would be a shame to chase away such a magnificent lion. It would actually be wonderful for the two of them to have such a strong friend. How could the rabbit and the tortoise become friends with the lion?' Paul shrugs his shoulders. 'Tortoises are very clever animals', I continue, 'they observe things very closely and they don't overreact. How would it be if the tortoise were the boss and would decide when he needs the gentle rabbit and when he needs the strong lion? If the three of them could work together and each would contribute his own abilities, they could make a great team.' Paul nods in agreement. 'To help the three animals become a good team and help each one of them learn to contribute his own strengths—the tortoise his composure, the rabbit his gentleness and the lion his ability to defend himself—I would like to invite you into a play group. It should help you make these three animals into good friends.'

We then explain to the family in detail the way session functions and illustrate it with an example. Initially, we schedule five trial sessions in order to win over the children—who are usually not motivated to take part in the therapy—to co-operate with each other. In particular, children who have the feeling that they are being sent to therapy as a punishment or in order to be improved need to have the experience that they are allowed to decide for themselves.

Children who have had negative experiences in groups—and therefore react with fear and want to avoid any new group situations—also need to have enough freedom of movement to come out of their defensive position. This arrangement also gives us the chance to see whether a child will be able to develop in and benefit from this specific group constellation. It is only after these sessions that we draw up a therapy contract with the child and the parents. They commit to having their child take part in the group once a week (except during school holidays) for a period of one year (approx. 40 sessions).

2.4   Accompanying Work with the Family or Parents

It is important to carefully determine whether the parents are sufficiently motivated to regularly bring or send their child to therapy over a long period of time (for example, even in winter), and to take part in concomitant family or parent conferences. It has never proven constructive to accept a child into a group too quickly and without sufficiently clarifying and feeling out the parents' motivation, simply in order to fill the group.

Furthermore, the parents must agree to regularly take part in the child's therapy in the form of parent or family conferences. From the standpoint of Moreno's theory of the social network, the need to work together with the child's real social atom is self-evident. Therefore, where necessary, we request a release from obligations of confidentiality in order to co-operate with the child's nursery, kindergarten or school.

The External Framework

Walter Holl

3

Abstract

In this chapter, we would like to explain the way a group space for psychodrama therapy should be furnished and what materials are needed, as well as providing an explanation of the temporal framework.

3.1 Furnishing and Equipping the Group Space

Certain external conditions are required for group psychodrama work with children:

© Springer Fachmedien Wiesbaden GmbH 2017

A. Aichinger and W. Holl, *Group Therapy with Children*,

DOI 10.1007/978-3-658-15813-2_3

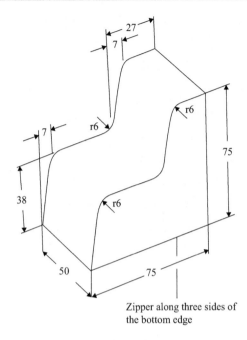

Zipper along three sides of
the bottom edge

First, there is the group room which, in our experience, should not be less than
30 m² (323 sq. ft.) in size. '…If it is too expansive, it encourages escape into silly
play and modes of behaviour which are reduced to pure physicality, and their
expressive content becomes lost; if it is too small, it limits the children's spontaneity and most of all, it can give rise to unbearable tension if the play stirs up
intense emotions' (Widlöcher 1974, p. 32). Since a room of this size should be
usable in a variety of ways, the question of furnishings is an important one: on the
one hand, it should accommodate the children's creative design ideas, but it should
also be suitable for work with families or groups of adults. As seating and building
elements, we use foam cushions (weight per volume: 0.30 kg/m³) in the shape
shown in the above sketch. They are firm enough to be used as chairs and can also
be used as very versatile building elements. Two chair elements can be combined
to form a block; we also have solid blocks of the same mass which are very stable.
In addition, we have large and small pillows; and in a cupboard (on which the
children are also allowed to climb) there are articles of clothing, cloths and hats.
The different colours of the variously sized cloths take on an important significance. For example, green cloths can be spread on the ground to represent a
meadow or used to create a jungle scene. Cloths printed with flowers may be used

to depict gardens; with blue cloths, we can create a river, a lake or the ocean. We can use old white curtains to construct snow or icy landscapes; red cloths are used to represent fire, etc. The cloths may also be stretched to form roofs or hung to create doors for caves, stables or houses.

The cloths are equally important for the embellishment of particular roles: a player can use a white sheet to dress as a ghost; someone can play a fire spirit using a red cloth; a golden cape lets someone play a king; with a green cape, someone can be Robin Hood, etc.

There are also baskets containing soft, finely woven, finger-thick perlon cords, between three and five metres long. Since we have hooks screwed into the walls, we can easily and quickly attach these cords to them, use clothes pegs to hang cloths over the cords and thereby create room divisions.

Equally important is the 'Baufix' building material which children can use to construct huge variety of utensils and weapons. Since the original perforated 'Baufix' components break easily, we have had special pieces built for us in a workshop for disabled individuals: these are made of beech wood, 7 mm (0.28″) thick. A number of soft toy animals complete our collection of materials.

This assortment of materials has served us well over many years. We do not allow the children to bring toys or materials from home. The necessity of managing with the materials at hand fosters their ability to negotiate and supports the group process. 'An overly abundant or realistic supply of stage properties entices the children to play around with the materials, which always causes the dramatic representation to suffer' (Widlöcher 1974, p. 33).

3.2 The Temporal Framework

People sometimes ask us: Aren't 60 minutes too little time for a group session? This is what we also assumed in the beginning, and in the first few years, we worked in 90-minute sessions. Today, there are several reasons why we believe that 60 minutes are completely sufficient: the children adjust to this time period and the process becomes more compact. Disappointment and anger that the session is at an end are not a product of its length, but rather of the inevitable end of the regression that takes place during the symbolic play. This enforced revocation of their fantasies of omnipotence irritates the children. A longer playing period would not change this fact: on the contrary.

If, in a specific case, there really does not seem to be enough time for a game to develop, this is usually because of some form of resistance that needs to be worked through. An unresolved end to the session would not be helpful. Even in terms of the therapeutic tasks of recording the group process, understanding the occurrence of transference, intervening appropriately, keeping track of what one's colleague is doing and also taking note of what is going on inside oneself—60 minutes are still a long time.

As far as the time of year that a group should begin is concerned, one should take care that the long school holidays do not begin after only ten sessions have taken place, causing the process to be interrupted.

Furthermore, the regular presence of both therapists is not unimportant; therefore, conferences, training courses etc. should be taken into account when planning the day of the week that the group is to meet.

We do not continue to conduct any group work during school holidays if the participation of all the children cannot be guaranteed. It happens often enough already that one child or another is absent due to illness, which can also affect the consistency of participation and the group process.

The Structure of a Psychodrama Session and Therapeutic Techniques

4

Alfons Aichinger

Abstract

In the following chapter we would like to describe the structure of a group session and the therapeutic techniques which may be applied. Each individual session is the creative product of interaction between the children and the two leaders and therefore cannot be planned in detail ahead of time. Every session is 'unique, the first time, not repeatable' (Moreno 1973, p. 64). Despite all of the freedom that is allowed for spontaneity and creativity, the structure of each session is nevertheless defined. The process is structured into three phases: the initial phase, the play phase and the closing phase. Especially in therapeutic work with children, it is important to introduce this structure from the very beginning and also to maintain it. The regular repetition of the three phases in every session provides the children with a secure reference framework which they are soon able to internalise. This 'container function' that the setting provides offers the children safety and support. If we handle a structure too loosely, we will pay for it bitterly in the form of chaotic and destructive group processes. At a later point in time when, in the security of the group setting, the children rebel against the leaders' orders, it will be almost impossible to restore it.

4.1 The Initial Phase

Every psychodrama session begins with a warm-up phase, the aim of which is to stimulate the development of spontaneity, openness and readiness to take action in the game. According to Moreno, the warm-up phase for children's psychodramatic

© Springer Fachmedien Wiesbaden GmbH 2017
A. Aichinger and W. Holl, *Group Therapy with Children*,
DOI 10.1007/978-3-658-15813-2_4

symbolic play is an intrapersonal and interpersonal process which has many interconnected goals. First of all, each individual child should be ready to participate in the play and become aware of what he or she is experiencing and what themes she wishes to act out in this session. This intrapersonal aspect of the warm-up usually only needs to be supported in inhibited children. In contrast, the other children often need to be stopped from immediately translating their ideas into actions. The interpersonal aspect of the warm-up, on the other hand, calls for greater attention to all of the children. Since each child's action in his or her role is connected to the actions of the other children in their roles, the children must pay attention to the sensitivities and emotional relationships between each other. Furthermore, they need to make a mutual and consensual decision about the scenario they want to create in the symbolic play through co-operative psychodrama (cf. Schwinger 1994, p. 7).

In the case of extremely restless and hyperactive children, for whom the open group room can easily become a space for fighting or blustering around, it has proven useful to separate the work on the 'playing stage' (Pruckner 2002) from the work on the 'meeting stage' and to carry out the work of deciding on a subject not in the group room, but in another room where it is less tempting to become active.

It is the task of the leaders in the initial phase to facilitate and structure this warm-up process and support the attainment of these goals. In therapeutic work with children, warm-up techniques or pre-fabricated, 'canned' warm-ups are rarely needed for this purpose. With the exception of the first session, in which a warm-up game smooths the children's entrance into the action of the game (cf. 5.1), we do not suggest any warm-up games for them. Whereas in work with adults, it is often necessary to first awaken a state of spontaneity, children are usually so fascinated by the symbolic play after the first session that this, in itself, has enough of a warming-up effect. They almost always enter the group room 'hungry for action'. Like Schwinger (1994, p. 11 ff), we have observed that planning the implementation of warm-up techniques ahead of time increases the risk that the chosen technique will take priority over the actual, current situation in the group. In our first experiences in working with groups, we also found that in the course of the group's development, children started having fun derailing the 'canned warm-ups' which they considered 'dumb' or 'boring'. In group work with children, the leaders do not so much require a rich inventory of ready-made warm-up techniques like those that can be found in Shearon's (1980) work—not so much colourful animation—rather, they need a psychodramatic and sociometric view of the current states of the individual children in the group. In our experience, this is a better way to achieve the goal of the warm-up phase: namely, finding a consensual decision in favour of a symbolic scenario that the group of children can sustain. We will now describe in further detail the ways in which the leaders can support these general goals and what structuring is necessary for the warm-up process.

Step 1: Opening of the group session and exploration of themes
We begin each session seated in chairs, asking the children to sit together in a circle. Whereas in adult psychodrama, scenes from the real lives of the group members are acted out, Moreno recommends the method of symbolic psychodrama for children (1973, p. 201 ff). We begin with the simple question of what the children would like to play together today. They can then suggest stories that they would like to act out. They can pick up on or create variations on the suggested themes, or they can develop a story—a group fantasy—together, which each child can use according to his or her need for ideational realisation or as a means of resistance. Even if the ideas that the children bring in are ostensibly only themes from television programs, for the children they always have a deeper meaning, a symbolic content. Behind the façade of what is often 'banal canned culture', they are able to develop their own individual stories, their inner images and group themes. In the process, each child's dominant developmental tasks and their personality structures—along with their coping and defensive mechanisms—form the framework as well as the filter for their thematic suggestions. In this way, stories and images from the media are individually and selectively incorporated and altered in order to work through and cope with current themes in the children's lives. According to Moreno, through the spontaneous act of role-playing, these ready-made roles become changed and created roles.

The leaders are often faced with a multifaceted and disjointed collection of thematic material. Since these different play ideas are to be viewed as part of a meaningful co-operative process—a shared scenario—the leaders must help the children to shape the different contributions of each individual child into a shared theme—to combine them into a shared story which contains the individual contributions. The children may also select a story which finds the most resonance among them and will be supported by all of them. Naturally, this does not happen without discussion and negotiations. Majorities cannot take the place of a search for a consensus: therefore, agreement between the children is what is necessary, and not the principle of majority rule. Like Basquin (1981, p. 149 ff), we operate on the assumption that the subject that is chosen and acted out will be one which deals with that theme which unconsciously preoccupies or repels the group the most—or that the child whose individual play idea also represents the shared theme of the group as a whole will prevail. Then, through his or her choice of a role and the form which his play takes, each child can shape the shared theme according to his individual biography. Therefore, symbolic psychodramatic play encompasses both the unconscious world of the group of children as well as that of each individual child. Petzold tried to sum up this complex group process in a scenic or theatrical model of the group: 'A participant in the group dramatic process brings along the scenes from his or her own history that are recorded within her. These extend into the new scenes that are created within the group and by the group—which, in turn, call upon old dramatic material—and are thereby condensed into a new drama. Reality and fantasy, the conscious and the unconscious are thus continually interlaced, with varying intensity and concentration' (1986, p. 141).

Example

In the second session with a mixed group of six-year-olds, various ideas are suggested: playing animals on a farm, as they did in the first session; being astronauts; or playing children who run away from home at night. After a certain amount of back-and-forth discussion, the children agree on this last suggestion—a compromise between the two desires, to be cared for and for independence. While two girls and one boy choose the roles of seven-year-old children whose parents put them to bed and tell them a bedtime story, Max chooses the role of a secret agent who lives next door to the children's bedroom. The other children accept his suggestion that during their nocturnal adventure, the children should fall into a deep pit from which he will free them in a difficult rescue operation. (Max came to our counselling centre with extreme anxiety following a dramatic accident. He was playing on a construction site where he had been forbidden to enter and fell into a deep shaft; he became stuck inside and could only be freed hours later in a difficult rescue operation.) In the next session, while the other children select the role of Eskimo children—who once again are cared for by their parents, but also secretly engage in dangerous activities—Max plays a little seal who lives in a cosy home beneath a thick layer of ice.

The first problems often arise during the discussion of a theme, meaning that the leaders not only need to flesh out the children's contributions with the help of questions about specifics and associations and focus the group on a shared theme, but they must also intervene actively in order to set a process of consensus in motion.

In the case of preschool-aged children, it frequently happens that in the first sessions they are still so anxious and inhibited from playing that they will not enter the group room without their mothers; they want to sit on their mothers' laps and do not give any response to the initial question. If the leaders were then to pressure these children to come up with ideas, they would only reinforce their fears and replace the warm-up process with a schematically manipulated opening question. The children have permission to be as inhibited and unspontaneous as they are at that moment.

Here, the leaders have to find a warm-up process that accommodates the children's current situation as well as possible. If the children do not offer any verbal contributions, the leaders can observe their actions and interactions and convert the sensitivities that they express through their play into concrete terms. By picking up on the situation, translating it into actions in play and thereby expanding on it, they can help the children warm up to participating in the play session.

Example

In a mixed group of five-year-olds, four of the five children were not ready to enter the group space without their mothers in the first few sessions. They sat on their mothers' laps, clinging to them anxiously, some of them turned away from the leaders. The only child who reacted to our opening question was Hans, who was also the only one who had come into the group room without his mother. He said he wanted to be a cat. Julia whispered into her mother's ear that she would also like to be a cat. The other children said nothing; instead, when we asked them questions, they burrowed deeper into their mothers' clothing. Since a great deal of tension was building up, the leaders simply began the game: the female therapist pretended to be a farm woman while the male therapist played the role of a frightened mouse. While the farm woman expressed her thoughts about the animals—who were behaving very quietly and anxiously—and prepared some nourishing food for them, the mouse crawled around the room, full of fear and insecurity. He carefully peeked inside the nests (this is what he called the mothers' laps) and wondered aloud what kind of animals might live there. He wondered whether these were large animals—or perhaps very small ones like himself, who still needed a lot of protection. In a reversal of roles, he adopted the threatened position and acted out the children's fear so that more and more, the children took over the other, more powerful position and were threatening to the mouse. When the leader acted as an auxiliary, reinterpreting every one of the children's movement, gestures or expressions in a positive way, it was possible to reinterpret the definition of the relationships. Thus, when a child did not react to his actions, the leader would say: 'This animal doesn't seem to want to have anything to do with a little mouse. I guess it is much too small and weak for her.' He reacted to another child's arm movements by wondering whether this animal wanted to eat him. When the cat started following him, he asked the other animals if they would hide him in their nests; most of the children refused him with great amusement. In this way he slowly warmed the children up to a shared scene—even if it was a very sparse one—by getting them to participate through their expressions, gestures or even a few words, without leaving their mothers' laps. As the end of the session approached, they were no longer the frightened, withdrawn children, but animals who instilled fear in the mouse and who laughed at him.

With younger children, one should also keep in mind that in response to the initial question, they often simply name the role that they would like to play without describing the scenes that would go along with it. Here, the leaders need to ask further questions and suggest alternative possibilities in order to determine what scenes are associated with the roles and then combine them into a shared story in which the children can play out their roles. If we did not come up with a mutual theme, the individual roles would remain unrelated to one another and only disconnected individual scenes would take place. In this context, Widlöcher's (1974, p. 61) distinction—between the spontaneity of imaginary play in which children, if left to freely improvise, will lose themselves in anarchy and creative spontaneity, which is the result of psychodramatic improvisation—becomes important. Psychodramatic play places the children in fixed roles in the dramatic sequence of events and thereby obligates them to adjust to this situation and these roles. They may only bring in as much from themselves as the situation allows.

Example

In a group of six-year-olds, Anna responds to the initial question with: 'I am a cat again.' The leader asks: 'Where does the cat live? On a farm? Or does it roam about?' Anna: 'On the farm.' Then she immediately wants to build an oven on which she can lie down. The leader slows her down; she has to wait until the other children have chosen their roles. Then Eva says: 'I'm also a cat.' The leader: 'Do you live on the farm too?' Eva: 'No, I don't want to live on the farm anymore.' Leader: 'Why not?' Eva: 'Because the farm woman treated me so badly.' Leader: 'Where will you go then?' Eva: 'To America!' Martin joins in: 'I'm going to America too.' Leader: 'What are you?' Martin: 'I'm also a cat,'—to which Karl responds: 'I'm a gang of cats that run away.' Then the other children chime in: 'Oh, yes, we're a gang. We're going to America!' They stand up from their chair cushions and want to take off. The leader stops and asks: 'How will you get to America? On a ship or on an aeroplane?' After some discussion, the children agree on an aeroplane. The leader then asks: 'Are you sneaking on board in secret—maybe as stowaways? For example, when the mechanic who puts fuel in the plane is looking away, or when the people who load the baggage are taking a break?' The children answer: 'Yes, no one on the plane notices anything.' Leader: 'Could it be that the animals get hungry and secretly take some of the good food that is meant for the passengers? And maybe the flight attendant doesn't even notice when there is suddenly less food—less ham and chicken?' The children: 'Oh, yes—she doesn't notice anything.' Leader: 'Would the flight attendant think that the plane is haunted, or that they have altitude sickness? Or maybe she would suspect the other passengers?' Children: 'She would be all mixed up.' Leader: 'And would someone complain that there suddenly wasn't enough food? Maybe an important person?' Children: 'Yes, the King of England. He would scold the flight attendant terribly. We would secretly eat everything on his plate and leave an old rotten sausage in its place.' Leader: 'Will the cats be discovered?' Children: 'Yes, but only later. Then the flight attendant wants to throw us out. But the King thinks we are so cute, and he takes us with him to his castle.' Only through this repeated questioning was it possible to work out what should be played together in the scene.

However, the individual problems of specific children as well as the group dynamics can keep the warm-up from functioning according to a set pattern. Thus, inhibited children are often not capable of contributing their own suggestions in the initial phase. It can be enough to ask them whether they are willing to go along with the story that the more dominant children have suggested. Expecting more of them would place them under pressure because they are not able to demonstrate, at the start of therapy, the spontaneity and creativity that are actually one of the goals of that therapy. Waiting too long or asking them too many times would place them in a position in which they would be rejected or attacked by lively and restless children because they are standing in the way of the latter's desired play.

In the initial phase, inhibited children usually do not contribute much to the determination of a theme; usually they simply go along with the suggested play. However, within the play itself, they adjust the chosen theme according to their own needs.

If the children reciprocally block one another in the process of determining a theme by devaluing the ideas of others out of a sense of rivalry and introducing an opposing wish, the therapists must address this conflict of group dynamics or intervene in roles they choose themselves (for example, in the opposing position; on this subject, cf. 7.3.1, p. 157).

If children who were eager to play in the previous sessions suddenly react without imagination and are unable to come up with any ideas for play, the leaders need to uncover the cause of this resistance to playing, either as play leaders or from the position of an interviewer in roles such as newspaper reporters or doctors (cf. 7.1, p. 142).

However, agreeing on a shared theme for play does not mean that the children must always play together: only that they should bring the various suggestions down to a common denominator. Thus, in mixed groups, it very often happens that the boys want to play something very different than what the girls wish for. If we define agreement on a shared game too narrowly, the girls will be in danger of being dominated by the boys and having to subordinate themselves to the boys' suggestions. This situation can be avoided if the conflicting wishes are taken seriously and the group looks for possible ways to connect the different play ideas—even if this can only be made possible through the therapists' participation in the game.

Example

In a mixed group of nine-year-olds, the boys want to play aliens, while the girls want to play children on a farm with the therapists as their parents. Each party thinks the other's play idea is stupid and does not want to play with the other side under any circumstances. They reject the idea of a mutual game. In order to forge a connection between the two parties, the leader suggests that he could be a farmer who is also a ham radio operator: by chance, he makes radio contact with the aliens. Initially, the play then proceeds in separate directions. The boys, as aliens, fly through the universe in their spaceship. The girls, on the other hand, are children on a farm who become ill and require a lot of care from their parents. Only when, in the course of the game, the farmer makes radio contact with the aliens and—since the girls are becoming increasingly sick—asks them for their advice, does a connection take place. At the farmer's request, the aliens land on the farm and bring along a laser injection that will heal the girls. The girls protest this idea, but then agree to be healed by the aliens' laser rays. In return, the aliens have to fall ill and can only be healed by receiving blood from the girls. Even though the play was divided for a long period of time, and a connection was only possible with the help of the therapists, the session ends with shared ideas for play and shared actions.

Once children have found a theme through which they can act out their longed-for or feared scenes, it is frequently the case that they will play out this theme over the course of many sessions in different variations. Often they agree to continue the game while they are still in the waiting room, making the initial phase brief. On the other hand, if competition within the group increases, the consensus process can take a long time.

However, it is seldom the case that children remain seated quietly in their chairs like adults and wait until the decision on a theme and the consensus process are completed. They want to spring quickly into action and interaction; therefore, they wriggle around restlessly in their seats and call out: 'When can we finally play?'—or they simply start building the scenery or setting up the props. If we give in too hastily to this pressure from the children to accept the first play suggestion that comes along and abbreviate the consensus-building process in order to satisfy them, we will pay for it later in the play phase. It is up to the leaders to find a path in between the Scylla of yielding to pressure from the children to move into the play phase too quickly and the Charybdis of wanting to clarify too much ahead of time, and to expeditiously reach a clear decision on the play scenario in which the children's ideas are related to one another. Sometimes, out of fear of becoming overly pedagogical or restricting the children the way their parents do, the therapists give way too quickly and do not require the children to listen to one another and persist in searching for and negotiating a shared idea for play. This overly hasty false solution then results in chaos and conflict during the play phase. On the other hand, overly detailed negotiation can dampen the children's desire to play or may easily lead to a power struggle between the children and the therapists. Furthermore, it is always fascinating to observe that children who demonstrate their entire repertoire of problematic behaviour in the opening phase will subsequently, in the play phase, display their resources and anticipate their own possibilities for development: in the protected space of symbolic play, they experience how it could be if their restricted creativity were transformed into free creativity.

For a wide variety of reasons, however, many children are not able to get through the negotiation process. They wriggle around restlessly in their seats, push each other off and generally fool around, and therefore require the help of the leaders. Precisely in this area, psychodrama offers a wealth of possibilities for intervention that can transfer this restless activity on the part of the children into mutual play. Nevertheless, in order use these initial techniques to help find the subject that is relevant for the group and deal with it through psychodramatic play, the leaders need to understand the reason for the children's physical restlessness. Under no circumstances should they accept purely physical release without any symbolic significance (i.e., pillow fights); otherwise, as our early experience has taught us, they will simply have a mob of rampaging children.

Interventions at the verbal level—verbal starters
First of all, we need to understand the actions and the ongoing group process. For this, we require a special form of seeing, hearing and perception which Petzold (1986, p. 142 ff) called 'scenic comprehension and understanding' and understood as perception with the 'entire sensory organ of the body'. If the leaders can intuitively deduce the meaning of the action, they can try to translate it into a symbolic event which inspires the children to dramatic action.

Example

In the initial phase with a group of eight-year-olds, the children are still very tense and excited. During the discussion of themes, this tension expresses itself in physical agitation. First, two boys let themselves fall from their cushions; soon they have incited the other children to do the same. They jump around on their cushions and kick at each other with their feet. In all of this tumult, they are no longer capable of discussing a theme. If, in this situation, the leaders had insisted on continuing a discussion round, the children's agitation would have only escalated, with the result that the leaders would become more and more annoyed and the children still more excited and restless. Instead, the female leader describes this scene as follows: 'It seems as though horses are galloping back and forth restlessly inside a paddock, rearing up and kicking their hooves'. The children are able to pick up on this image and make the suggestion that they can be wild horses who have been captured by horse thieves—the therapists. After they have set up the scene, the children release their tension physically in the roles of horses. They act out the threat they feel from the therapists, and in the opposing role of beautiful, strong horses, they assuage their fears by breaking out of the enclosure and trampling the horse thieves.

Interventions at the action level—active starters As actors, the leaders take on a supportive or auxiliary function in order to strengthen the underdeveloped abilities of one or more of the children and to thereby prevent any child from reproducing previous experiences in the group therapy setting due to a compulsion to repeat. By setting boundaries and ensuring stability, they assume the function of an auxiliary in areas where the child's ego organisation is not yet sufficiently developed. Only in a supportive relationship can a child develop the stability he or she initially experiences externally into internal stability, and thereby internalise the supportive environment.

Example

Ten-year-old Franz, who was adopted as a four-year old following very early experiences of being rejected and cast out, reproduces these experiences in the group. During the opening round, he simply runs around screaming and insulting the leaders with obscene phrases, hindering the group in its discussion of a theme. Both the leaders and the other children become increasingly annoyed with him, which only leads Franz to provoke them further. After the session, the leaders reflect on what has happened: through scenic understanding, they realise that Franz is reproducing a scenario that he has experienced and pushing them to repeat the reactions of his earlier interlocutors. In the next session, they give Franz a different answer. They gently tell him that they do not wish for him to have the same experience here that he has had in the outside world. However, they understand that he is not yet able to behave differently. They want to look after him and hold him so that he does not encounter rejection again here. The male therapist sits down beside him, and by holding onto him without hurting him, prevents him from hindering the development of group play by raging around. When the therapist offers his body as a holding space—as a container—this allows Franz's emotions from his situation of deprivation and his longings for the protection, stability and security that he has missed to come forward and be expressed in the play process.

Alternatively, however, the leaders can have a therapeutic influence on the group process using the children's symbolic language by adopting a position which they either choose based on therapeutic considerations or allow themselves to be assigned based on the children's unconscious expectations for the role (cf. 6.1, p. 142).

Once the children have agreed on a mutual play scenario, we allow them to roughly sketch out the storyline—or in most cases, only the beginning of the game. This brief process of imagining what could happen in the story often opens the children's minds up to more new ideas for roles and plot lines. Nevertheless, during the game, the children have the freedom to improvise. The game does not need to conform to the story that was suggested, since the dynamics of interaction as well as the children's individual dynamics often lead to a different sequence of events than what was originally sketched out. However, in order to maintain a shared storyline, the children must agree on any changes in the dramatic sequence of events and coordinate their roles with one another. Widlöcher (1974, p. 11) sees this joint effort of 'co-improvisation' as an important therapeutic effect of psychodramatic play.

Step 2: Choosing roles
After a subject for play has been chosen, we let the children choose and briefly describe the roles they would like to play in the game. In order to flesh out each role as vividly as possible, the leaders need to ask questions, for example: 'Are you a little wolf or a big wolf?' 'Do you have strong fangs?' 'Then you must have beautiful, soft, cuddly fur.' 'Then you are also good at growling and howling.' However, these questions must not take too much time, since the children usually can hardly wait to start playing. The important thing is to work out important characteristics of the chosen role with just a few questions.

Furthermore, descriptions from the leaders can help the children warm up to their chosen roles; for example: 'A wolf like that can sneak around very quietly' or

'A little wolf like that has very cuddly fur.' In the initial phase, inhibited children are often not capable of choosing a role. The leaders can help them find one by describing possible roles—for example: 'In the rainforest there are lots of wild animals, like crocodiles, tigers and snakes; or animals that are good at protecting themselves, like porcupines or tortoises; or animals that are very fast or can fly, like monkeys and birds'. Or the leaders may simply suggest alternatives, such as, for example: 'Would you rather be a person or an animal?' or 'Would you rather be a dangerous animal or a peaceful one?'

In the case of certain role choices that have to do with exerting power or making decisions for others, it is important to let the other children agree about whether or to what degree they are willing to take orders from a leader or submit to magical powers. If a child wants to be a wizard, the leaders ask what magical powers he or she has and whether the other participants will consent to having spells placed on them if the magical powers are directed toward them. These consultations are necessary so that children will play along in the game and fierce conflicts do not arise during play. It is also important to coordinate the roles in such a way that relationships are created between the different roles. Thus, for example, a child who chooses the role of a doctor will need other children who are willing to become ill or injured in the play scenario. Moreno repeatedly stressed this con-figurative character with regard to the roles. Without an interactive context, the actional roles are not comprehensible.

Television series like *Ninja Turtles* and *Pokémon* or *Police Academy* increasingly lead to situations in which the children no longer want to acknowledge the limitations that are associated with every role. If they are animals, they can do anything; if they are police, they can do anything. There is no longer any role definition. Therefore, it is more and more important to point out the reality and limitations of the respective roles to the children—for example, that a tiger has strong teeth and can leap very far, but it cannot fly; or that a police officer can chase and arrest a criminal, but he or she cannot do absolutely anything she wants. If we allow children to do anything at all in their chosen role, or let them play an exaggerated caricature, we then rob them of the experience that every role comes with possibilities but also with limitations. Otherwise, any differences are erased and the role that a child chooses becomes unimportant. Then there is only one rigid role that remains—that of an omnipotent character that can do anything and whom no one needs. Mutual play becomes impossible; then there are only isolated, egocentric individual games. However, do not exercise these limitations too rigidly. Naturally, for example, we let children speak in the roles of animals, or do things that real animals cannot do, if they want to communicate something important to us in this way.

If one child wants to suggest roles for other children that will accommodate his or her intentions for the game, we accept his suggestion, but we remind the children of the rule that each child can decide for him or herself which role she wants to play.

If a child wants to switch roles during play, we only allow this if the new role will contribute to making a change—for example, if the child can find a better relationship to the other children through this role or can step out of a rigid behavioural role and discover possibilities within him or herself which he was previously not able to develop. After all, according to Moreno (1946, p. 18), the task of psychodramatic treatment is to bring the children to a point at which they can discover experienced and not-yet-experienced dimensions of their inner world and integrate them into their Selves. However, we rein in children who switch roles whenever they find themselves at the limits of their current role and realise that their omnipotence has an end—who, in misinterpretation of spontaneity, display problematic 'canned' behaviour in the guise of something new. We then frankly tell them the reason why it is not good for them to choose a new role at this time and why we want them to remain in the role they originally chose for this game.

If children repeatedly choose roles that will bring them into conflict with the other children in the course of play and are not able to discover a different choice of roles for themselves based on this experience, we advise them at the role selection stage about the difficulties that might once again accompany such a role.

If the selection of a theme has taken too long and it is no longer possible to hold the children back, we can ask the more specific questions about the children's roles while the scene is being set up: the leaders walk around to the different children and ask them about their roles while they are building the scenery. It is important that they then describe all of the roles out loud at the beginning of the game so that the children are aware of each role's characteristics.

This questioning about roles can also be conducted in a playful way. For example, at the beginning of a scenario about knights, the leader can warm the princesses and knights up for their roles by asking questions in the role of a scribe for the royal chronicle.

When all the children have chosen their roles, they decide together on which roles the two leaders should portray. If one child suggests a role, the leaders ask the other children if they would also like that one, or whether they have other ideas. Unlike in adult psychodrama, where the leader does not play a part in the scenario, we—along with Anzieu (1984)—have switched over to an approach in which both leaders generally participate in the play, thus allowing the children to fully act out their parental transference as well as any desires for splitting. In order to portray the children's projections in our roles, we gather precise details about the character and behaviour of the roles we have been assigned to play. Thus, for example, the leader who has been given the role of a teacher will ask whether he should be a strict, authoritarian teacher or a kind, caring one. These specifications from the children also act as a protection from the leaders' own transferences and provide the latter with important instructions for action in the play.

If the children have assigned the leader the role of a strict teacher, then he must assume this position with regard to the pupils and treat them strictly. If uncertainties arise during play, the leaders have to keep asking the children about how they should behave in their respective roles. In order that the leaders do not act out their own conflicts in the course of their participation, personal therapy focused on reflection and processing of the therapists' own childhoods is absolutely necessary.

However, in the case of children who have too little structure—who are uncontrolled and overly rigid in their repertoire of roles, with the result that they can only demonstrate chaotic and destructive play behaviour—one of the two leaders will refrain from taking on a transference role; rather, he or she chooses an auxiliary role for herself (cf. 6.2.2, p. 137).

In the assignment of roles, we pay attention to which roles the children want to impose on us and what relationships they are unconsciously trying to forge between themselves and us. We ask ourselves whether we are being pushed into taking on roles in which we feel the way the children did in earlier scenes or in the current one—or whether we are being given roles in which we should react as interactive partners for the children. Expressed in the language of object relations theory, the children project self or object representations onto us, and our task is to partially identify with these projections and to act them out.

Step 3: Setting up the scenery
Since there is no audience in children's psychodrama—for Moreno, this was also out of the question—there is also no stage in the true sense of the word. The entire room becomes the playing space, where no one outside the psychodramatic play can remain. In this room the children can set up the scene or their action using the cushion elements and the existing materials. In order to create a spatial structure in the playing space that fits the representation of the story, the room first needs to be divided and partitioned off with cushions and cloths.

Example

After the children have agreed to play a game about robbers and have chosen their roles, the female leader asks them where the robbers' lair is located in the

room. The children choose a corner of the room for this purpose. The castle is to
be built in the opposite corner. When asked further questions, they then decide
that a dark forest lies in between these two places; near the castle is a meadow
with bushes, and a deep moat is located directly in front of the castle.

Once the room has been divided, the children can begin building their scenery
using the existing materials and sketching out the locations they have delineated
using cloths, cushions, etc. At this stage, arguments over cushions and materials
can arise quickly. With the help of the leaders, the children learn to negotiate about
who needs what building material and how it should be divided up so that those
children who are dominant or very fast do not grab all the material for themselves.
The children often need a fair bit of time to build the scenery. If children only want
to build a little bit, we encourage them to give the scenery structure and open up
possibilities for play at the same time. An unstructured space quickly leads to
chaos. Furthermore, the game is over very quickly if, for example, the robbers are
able to steal the king's treasure with one leap over a cushion and do not have to
first ride through the forest, sneak across the meadow in front of the castle, hide
behind the bushes, make their way across the moat and over the castle walls and
pilfer the key to the vault from under the king's bed before they reach the treasure.
For children in particular, a 'description of the configuration of the location which
is as concrete as possible … [is] indispensable' (Moreno 1969, p. 132), 'with as
many details as possible' (Moreno 1946, p. 185).

The leaders must also build their scenery in detail in order to open up play
spaces for action and to provide unstructured children with the necessary boundaries. Thus, for example, when they build a castle, they need to clearly identify
where the throne room is; where the vault is located (and the fact that it is protected
by heavy iron doors); where there is a window that the robbers might be able to
climb through; where the royal couple's bedroom is located; where the key to the
treasure chest is hidden, etc. This detailed construction not only helps to structure
the game so the children are forced to take walls or doors seriously. It also opens
up new ideas for play: for example, if the leader has also built a dungeon into the
castle, the children—in their roles as robbers in the game—can exert their wrath on
the evil king and pay him back for all his injustices by locking him in the dungeon.

In addition to providing structure, the process of setting up the scenery also
serves as a further warm-up. If, for example, for a jungle game, we pull the blinds
down to make the room dim, cover the cushions with curtains or cloths to make
them look like lianas or spider webs, lay down a few ropes to represent snakes,
spread out blue cloths for a lake and black ones for a swamp—then we create an

atmosphere that will lead the children further and further into the world of the rain forest and thereby warm them up to playing a scene in the primeval jungle.

While the children are building the scenery, the leaders can go around the room and ask questions to make the symbolic world more three-dimensional for the children. For the robber scenario, for example, they can ask: 'What does your robbers' lair look like? Is it very dark inside? Is it a hole in the ground or a stone cave? Is it comfortable in there? Where is the fireplace?'

In addition, the children have the option of making costumes for themselves using the cloths and hats from the cupboard, or using Baufix to build the props that they need—for example, daggers, pistols or swords. The leaders should also use cloths and hats to indicate their roles: for example, as the king and queen, they can decorate themselves with beautiful cloths; they can use colourful Baufix cubes to make diamonds for their treasure trove and pillows to represent bags of gold. Costumes and props also help to warm the leaders and the children up for the play and during play, allow them to insist on certain structures. Thus, for example, the children playing the robbers cannot simply say that they have stolen the key to the vault. Rather, because the leader—in the role of the king—has chosen a Baufix element to represent the key and hidden it under his bed, the robbers have to sneak up to the king's bed, pause for a moment in suspense because, perhaps, the king starts up briefly and moves in his sleep, and then carefully slide the key out from under the pillow of the sleeping king. This also creates a greater arc of suspense in the game—something that is particularly important for children with a low tolerance for frustration.

Sometimes children want to bring their own properties—particularly weapons —because they are not satisfied with the representations. Here, we limit the children and remind them that they have to make do with the existing materials.

Once the children are finished with the construction and decoration, we describe the playing space before the play starts. Alternatively, we let each child describe his or her existing or imaginary scenery so that all the children's powers of imagination are stimulated and all of the children know what the pillows, cushions, cloths, etc. represent. In this way, in the subsequent play phase, they can move about in the room as if the furnishings that have been described actually existed. At the same time, we also ask the children, for example, when their lair is closed and who is not allowed to come in. We also remind them that a solid stone cave cannot simply be knocked over, even if the cushions are somewhat wobbly. Having the opportunity and the security to retreat into a safe place—which is respected by everyone—is particularly important for insecure, anxious or traumatised children. Such possibilities for withdrawal also allow children to insert quiet phases into the play session.

4.2   The Play Phase

Following this building phase, the play begins with a ritual of transformation. In order to ensure a shared start to the play, we ask the children to go into the dwellings they have constructed—their caves, nests, castles or spaceships. Then, with the rustling sound of a rain stick, we initiate the transformation into the chosen roles of animals or heroes. It is still night time; the animals or heroes are still resting or sleeping. Then we let the dawn come, and the animals or heroes awaken. With younger children, we accentuate the start of the day with animal sounds (the crowing of a cock in the farmyard or the calls of monkeys in the rainforest).

During play, the children have the freedom to improvise. The actual play does not have to correspond at all to the story that was suggested, and it is rare that children adhere strictly to their original plan of action. The first descriptions simply serve as an outline. The dynamics of interaction often lead to a different sequence of events. Nevertheless, in order to ensure a shared storyline, they need to agree on and coordinate the changes in the dramatic sequence.

In the course of the play, a space for development emerges. In this 'potential space', the children can repeat 'bad scenes' that they have had to endure in new re-enactments and bring longed-for scenarios to life. They depict emotionally distressing experiences and repressed feelings and free themselves from the scenes' threatening character through cathartic action. When a child embodies symbolic figures in play, 'then they not only lose their power and magical force over him, but he also takes on their power for himself. His own ego has the opportunity to discover and reorder itself; to bring together the elements that had been kept separated by the damaging forces, assemble them into a whole and gain a sense of power and relief—a catharsis of integration; a cleansing through completion' (Moreno 1973, p. 83). This facilitates the breakdown of psychological disturbances and the formation of a healthy self-acceptance.

Here, touch is a significant element of children's psychodrama. Through touch—the most elementary form of contact—we can address the child's early, preverbal experiences. Through this physical experience, the child then undergoes a new, healing experience—a healing answer to his or her trauma or experience of deprivation. The child has an immediate experience of being held and protected, comforted and supported. In this new relationship experience with the therapists and the other children, previously unfulfilled physical needs—to be touched, stroked, comforted and held—are answered with empathy and acceptance, and suppressed and blocked emotions are set free. Through this embodied corrective experience, the child feels nourished and supported. For the therapists, this means that they must embody the thing that was missing. As Petzold (1995) emphasises, they must touch the child where he or she has not felt any caressing hands; look lovingly at her where there have been looks of contempt, and acknowledge her with kind words where there has been silence or criticism. However, the aim of this 're-parenting process' (Petzold 1995, p. 440 ff) is not to replace a missing parent and compensate for past suffering through symbolic wish fulfilment. Rather it aims—through an alternative personification and the creation of a corrective atmosphere—to provide the child with new paths for experience and behaviour and to free her constricted creativity. Through the experience of being touched, a feeling of being accepted emerges which, through a change in the child's self-image, leads to an altered self-confidence. Nevertheless, when accepting a negative transference role, the therapist in question must also give the child space for her pain and anger (cf. Aichinger 2008).

Since the play is also fun, the children can always find an enjoyable approach to their vital processes of living and creating.

During the play process, there are various possibilities for intervention available to the leaders, through which they can support and stimulate the children's process of self-healing. These techniques for action are 'directorial aids' which help structure the storyline, intensify the symbolic events of the game and facilitate experiences, insights and changes.

4.2.1 Attunement

Even though children usually make the transition from reality to the semi-reality of psychodramatic play quite easily, preschool children in particular, and children in the beginning phase of group therapy need a warm-up or attunement process in order to better imagine the time and place of the scenario they are acting out. If, at the beginning of the game, the leaders describe the opening scene as vividly as possible or use sounds (for example, animal noises) to fill the scene of the action with life, they will create a playing atmosphere and warm the children up for the play that is about to begin. Restless or impulsive children in particular require this period of attunement in order to give themselves enough time to find their way into their roles and not simply explode immediately into action.

> **Example**
>
> In the initial phase with a group of ten-year-olds, the children agree to play the roles of explorers discovering an unknown island. The female therapist should

be a native of the island who welcomes them into her village and cares for them; the male therapist, on the other hand, is a cannibal who lives deep in the rainforest. In the next step, they construct the rainforest. Since the boys are still very restless and excited, the female therapist suggests that they begin the game with a scene of the explorers lying in their hammocks in the village; it is still the middle of the night. The male therapist darkens the room and then attempts to use sounds—for example, parrot calls, the squeals of monkeys, the hissing of beasts of prey and the drumming of the native villages—to create an atmosphere that will help the children get into their roles and warm up for the game. After a little while, he slowly raises the blinds, saying that the sun is now rising over the village, and the villagers are waking up.

4.2.2 Instigation

Most of the children who come into the therapy group are impaired in terms of their spontaneity and creativity, and they must first learn how to play again. This is why they need the therapists to play with them. Through the leaders' example—through the sincerity with which they play their roles, through their emphasis on expression, gesture and movement—they show the children what is possible in this 'as if' game, and incite them to imitate their actions. In this way, they demonstrate that play is an integrated event. Older children in particular observe very closely whether the leaders are participating earnestly in the play, or simply pretending to do so—whether they remain at a superficial level in their roles or whether they are experiencing them from deep inside and using their entire bodies as a means of expression. Moreno repeatedly emphasised this factor of physically embodying the role.

Inspired by brain research, calls to increasingly integrate the body into psychotherapy are becoming more and more frequent in recent years; psychotherapy without the involvement of the body no longer corresponds to the current state of scientific knowledge (cf. e.g., Gottwald 2006; Grawe 2004). The body represents a simple gateway 'to all the phenomena and levels of experience and behaviour: that is, sensory perception, affect, motor impulses, emotions as well as memories from all stages of life' (Gottwald 2005, p. 140).

Psychodrama took the interaction between the body and the psyche into account from very early on. In Moreno's view, human beings are first and foremost physical creatures; therefore, a scene is shaped by the physicality of all the participants. According to Hutter, Moreno embedded these ideas into his philosophy by emphasising that every role is based on physical role elements and that every encounter is first and foremost an encounter between bodies (Hutter 2000, p. 134 f). His concept of physicality is also connected to his theory of creativity and the release of bound-up life energy.

Therefore, anyone who works with children must also take the body into account—both his or her own body and those of the children—because during play, children are engaged in their entirety, both mentally and physically, with all of their senses. According to neuroscientist Hüther (2005, p. 23) such physically-oriented experiences also make it possible for a child to 'rediscover an integral experience that he or she had in very early life: my body—that is me!'

Children's psychodrama, which is based on the anthropology of the human being as creator, considers the fostering of an expressive, creative personality to be its central purpose; therefore, it integrates all of the sensory organs, as well as affect and physicality, in order to facilitate the free expression of emotions and physical impulses. With reference to children's therapy, Nicole Gäbler rightly calls for a 'return to the body-oriented senses': 'By integrating the body-oriented senses into psychotherapy with children, we gain experiences that correspond with the developmentally and psychologically relevant, naturally-occurring needs of the child' (2006, p. 802).

Through their own participation, the leaders can help small children and children whose creativity is buried—whose play would otherwise quickly come to an end—to develop their roles and keep the game going. Therefore, the leaders must be capable of assuming and embodying any role. Yet despite their lively participation, they must not become completely absorbed in their roles; rather, they must pay close attention to the children's playing. In order to ensure that they do not play their roles based on their own projections but rather according to the children's descriptions, the therapists continually ask the children how they should portray their roles. Questions such as: 'As the farmer, would I scold the animals now, or would I be very forgiving when I discovered them in my larder?' will bother the children very little when they are immersed in play. They are accustomed to oscillating between levels of communication and giving each other similar instructions in the course of their normal role-playing games.

In the symbolic play with the therapists, the children construct their own inner scenarios again and again in order to find solutions to the tasks, conflicts and problems they contain. In order to comprehend this world of the children's experiences, the therapists must immerse themselves in the atmosphere and the scenarios along with the children, become participants in their scenarios and experience their feelings along with them, in the same way that they do, 'in order to then gain an overview by shifting into an inner distance through "partial engagement"', from which their respective interventions can emerge (Petzold 1987, p. 391). It is precisely in the act of earnestly playing this transference role that they will gain a sense of its significance and possibilities. They must also take the roles of the children seriously and discover the symbolic content behind the façade of the 'canned' television characters—a content which extends beyond the media template. If they apprehend their own roles and those of the children with all of their senses, they will be able to understand the messages contained in the symbolic actions. On the other hand, however, if they remain stuck at the level of the media template—the superficial content—and do not comprehend the underlying meaning of the scene, they will not be able to achieve the symbolic-dramatic interventions which, if they engage in the play in earnest, will emerge practically on their own.

Example

In a mixed group of eight-year-olds, the children choose the roles of animals in the rainforest. Anna wants to be a human child who lives alone in the jungle with the wild animals; she calls herself Mowgli. The female therapist is to play an animal researcher; the male therapist a giant snake. Anna calls him Kaa; she likewise assigns the other animals names from *The Jungle Book*. Although the other children resist it, the two therapists remain mentally stuck on the film version of the story. Only in supervision are they able to recognise how this has kept them from understanding the children's communication. For example, if the female therapist had taken her role and those of the children seriously, she would have realised with horror—in her role as the animal researcher—that a child had been abandoned alone in the rainforest without human protection and was threatened by a giant snake. She would have sensed the fear and dismay that Anna was fighting off in the play scenario. She would have recognised the danger that the child was in and the necessity of rushing to her aid. However, since she only saw the symbolic play as a repetition of the television version, she did not understand the coded message that the little girl wanted to communicate.

For this purpose, the therapists need to have 'a flexible Self which has access to the archive of the body's memory, which makes regressions possible' (Petzold 1987, p. 361), so that they are able to feel and think the way children do—as well as an ego that also repeatedly allows them to become restabilised. This immersion into the children's scenes certainly allows the therapists to more fully understand what the children are experiencing. However, there is also the danger that the therapists could be overcome by their own feelings and memories. When their partial engagement with the children becomes a deeper involvement with them, the therapists may lose the necessary broader view of the process and no longer be able to intervene properly. Therefore, a great deal of working through and reflecting on their own childhoods is a prerequisite for the leaders to participate in psychodrama play with children. The scenarios often contain negative roles which are difficult to maintain. Since great dangers lurk the regressive undertow of participation in the play, constant reflection after each play session is necessary in addition to self-analysis. In supervision and training groups, we often have the experience that due to their own set of problems, the leaders do not take their assigned roles or those of the children seriously and thereby block the children's further development.

> **Example**
>
> In a group of six-year-olds, the children chose the roles of wild animals; the two therapists were given the roles of animal catchers. When a powerful lion, played by a delicate, inhibited boy, suddenly appeared in front of the female animal catcher and hissed at her, the therapist did not see the lion. Rather, she saw the inhibited little child; she stroked his fur as if he were a little cat instead of trembling in fear and shock or making a quick run for safety. Thus, due to her own difficulties with aggression—which were revealed in the context of supervision—she thwarted the child's first attempt to deal with his underdeveloped aggressive side. She made him 'tame' again, thereby reproducing his parents' upbringing strategy.

It is equally detrimental when the leaders lose themselves in the play scenario and play their roles to an extreme, with the consequence that they no longer see that their behaviour in the role represents a 'role response' to the children's transference. The result is then inadequate answers, because in the intensity of the game, the leaders lose control over their own affect or they no longer register their own defensive behaviour.

> **Example**
>
> A group of eight-year-old children chose the roles of American Indians and gave the leader the role of a bison which they wanted to hunt. Instead of allowing himself, as the bison, to be defeated in the battle, the leader was overcome by his own difficulties with aggression: he behaved like a real wild bison, repeatedly trampling over the children, even though they gave him the direction that he was gravely wounded and had to fall down. The children became more and more frightened, until they stopped the game and said that they no longer wanted to play.

These examples show that while the leaders definitely need to participate in the world of the children's experiences, they must not give up their adulthood—which, after all, the children rely on—or lose sight of it in regression. 'The golden mean of psychodramatic behaviour lies between lively play and precise attention to the child's imaginary world' (Widlöcher 1974, p. 139).

Because—in contrast to work with adults—it is not speech, but play that is the primary medium of therapy, the leaders must direct their attention to the nonverbal processes; they must understand an analogous form of communication and be able to answer analogously. In this way, they can help the children achieve intensive play and stimulate therapeutic processes. Schmidtchen (1995, p. 15 ff) demonstrated the importance of immersion in play which, in combination with other variables, encourages healing.

4.2.3 Structure

In order that a game does not quickly peter out or escalate into chaos, the leaders intervene to provide structure as play leaders—particularly in the case of preschool children or with impulsive, aggressive children—and support the children's sometimes underdeveloped capacity for self-direction in a 'holding function'. These structure-oriented interventions are intended to strengthen the children's egos and thereby enable them to regulate themselves and their relationships.

(a) Children need to be reminded of the limits of their roles and be presented with options which provide structure and open up new possibilities for behaviour.

Example

During a rainforest play scenario, an eight-year-old boy—in the role of a black panther—attempts to enter the helicopter into which the leaders (in the roles of animal catchers) have fled. When the leaders set a boundary for him, telling him that the helicopter door is locked and he cannot simply come in, he answers that he has a laser gun with which he can shoot off the bonnet of the helicopter. At this point, the male leader briefly steps out of his role and reminds the boy that a panther could not do this. However, panthers are very clever: for example, he could find a good hiding place and wait until his victim thinks it is safe and carelessly exits the helicopter; then he could take the animal catcher by surprise and attack.

(b) Sometimes they also need the help of the play leaders in order to react appropriately to the roles of the other children or the leaders.

Example

In a mixed group of children, the boys are playing dangerous Indios, the girls are rainforest animals, and the two leaders are adventurers who want to steal Inca treasure. One aggressive boy does not take the girls seriously in their roles as animals. When he makes fun of the wild cats, a girl playing the role of a giant snake grabs him by the leg and says that she has wrapped herself around him and he cannot get away. However, the boy does not react to her as a giant snake: he uses his superior physical strength to kick her away and escape. At this point, the leader quickly steps out of his role and reminds the boy that without a weapon, he would have no chance against a giant snake. He might perhaps be able to call for help or attempt to distract the snake with a clever trick. The girl then says that she never wanted to kill the boy; she only meant to knock him unconscious, and then she would disappear again into the jungle. When the leader asks whether he is willing to go along with this, the boy briefly concedes the girl's strength, allows her to twine around him again and pretends to be unconscious until the snake slithers back into the rainforest.

(c) It is necessary to repeatedly set boundaries in order that the children take the reality of the scenery and props seriously.

Example

A group of six-year-olds are playing bank robbers who want to steal from the bank director's safe. Even though, before the start of play, she clearly stated that alarm systems and video cameras are installed in the back, the children simply march in and take the diamonds. The leader interrupts the game briefly and says that the bank robbers cannot simply enter the bank so easily. They first need to disable the alarm system and the video cameras—for example, by cutting the electrical cables, opening the door of the bank with keys which they have copied and breaking open the safe with a welding device.

These suggestions for structure open up new play possibilities and create a greater arc of suspense, particularly for those children who otherwise react quite impulsively and cannot tolerate a great deal of suspense. Nevertheless, it is important to remain flexible when insisting on the reality of the scenery. Thus, in the case of an inhibited child who, in the role of a cat, dares for the first time to steal a sausage from the farmer's larder, the leaders would not insist that the door is locked and that the cat can therefore not sneak in. Using words like: 'Oh dear, we didn't lock the door properly. And this little cat, who always watches everything carefully, noticed it right away', they can encourage the child to act on his wishes to take things for himself. With an uncontrolled child, on the other hand, they would set limits and insist that the door is locked and a cat cannot get through locked doors. However, when setting limits, they should also offer an alternative that can increase the child's low tolerance for suspense, for example: 'Hopefully the cat won't lie in wait for a moment when we aren't paying attention and accidently leave the window or the door open.'

(d) In addition, it is necessary from time to time to interrupt the children's play, 'freeze' the action and help the children to deal with their conflicts with one another and search for solutions to those conflicts.

Example

In a mixed group of ten-year-olds, the boys are playing aliens; the girls want to be children, with the leaders as their parents. During the night, the aliens suddenly land in the girls' bedroom and want to kidnap them; however, this had not been discussed ahead of time. Here, the female leader interrupts the play briefly and clarifies the conditions under which a shared game could continue. The girls make the concession of accommodating the boys' desire to be powerful aliens. They let the boys capture them and take them away to a strange planet. In return, however, the girls request that the boys let them steal the spaceship so that they can fly back to their parents, who are nearly dying from worry. This reciprocal arrangement allows the play to continue constructively and leads the group to surmount the boys' solidified, 'canned' mind-set of only playing the roles of the powerful figures.

(e) When children begin to simply act out differing play ideas without discussing or agreeing on them with each other, the leaders must briefly interrupt the play and ask how the game should continue. Even when one child gives a particular direction to the leaders in their roles, they ask for the consent of all the children. For example, if one child says to a leader: 'Now you are dead', the leader asks the other children if they assent to this idea and if so, how long he should stay dead—how many seconds should he count. If it is not possible for the children to agree, the leaders can also behave in different ways, according to the wishes of individual children. For example, with an anxious child, a leader playing a dragon could be less dangerous; with the others, she might be more aggressive.

(f) If children overstep boundaries or rules, we remind them briefly of the rule of 'as if'. If children hurt or insult one another, the leaders quickly step in and set limits. Out of fear of resembling a negative parental image or seeming overly authoritarian, many leaders postpone this intervention as long as possible instead of pronouncing 'No more of this!' This establishment of boundaries is particularly necessary for children who act out strongly—in order to protect them, hold them and support them.

However, the leaders may not only introduce structures as leaders—by stepping briefly out of their roles in a quick-change act and intervening as themselves—they may also do so within the roles that they are currently playing. Since this version of structuring—within their roles—does not interrupt the play but rather influences it in the context of the symbolic language, these interventions are preferable.

Example

A group of twelve-year-old boys has decided to play that they are gladiators. The female leader should be the empress of Rome; the male leader is a masseur and the supervisor of the gladiators. While the other boys prepare for battle and carry out various test fights, Thomas—who is otherwise very constricted in his creativity and has a limited repertoire of roles—plays a drunk: he staggers among the fighting gladiators and disturbs their earnest battle play. The other boys are annoyed at the disturbance and they scold him—especially because he is paying too little attention to the scenery (such as the Colosseum wall) and knocking it over. In the role of the supervisor, the male leader wonders aloud what is the matter with this gladiator. He is in danger of being laughed at by the audience; or the empress might fire him in shame and disgrace. The supervisor wonders what would happen if this gladiator were to stop displaying such peculiar behaviour: instead, he could surprise the empress by letting himself be rubbed with oil or dressed in elaborate armour like the most famous gladiators and, using only his own physical strength, fight against a giant black bull or face the hungry lions with a net. This intervention opens up new play ideas for the boy and stimulates his sense of possibility. He stops playing the drunk and orders the masseur to oil him down and dress him in an elegant red cape. He then enters the arena as Spartacus and fights against the black bull, which the male leader must now portray.

When conflicts arise, the leaders can also intervene in an appropriate role.

Example

In a group of six-year-olds, each child wants to build his or her own rocket with which they can fly to the moon. The teachers are assigned to be workers who have to build the rockets according to the astronauts' instructions. When Johannes takes away a cushion that Florian had already built into his rocket, the male leader changes his role. Rather than intervening as the leader, he says that he is a member of the airport police and needs to investigate an act of sabotage. A part was dismantled from one of the rockets during the night. Johannes first accuses other astronauts. However, when the police officer discovers the stolen rocket part, Johannes says that a spy must have planted this part at his place in order to cast suspicion on him. The others then decide that the female leader should be a Russian spy who has stolen this important computer. The boys, who have played separately up to now, join together and set out to catch the spy.

Entering the game as a police officer who wants to write a report on a conflict; appearing as a reporter looking for witnesses to an incident or intervening as a sheriff who is concerned about keeping order in the city can prevent the children from simply talking and blaming each other. Instead, it can lead them to find solutions within the play scenario. This will also open up new ideas to children who have a limited repertoire of roles.

Another option for intervention consists of describing a child's rule-breaking behaviour using an image that could trigger a new storyline.

Example

When a boy playing in a scenario about knights steals a pillow from another boy, the leader—in the role of a servant—wonders aloud whether the red knight has become a robber baron. When the boy confirms that he has, the other boys also become robber barons. The therapists are assigned to be rich merchants whom the knights attack and rob.

All of the familiar and important psychodramatic action techniques used during the play phase—such as role reversal, permanent doubles, doubling, the psychodramatic mirror and the soliloquy—are employed in children's psychodrama, if perhaps in a modified form. These psychodramatic techniques are possibilities for action and behaviour that are derived from role development, a natural developmental process (cf. Mathias 1982, p. 228).

## 4.2.4	Changing Roles and Role Inversion

Pruckner and Schacht (2003) clarified the confusion of terms between changing roles and role reversal: they define a change of roles as a one-sided, linear occurrence; role reversal, however, is a two-way process in which two people exchange their respective roles and each individual plays the role of the other. According to this definition, only a change of roles and role inversion come into play in children's psychodrama—since, on the one hand, role reversal represents a complex task which can only be mastered in adolescence (Schacht 2003); and on the other, children refuse to engage in role reversal at the real-life level (as Pruckner (2003) also emphasises), since they experience role reversal as a form of discipline and reproach.

Like Anzieu (1984), in the context of therapy, we allow the children to perform role changes of their own accord, unconsciously and without explicit instructions. This unconscious change of role can, on the one hand, take a form in which the children update or restage past or current conflicts in the act of role transference, but they do so through a role inversion: they turn the tables, so to speak, and assume the position of the powerful adults while assigning the therapists the roles of the powerless children. Expressed in the language of object relations theory, the children project their self-representation onto the therapists and in doing so, force the therapists to identify with these projections. In a process of concordant iden- tification, the therapists then feel as anxious, powerless, ashamed and helpless as the children felt or feel in their past or current interactions. By frequently assigning the therapists the roles which they themselves otherwise embody real life—and, through this role inversion of the original object relationship, inflicting their own unpleasant experience onto the therapists—the children are able to communicate their conflict. They can then deal with these issues by assuming the role of the active perpetrator and newly experiencing their effectiveness and capacity for control over the past events. This experience of strength and control has the effect that the children no longer see themselves as victims or passive, defenceless creatures in relation to their environment, but rather as active, creative individuals. This fundamental need for control is also closely connected to good psychological health (Grawe 2004).

Example

In the initial phase with a group of eight-year-olds, the intense anxiety at the beginning of treatment becomes a theme within the group. Fantasies of appro- priation, subjugation and injury arise, as well as the fear of shame, exposure and humiliation. As a way of dealing with this group theme, the children decide on a rainforest play scenario. However, they change their roles and adopt the roles of wild, dangerous animals who know their way around and are very much at home in the jungle. They assign the therapists the roles of researchers who are coming to the rainforest for the first time, do not know their way around and are too stupid to get their bearings. In the game, the researchers are then attacked by tigers, panthers and other dangerous animals who knock them over and injure them. According to the children's direction, the researchers must then be completely terrified, go nearly crazy and cry that they want to go home. They walk around in circles and cannot find their way out of the jungle. The animals then laugh at the researchers' frightened and stupid behaviour. Finally, the researchers are forced to take off their clothes and are filmed in their fear and shame using a purloined camera. Since it is important that the children play out their fear of humiliation in this role change, the leaders do not point out the reality of their roles—that animals cannot use a film camera.

Another possibility for role changing consists of the children projecting the object representation onto the therapists and, through role transference, forcing them to identify with these projections. Through complementary identification, they must then behave and react in the way that (from the children's point of view) earlier or current attachment figures behaved or behave. However, they do not simply repeat these unpleasant scenes; instead, in the play scenario, they reverse the behaviours and emotions associated with the roles. In an inversion of roles, the therapists—in the powerful roles of the attachment figures—are made powerless and helpless, while the disadvantaged children become powerful and capable of action and can therefore enact the old scenes with an altered and inverted power balance.

Example

A mixed group of twelve-year-olds—some of whom have experienced severe neglect, abuse and violence at the hands of their parents—agrees to act out a circus scenario. The children choose the roles of animals; the female therapist is assigned to be the circus director and animal trainer; the male therapist is a television reporter who is broadcasting the performance live on a Eurovision programme. The female therapist is given the instruction to be very strict with the animals, to hit them and give them nothing to eat. During the performance, however, she should feign being very kind to them. After the therapist has acted out this behaviour and mistreated the animals, the day of the premiere is at hand. The reporter tells the television audience that in just a few minutes, an extraordinary, never-before-seen animal performance will begin. However, during the wildcat performance, the tiger suddenly falls down dead. The tiger is portrayed by Tanja, a girl whose mother is addicted to drugs, and who has experienced neglect and violence. The reporter is horrified by the sudden death of this beautiful animal, and wonders what has caused it. Here, Tanja changes roles and approaches the reporter in the role of a jaguar. Tanja, who was very shy and has barely spoken up to this point, communicates to the reporter (using animal language in her role as a jaguar) that the tiger has died because it was chained up and abused. When the reporter asks who has done this, she points to the animal trainer. The reporter immediately tells the television audience about this abuse of the animals. Then all of the animals, who had previously been cowering, run at the trainer, attack and bite her and then lock her up in a cage. The animal trainer must then wail and complain that her misdeeds have been brought to light. The animals, on live television, then tell the reporter that the trainer has poisoned other animals and fed them alcohol. Thus, the abuses are made public, and the animal trainer—representing the negative side of the mother—is finally sentenced to life in prison.

Children can also switch between the role of the active perpetrator and the suffering character within a play scenario without being ordered to do so. In this way, the change of roles leads to a playful alternation of portraying both the object and the subject of a conflict and to interactive confrontation: thus, the conflict is played out within the scene.

Example

Fritz, an eight-year-old boy whose mother had tried to abort him, repeatedly acts out scenarios in which adults—be they his teachers or even the group therapists—would like to get rid of him. He stages his trauma in the group play scenario as well. In a scene based on the television series *Daktari*, the children play injured animals at a veterinary clinic at the edge of the rainforest. The therapists are assigned to play a game warden and an animal caretaker. In the game, the caretakers rescue Fritz, who is playing the role of a little lion, from a snare just in time to save his life; they bring him to the animal clinic and care for him. When night falls, he changes his role. Now he is the jungle native who set the trap; he breaks into the clinic at night and shoots the little lion. However, the lion is not quite dead, as the hunter believes. After committing this act, Fritz switches roles again and plays the injured little lion. The caretakers must waken with a start from the gunshot; they run to the clinic and perform emergency surgery on the little lion. They are not able to catch the perpetrator; he has disappeared in the darkness. Now the other animals say that they have been injured as well, so that the caretakers have to heal and care for all the animals at the clinic. They express their outrage that a stranger would want to kill such beautiful animals; they are happy that the animals are so strong and have been able to survive. They keep a night-time watch in order to protect the animals. In the next session, the children want to continue this scenario. Now Fritz suggests that the female therapist should be an evil native who wants to kill the animals. The other children agree. They also agree that they will not be injured or killed this time, because the game warden will catch the hunter in time. The warden lies in wait and surprises the hunter during the night, just as she is taking aim at the animals. Now all of the animals jump on her and release their anger by mauling her. In order that the result is not simply an aggressive abreaction, but that a reconciliation with the introject can also be initiated, the caretaker asks the native woman why she would carry out such horrific acts. She answers that she did so not because she hates animals, but out of fear that people and animals could not survive side by side. She is afraid that the animals might eat up the crops she has planted and that she then would not have enough to live on. The caretaker then consults with the animals and considers how the wild animals and the native humans might be able to live side by side without posing a threat for one another.

Children also engage in unconscious role changes when processing an unconscious conflict between impulse and resistance. In a play context, unconscious impulse and object representations connected with the tension of a conflict can be reciprocally embodied by the child and a therapist. The internal, psychological representations—now personified—strive for balance and reconciliation, for a compromise. If the child embodies both sides of the conflict through an exchange of roles, it is possible to integrate parts of the personality that have been split off.

Example

An inhibited ten-year-old boy plays the role of a gamekeeper in a scenario in which the other boys are playing knights. While the other boys boast about their strength at a tournament and present themselves to the queen (played by the female therapist) for admiration, René goes off on a hunt and kills one wild animal after another. The male therapist must take over the roles of a deer, a wild boar and a bear. René then brings the meat from his catch to the queen for a banquet. When the male therapist, in the role of an animal, wonders out loud why the gamekeeper is shooting all of these wild animals ('after all, they have a right to live'), the gamekeeper replies: 'The wild animals are destroying all of the queen's fields, so they must be exterminated.' In the severity with which he acts against the animals, he demonstrates the strictness of his superego introject. In the next session, when the other children want to play knights again, René says that this time he wants to be a wild boar, and he destroys all of the queen's cultivated fields. Now the male therapist should play the gamekeeper, who chases the boar but does not catch him. The gamekeeper goes to the queen and tells her about the destruction. Following René's instructions, the queen becomes very angry, scolds the incompetent gamekeeper and orders him to hunt and kill the wild boar. The gamekeeper then changes his role and intercedes with the queen: 'The boar is such a beautiful animal; I cannot kill him. Your majesty, you have so many forests and fields. Perhaps you could build a large game preserve where the boar can root around without destroying your fields.' The queen listens to the gamekeeper's arguments and changes her mind. She then orders him to simply fence in her fields so as to protect them from the wild boar. In these two sessions, René confronted his suppressed aggressive ego states by alternatively playing the roles which suppress them as well as those which embody them. In order, however, to free himself from his strict superego, he requires the modulating intervention of a mild ego ideal, which the therapist embodies in the role of the gamekeeper.

However the leaders, too, may change their roles of their own accord, without direction from the children, and take over the sides of the children that they repel or reject. With this change of roles, the children and the therapists can then work through the conflict in complementarily opposing roles. This interactive confrontation can help the children achieve better self-integration.

Example

In a mixed group of twelve-year-olds, the three boys want to play omnipotent gladiators; the two girls choose to be elegant ladies from the imperial family. The male therapist is assigned to be the gladiators' opponent; the female therapist is the empress. In the gladiatorial battles, the male therapist must fight with each of the gladiators and lose. In the process, as a strong gladiator, he verbalises all of the feelings which the boys resist in their fantasies of omnipotence. Before the battle, he expresses his fear of being defeated and the pressure of constantly presenting himself as strong as well as the stress of moving from one fight to the next. During the fight, he uses a soliloquy to express his wish to receive the spectators' cheers and adulation as the victor and his fear of being laughed at and humiliated as the loser. The boys do not want to listen to these suppressed feelings at all; they quickly silence the gladiator by stabbing him with their swords.

In addition, cotherapy offers a possibility of representing a child's conflict in such a way that the female therapist expresses the child's wishes, needs and impulses while the male therapist expresses his or her defensive or resistant side. Through this change of roles, the child can see his conflicts in the scene played by the therapists as if he were seeing it in a mirror. This 'immanent mirror' (Krüger 1989, p. 33) can be a means of removing resistance through denial.

Example

Prior to the therapy session, Max's mother reports that due to a severe heart defect, Max has fainted during gym class. Therefore, he must be careful during the session and avoid exerting himself too much. In the therapy session, the children agree to continue acting out the storyline they started the last time, in which the leaders were dinosaurs on the planet Pluto and the children were astronauts. Since, despite his mother's warning, Max is wearing himself out physically during the session, the therapists attempt to address his conflict within the play scenario. Withdrawing into their dinosaur cave, the female dinosaur speaks with her husband: 'You really must stay calm. You know that you have a lung that is too small and you can't get enough air. It is very important that you take care of yourself.' The mail dinosaur replies: 'I can't afford to be still. I have to keep fighting. Otherwise, what will the other dinosaurs think of me? They are sure to laugh at me.' His wife answers: 'Don't let it bother you. Let them go ahead and laugh, and don't pay any attention. Your health is more important than the other dinosaurs' approval.' Nevertheless, the male dinosaur doubts that he will be able to hold himself back. Then the astronauts arrive; they laugh at the injured dinosaur and taunt him, calling him a 'chicken'. The male dinosaur rages: 'I'm bursting from anger! Now I can't hold back—I have to show them that I'm not a coward!' The female dinosaur tries to calm him down and reminds him of how dangerous it could be for him to fight again. Now Max interjects: 'You could say, I won't be responsible. It's your own fault if you don't feel well.' The therapist then asks the children whether he should heed his wife's warning and avoid exerting himself. Max says no, the dinosaur should keep fighting and fall down in a faint. The other children agree. Hereupon, the dinosaur leaps out of his cave, runs after the astronauts, and collapses from the exertion. The female dinosaur drags him back into the cave and scolds him. After this fight—in which Max participated vigorously and paid no attention to his handicap—he does push-ups, declaring that he needs to stay fit. Now the therapist changes roles briefly: from the space centre in Houston, he calls the command centre on Pluto.

The control units show that oxygen is becoming scarce. The astronauts should take it easy and consume less oxygen. Max then replies that the space centre should send up a rocket filled with oxygen. The children then ask the therapists to repeat the scene that they have just played. The female dinosaur should be asleep; the male dinosaur should sneak away because he cannot stand to sit still and feel ashamed; he should start fighting again and collapse. After the male therapist has played out the scene according to these directions and is once again rescued by the female dinosaur, Max is able to retreat. He tells the other children that he has a heart condition. He corrects himself and says that he is an astronaut with a heart condition and he must return to the spaceship to take a rest. At first it is difficult for Max to tolerate when the other children continue to play. He wishes they would return to the spaceship as well. However, when the other children attack the dinosaurs again, Max stays inside the spaceship and watches. The other children then secretly install a loudspeaker in the cave. They disguise their voices so that the dinosaurs will think they are the leader of the dinosaurs. As the dinosaur chief, they ridicule the sick dinosaur. However, the sick dinosaur does not allow himself to be provoked; he continues to rest in his cave. In the role feedback during the closing round, the leader then says that he realised how difficult it is as a dinosaur to admit to his weakness and accept the fact that others laugh at him.

As the previous example has shown, closely related to role changes are the techniques of mirroring, soliloquies and dialogues.

4.2.5 Mirroring

According to Moreno (1973, p. 87), the psychodramatic technique of mirroring as an agent of information about oneself corresponds to the stage of self-recognition. For him, it is a method associated with the natural process of self-awareness. 'We are all familiar with children's continuous astonishment when they see themselves in a mirror … When the child finally realises that the image in the mirror is his or her own, a turning point has been reached in her development—an important step forward in her understanding of her Self.' When we use the mirror technique in psychodrama, we draw on these fundamental experiences from the children's lives (Schacht 2003, p. 115 f). Whereas, when we use mirroring in therapy with adults, the protagonist is confronted by an auxiliary who imitates his or her behaviour and sees himself in the mirror as a spectator, in children's therapy, the children are reflected in their situation through the participation of the therapists. In the role-playing process, the children dramatize scenarios which resemble real scenes they experienced earlier in their own lives—except that the balance is reversed. The children play the powerful and punitive roles; they transfer the passive and suffering roles on to the therapists. If the therapists then become truly engaged with their transferred roles, they can experience the feelings of anger, sadness, powerlessness and helplessness that arises within them and thereby understand the children's feelings. Then, in the play scenario, they can reflect—for the children to see—the distress, desperation, helpless anger and fear which the children are no longer experiencing themselves but which they have incorporated into their symptoms.

Just as when, in parental affect mirroring, the infant will not mistakenly attribute the reflected feeling to his or her mother if she 'marks' her reflected expression of affect and thereby differentiates it from her own actual feelings, the therapists in this 'as if' game must express these feelings congruently, but in a somewhat exaggerated manner. Appropriate mirroring must not be too strong, but it should also not be too weak—and it must be marked in such a way that the child is able to realise that this is not the therapist's actual feeling, since this would trigger fear in the child.

This reflection of behaviour and emotions in mirroring play is highly significant for therapeutic work. However, the therapists can only appropriately understand the children if they become resonating bodies and accurately embody what the children have transferred on to them in their roles. Therefore the therapists' countertransference plays an important role as an empathetic reaction. If the therapists reflect the emotional reactions that are triggered in them, they can achieve an understanding of the children's internal images. Only through this 'scenic understanding' can they discover an appropriate role response and set a supportive dialogue in motion.

However, they must repeatedly create space for this self-reflection. For example, by giving the direction: 'Now night is falling; the animals retreat into their lairs and the researchers lie down in their tent to sleep', they can create suitable conditions. Then they can quietly reflect on their emotional reactions and speak them aloud in a soliloquy or dialogue. In this quiet phase, the children are also in a better position to direct their attention to the therapists' dialogue.

Example

In a mixed group of seven-year-olds, the children are pretending to be wolves; the therapists are to play animal catchers who want to capture and train them for their zoo. The animal catchers let themselves be lured into the traps they laid themselves and be captured. Under threat of being beaten, they must imitate everything the wolves show them how to do. They have to howl, bite through bones, and do things that human beings do much more poorly than wolves can. Every time they make a mistake, the wolves punish them by biting them and laughing at them. They are then placed in the zoo in which they wanted to put the wolves on display. The wolves tie ropes to the animal catchers' arms and legs. Two girls switch roles and play children who pay 1 DM for the chance to pull on the ropes so that the animal catchers move their legs like jumping jacks. The children and the wolves enjoy themselves immensely and roll around laughing. In their roles, the therapists experience shame, helplessness and dependency, and they express these feelings aloud in a dialogue. Then the wolves cry out indignantly: 'And that is what you wanted to do with us! Do you think we would have liked that?' The animal catchers reply: 'We thought that it is different for animals. It doesn't bother them.' Filled with rage, the wolves cry, 'Poo—we want to be free, too. And we only became wild because you treated us so badly and beat us.'

Alternatively, as the example with the dinosaurs illustrates, the leaders can—on their own initiative—alter their roles in such a way that they mirror the behaviour of one particular child and express his or her thoughts and emotions through a soliloquy or dialogue.

The leaders can also assume mirroring roles—for example, as radio or television reporters—in order to make a child aware of his or her behaviour and its interpersonal consequences. In this role, they describe the child's behaviour out loud and provide him with an image of himself at the symbolic level. Particularly children who are conscious neither of their behaviour in the present moment nor of its impact in the current situation can receive important feedback in this way.

Example

A group of ten-year-old boys choose to play the roles of a US special military operations unit in Vietnam. A very dominant and aggressive boy declares himself the commander, and calls himself Terminator. The leaders are assigned to play Vietcong. First the boys play that they are in a camp preparing for their mission. The commander shouts at the others more and more, bullying and insulting them with the foulest of language. Here, the male leader changes his role and says that he is an American war reporter who wishes to write a story about the training camp. He walks around the camp and writes down what he observes, speaking aloud to himself. He remarks on how severely the Terminator treats the other soldiers—that they cower in front of him but complain about him behind his back. With his rough treatment, he has succeeded in making the soldiers afraid of him, but the price for this is that he is becoming more and more disliked.

The therapists can also describe the ongoing process of group dynamics and explain its effects by verbalising their observations, either through mirroring or transference roles.

Example

In recent sessions with a mixed group of ten-year olds, conflicts increasingly arose between the boys and the girls because the girls resisted the boys' desire for dominance. In the current session, the boys want to play aliens flying through outer space in a space station. The girls agree to be the American crew on a spaceship. The leaders are assigned to play scientists at the control station in Cape Canaveral. When, in the play scenario, the aliens approach the American spaceship, the scientists describe aloud what they observe on their monitors. A foreign object is coming near the spaceship. They wonder what this foreign object's intentions are and how the American crew will react to it. They comment on the interaction by adopting differing positions. The female scientist expresses some fear that a conflict might arise. Already on earlier missions, there have frequently been aggressive encounters between aliens and humans. They must warn the crew immediately and call them back to earth. The male scientist, however, is more optimistic, believing that the aliens only want to investigate the human beings—or they might even want to enter into a friendly relationship with these foreign creatures. Furthermore, the American team have proved their abilities in many difficult missions. When the aliens simply dock on to the American spaceship, the girls complain and call the boys 'stupid'. However, the leaders do not intervene in the roles of play leaders; instead, they remain in their roles and wonder aloud whether the aliens always make contact in this way—simply butting in on a foreign spaceship without asking whether they might visit. Perhaps it is not clear to them that this kind of behaviour would be interpreted by humans to be aggressive. In addition, they send the American spaceship a message that it is pointless to be outraged at the aliens. Perhaps they need some tips about how to interact with human beings. Thus, it might be better to send a radio signal saying that Americans will interpret this behaviour as a hostile assault. If they are coming with peaceful intentions, to do research, they will need to get permission from the American crew. When the girls begin arguing about whether or not they should let the aliens in, the therapists once again describe their dynamics out loud. Among the American crew, they say, there are some astronauts who want to explore the unknown very daringly, even if it is dangerous. Others, they say, have a more cautious attitude; they do not want to take too many risks and would rather forego discovering and studying something unknown. In addition, the therapists try to reinterpret behaviour in order to initiate positive interaction. When one boy, who also has trouble observing boundaries in other situations, immediately seals up the Americans' spaceship with lasers, the researchers make a call to the Institute for Extra-terrestrial Peoples and ask what this behaviour might mean. Speaking out loud on the telephone, they ascertain whether the experts are truly convinced that this behaviour on the part of the aliens does not need to be considered so dangerous; they determine that there are certain aliens who appear more aggressive than they really are—who do not know that one needs to respect boundaries. They find out that it is essential not to attack these aliens, since they would then become extremely aggressive. By using such descriptions and commentaries, the leaders can help the group to discover new forms of inter-action and slowly break down the boys' rigid pattern of always attempting to overpower the girls.

Furthermore, the mirroring role provides the opportunity to express admiration, to demonstrate the 'sparkle in a mother's eyes', and through symbolic wish fulfil-ment, to strengthen the self-esteem of children who have been made insecure in their self-worth—to use the 'power of a loving look' (Petzold 1995, p. 21). Indeed, infant research shows that self-worth and self-esteem are dependent upon whether an infant's early competence is acknowledged in interactive dialogue with the parents and vividly mirrored. It is only on this basis that positive self-perception can develop (Dornes 2004).

This act of responding with admiration to children's fantasies of omnipotence is especially important in the case of children with poor narcissistic development, as is frequently seen in aggressive children. The fantasies of omnipotence that these children act out provide them with the possibility to deal actively with threatening aspects of helplessness, powerlessness, abandonment and devaluation through fantasies of complete power. The fantasy play helps them to overcome their fear of their split-off feelings. In order to strengthen these children's sense of self, it is important that the therapists, as 'parental figures', mirror the children's grandiosity, thereby reinforcing their feelings of self-worth. The therapists must accept that the children will fight back against any confrontation with their illusions of their own grandeur for a long time, and avoid narcissistic injury and humiliation. Only in this way can they draw closer to the vulnerable children and make it possible for them to slowly alter their false, grandiose sense of self.

For severely traumatised children in particular, the therapist can use the admiring mirror technique to act as a counterforce 'against the merciless inner voice of condemnation and the inner "disapproving eye of disdain" … Both inwardly and outwardly, the evil eye may then be gradually transformed into a shining countenance' (Wurmser 2004, p. 13).

The desire to act out a circus scenario arises frequently in children's therapy groups. This game allows children to portray their fantasies of omnipotence and longed-for admiration very well. Since the circus stunts take place almost entirely in the children's fantasies—after all, they cannot walk on a tightrope or fly on a trapeze—the therapists have to mirror back the children's indicated movements as circus stunts and comment on them admiringly. In this process of correspondence, the children are able to view themselves positively because they are being observed with admiration.

Like Petzold (1996, p. 442 ff), we consider it important to enable children to experience omnipotence in order to strengthen them in their desires to make the impossible possible.

Example

A mixed group of seven-year-olds decide to play a circus scenario. The children, some of whom have quite poor motor coordination, want to play the roles of a tightrope walker, a trapeze artist, a dressage horse, a polar bear, a tiger and a clown. The male leader is assigned the role of director and animal trainer; the female leader is a spectator. In order to reinforce the admiration through a live broadcast on Eurovision, the female therapist asks whether she may also be a television reporter. The children want to begin the performance immediately. The television reporter begins by greeting her viewers all over the world: 'And now we say hello to our viewers in America, who have just tuned in. And now we welcome the people of Japan. In just a few minutes, the big event will start. The circus tent is filled to capacity. Everyone is excited and eager for the premiere to begin.' The circus director then begins to introduce the acts as sensational—unique throughout the world. However, since the children have very little idea of what they could do—they simply have the wish to be admired— they need the help of the director and the television reporter. The director opens up possibilities for play by elaborating on his announcements and describing what the audience is about to see. In this way, he stimulates the children's creativity. Since the children are barely able to fulfil their roles, the television reporter elaborates on her description of each act, complimenting and admiring each of the performers or animals. For example, when an overweight, physically uncoordinated girl appears as a tightrope walker, the reporter comments aloud: 'Ladies and gentlemen, like me, you will be enchanted by this beautiful performer. Look at her elegant costume! Observe the grace and skill with which she now ascends onto the tightrope! Hold your breath! She will now perform a trick at this great height without a net, without any safety ropes—a stunt that has never been seen anywhere in the world before. Watch how effortlessly she dances on the tightrope—what jumps she can make. Now she is getting ready to perform a back handspring. She did it! Bravo! Bravo! Extraordinary!' At the same time, the rather clumsy girl walks along a rope that is laid out on the floor. She experiences herself as an acrobat only through the leader's mirroring; and we can clearly see how, through the description, she resembles a tightrope artist more and more as she walks back and forth, glowing with happiness. When an inhibited boy appears on the stage in the role of a polar bear, the reporter describes him as follows: 'And now a gigantic polar bear is entering the circus ring. Look how his fur glistens! He rears up and shows his enormous body and his powerful paws. Listen to him growl! It makes shivers run down your spine! The spectators are enthralled at the sight of this powerful animal; they have never seen anything like it. I hope there won't be any accidents during this animal act: it is incredible that such a ferocious animal can be trained at all.' When another boy appears as a clown without having any real idea of how he could fulfil this role, the reporter mirrors him once again: 'The whole circus tent is roaring with laughter. Listen to how the tent is rollicking with amusement. What funny faces this clown can make! And now he is tripping over his own legs. The way he rolls around on the floor is hilarious. I can hardly even report on this funny scene because my belly is hurting so much from laughing!'

The children can scarcely get enough of these admiring commentaries from the circus director and the reporter. They play variations of this game over several sessions, relishing the reflection of their grandiosity.

4.2.6   The Soliloquy

In adult therapy, the protagonist is encouraged to speak freely in an aside about hidden feelings which he or she was not able to express in the corresponding past situation, or to reflect aloud on her new discoveries and insights (cf. von Ameln 2009, p. 52 ff). In therapy with children, it is not the children who speak the concealed feelings and thoughts aloud, but rather the therapists who, in a role reversal, are assigned to play transferred versions of the roles that the children have in real life. When (in their roles) they verbalise the feelings of anger, sadness and helplessness that arise in them through a soliloquy, the children become aware of what is moving and tormenting them inside and are thus able to gain more insight and connection to reality.

Example

A group of eight-year-old boys want to play astronauts and build a space rocket. The male leader is assigned to be a labourer; the female leader is a cook. The children boss the labourer around and bully him. While he assists in building the rocket—carrying the heavy building components (cushions), Daniel, a boy who soils himself, suddenly declares that the labourer has defecated in his trousers. He insults him, calling him a stinker and laughing at him for still soiling his trousers at his age. In a soliloquy, the leader expresses his shame, saying how awful it is that this happens to him—and worse yet, people laugh at him for it. He also expresses his annoyance. It stinks to be bossed around like this, be forced to do the dirtiest work and to be scolded at the same time. The other children pick up on this game; they boss the leader around even more and laugh at him for being a poopy-pants. The leader grumbles to himself that he is disgusted with this drudgery. Then Daniel comes over and welds the leader's behind shut so that he can no longer defecate in his pants. The labourer wails that he has no other choice but to openly put up a fight and rebel against this terrible treatment.

In order to make the children more aware of ambivalences and conflicts, both therapists can reverse their roles, with each of them representing one of the opposing tendencies in a dialogue, arguing in alternation and thereby revealing the conflicting feelings, wishes and tendencies—and then leave the solution up to the children (cf. the dinosaur scene in 4.2.4, p. 51).

4.2.7 Doubling and Permanent Doubles

The difference between doubling and permanent doubles lies solely in the duration of their usage. Whereas doubling is an activity of short duration, a permanent double accompanies a child for a longer period or throughout the entire play session in a supporting function. In a variation on its use in adult therapy—where the therapist or a member of the group stands behind the protagonist, assumes his or her physical posture, empathises with his emotional state and then verbalises the recreated feelings—in children's therapy, the therapists assume roles in which they can become an empathetic, supportive or exploring double or permanent double for the children. Moreno saw a parallel between the permanent double method and the relationship between a mother and child before and after birth (1973, p. 85). In a small child's first psychological universe, in which all actions and behaviour are determined by the symbiotic stage of identity, the mother is an auxiliary for the child. She tries to determine what her child needs and how he or she feels, and she acts for the child. Thus, the permanent double method offers the child that auxiliary function which the mother served during this early phase in order to provide him or her with ego support through warmth, intimacy and security—or to allow her to catch up on her ego development (cf. Schacht 2003), something which is especially important for children with insecure attachments. Doubling aims to reproduce the type of experience the child had during the symbiotic stage with the goal of supporting, encouraging and strengthening her in dealing with a reality that is too difficult for her; to give her the experience of having her own needs understood by the therapists; to offer her assistance in self-exploration and in summarising the situation through the verbalisation of emotional content (cf. von Ameln 2009, p. 60 ff). Particularly for children who have experienced early trauma and those with attachment disorders, this corrective experience is very important.

In order for children to better achieve these goals and to see the doubler not as an invasive adult but as a helping auxiliary, we do not double as leaders, but rather in transferred roles or roles that we select ourselves.

We make a distinction between different types of doubling: empathetic, supportive, exploring and ambivalent doubling.

1. **Empathetic doubling**

With this approach, the therapists attempt to enter into an inner dialogue with the child by empathising with him or her. The aim is to help the child to recognise and experience what is going on inside of him. In children's psychodrama, this usually does not take place at the level of reality, but at the symbolic level of role playing, where the child portrays his reality through the guise of fantasy. Here, the therapist does not double the child; rather, via a transferred role, he or she speaks to the child in his own chosen role.

Example

During the initial phase, a group of six-year-old children are playing animals in the forest. Two aggressive boys want to be a bear and a wolf; a third boy wants to be a fox, and an inhibited boy, Fritz, chooses the role of a hedgehog. The male leader is assigned to be a forest ranger and the female leader is a farm woman who lives at the edge of the forest. When the two aggressive boys begin fighting in their roles as the bear and the wolf—attacking and snarling at each other—Fritz becomes visibly frightened. He retreats into his lair and watches the fight fearfully, with a shocked expression. Now, the therapists could function as empathetic doubles in the style of adult therapy, by going to Fritz, standing beside him in his lair and verbalising: 'This is much too wild for me; this scares me; I think I'd rather hide.' However, for children it is easier to accept when the therapists double from within their roles. Thus, in this play session, the male therapist (as the forest ranger) walks past the hedgehog's lair and speaks aloud to himself: 'It looks like this fight is too wild for the hedgehog. Maybe he is afraid that the wolf or the bear might attack him. That's why he has crawled back into his den. But maybe he forgot that he has spines, so he doesn't need to be afraid of anything. The bear or the wolf would hurt their paws or their mouths on his spines. But maybe he is still being very careful and thinks that his den is still safer. Maybe he won't come out of his lair until darkness starts to fall. After all, hedgehogs usually come out at night when other animals are asleep. Hedgehogs have good eyes and they can find their way around very well.'

Through empathetic doubling, the children receive the therapists' empathy, which they need in order to be able to develop a feeling for themselves.

2. Supportive doubling and permanent doubles

The fostering of an expressive, creative personality is an important aim of children's psychodrama, which stems from Moreno's anthropology of the human being as creator. In particular, the technique of supportive doubling and the supportive permanent double offers a good opportunity to stimulate children's creative potential and—in cases where they have been limited and constrained—to help them to blossom again. If a child wants to try out a new role for which he or she has an insufficient performance repertoire, the leaders can start with the children's creative potential and through supportive doubling, actively support the child's intention—contributing to the development and portrayal of new themes and the expansion of the child's role repertoire and structures. As doubles, the leaders represent a need or longing which the child has not yet recognized or has suppressed. In this way, their doubling is equivalent to encouragement and approval, and contributes to the development of ego functions. 'Like a good fairy, they penetrate the psyche of the failed human being with their magic. Like good and bad poltergeists, they sometimes unsettle and arouse the patient; another time they surprise and comfort her' (Moreno 1973, p. 84). In this way, completely new emotional states and freedom of movement can secretly be revealed.

Example

In a group of ten-year-olds, three boys want to play the roles of Mexican bandits; two inhibited boys want to play adventurers travelling from Germany to Mexico. The therapists are assigned to play shady police officers whose actual adherence to the law is not certain. Contrary to their role selection, the two inhibited boys do not behave like adventurers; instead, they retreat into a hut, shut themselves in, and continually call the police for help over their walkie-talkies as soon as the bandits come near their hut. The police respond to these calls for help, hurry to the scene immediately, defend the adventurers and fight against the bandits. Without realising it, they take on the role of over-protective parents. They allow themselves to be drawn into the same constellation that the two boys have at home, where their parents shield them overprotectively from the evil outside world and from their classmates' hostility. Instead of paying attention to the progressive tendency the boys demonstrated in their choice of roles, the therapists react to the boys' performance in the roles—to the children's fearful behaviour. At the same time, they allow themselves, despite their assigned role description—that of shady police officers—to be pushed into a role behaviour and do everything for the two boys. Instead of supporting their ego development, they make the children more and more passive and helpless. Furthermore, they lead the two boys into the same difficult situation that they endure at school. Consequently, at the end of the session, the other boys complain that it was not possible to really play with these two boys: they were so stupid and would always simply call the police. In supervision, the therapists recognise that they have repeated a non-beneficial situation. Therefore, in the next session, when the children continue the same play scenario, they attempt to shape the roles differently. Once again, the adventurers very soon call the police for help. This time, the police do not respond immediately; instead, they remain at the police station and wonder aloud about the adventurers. They are surprised that these men, who have travelled to Mexico to experience adventures, are always calling for help right away. After all, they are adventurers who could take matters into their own hands and watch out for their own protection and safety. Other adventurers who have come to this region have fought against the bandits and had fun giving them the run-around. Some have them have even joined up with the bandits because the latter had so many adventures. They also wonder if in Germany—in the country these men come from—it is normal that police officers have to act like babysitters for adventurers. Besides, they don't feel like going out into the wilderness now, in the middle of the night. It is much too dangerous for them. Right now they would rather keep on playing cards. After all, they can also go out tomorrow morning and check on the adventurers. The result of this supportive doubling is that the two adventurers suggest that they will now sneak away without the bandits' notice and look for a place to spend the night. However, this will turn out to be the bandits' own hideout. Then they will be surprised when the bandits return home from their night-time prowling. The other boys agree to this idea. However, they also want to break into the adventurers' hut, find their walkie-talkie, disguise their voices and call the police for help so that they can lure them into a trap. The two anxious boys agree to this suggestion. As a result, a completely new interaction takes place between the adventurers and the bandits: near the end of the session, they even team up and overpower the dishonest police officers together.

Another possibility for supportive doubling consists of the therapists performing their roles in such a way that they strengthen the child's intention. As auxiliaries, they support the child's fragile ego and build up his or her low self-confidence through corrective play and by making alternative fantasies and experiences come alive for him. In this way, they foster the children's expressive behaviour and spontaneity as 'the appropriate response to a new situation or the new response to an old situation' (Moreno 1973, p. 34).

Example

A group of seven-year-olds are playing wild animals in the rainforest. The therapists are assigned to play animal catchers. Alexandra, a shy and inhibited girl, wants to be a puma. While the other animals attack the animal catchers and chase them away, Alexandra, in the role of the puma, remains sitting in her tree and watches with glowing eyes as the other children (playing animals) snarl, bite, strike with their paws and ferociously harass the animal catchers. However, she does not attempt any aggressive action herself. The animal catchers discuss this aloud: 'Did you see that female puma up in the tree? She is behaving very peacefully. But I don't dare cross her path. Earlier, when I saw her sharp teeth and powerful paws, a shiver ran down my spine.' The female animal catcher answers: 'And especially those sharp claws. I wouldn't want to get scratched with those. We had better make a wide circle around her, even if she is just lying up there peacefully like a little kitty-cat.' Alexandra beams from ear to ear at this supportive doubling; she hisses at the animal catchers and timidly shows her teeth and claws. Immediately, the animal catchers take to their heels in fear and horror. By taking the choice of role seriously, rather than the way it is played, and reacting to Alexandra as a puma and not as an inhibited child, the therapists comply with Alexandra's desire to express her aggressive impulses and help her to express the intention she demonstrated with her choice of a role.

Moreno described the permanent doubling method as 'the most important therapy for lonely people; therefore, it is also important for isolated and neglected children' (1973, p. 200). However, this ego-supporting technique must be altered in children's therapy. If an adult were to offer him or herself to a child as a permanent double, there is a danger that the child would not see her as an auxiliary, but rather as an adult who wants to patronise or set rules for the child. On the other hand, if the therapist intervenes at the symbolic level, in the context of a role in which she provides the child with help and support as a permanent double, then it is easier for the child to accept this healing, interpersonal experience of being understood and cared for. Supported by the therapist, the child gains the courage to take steps within his or her role which he would not dare to take in reality. Under the protection of the permanent double, the child learns to better care for himself—he experiences help in helping himself. Through this structural technique, aspects of the child's Self which have suffered early damage—his self-image, self-demarcation and self-guidance—are stabilised and his ability to focus emotionally on others and engage in emotional interactions are nurtured.

Example

A group of nine-year-olds are playing pirates. One boy, Franz—an outsider who is very anxious and shy—chooses the role of the lookout pirate in the crow's nest. The therapists are assigned to be admirals of the Spanish king who are sailing from America to Spain in their ship loaded with gold. While the other boys attack the Spanish ship, fight with the admirals, take them prisoner and then celebrate their victory with rum on their own ship, Franz remains seated for the entire time on a cushion which has been built up to be the crow's nest on the pirate ship. Supportive doubling from the therapists does not change anything, either. In their roles as admirals, they lie imprisoned in the belly of the ship and wonder out loud why the pirate up on the mast is not joining in the celebration, even though he was the first one to spot the Spanish ship. On the Spanish crew, the sailor in the crow's nest would come down after a battle, join in the celebration and sing along with the sea shanties. Still, Franz stays in his lookout post and appears very tense. In the next session, when the children want to continue the same game, assigning the therapists to play captains of a warship that the king has sent out to capture the notorious pirates, the female therapist changes her role. She asks the children if they agree to let her be a cat on the pirate ship. The children hesitate briefly but then agree. While the other children are back in action in their roles as pirates—for example, loading the cannons and raising the sails—Franz once again sits quietly in his crow's nest. Now the therapist, in the role of the cat, climbs up the mast and snuggles up at his feet. She admires him: 'How do you manage to sit up here all by yourself? I couldn't do that. Even though I love my freedom, I need other people from time to time, to play with or to cuddle with. Don't pirates need that too?' Franz shakes his head. Since he continues to simply sit on his cushion and not allow himself to be drawn into the game, the female therapist tries to integrate him into the play. 'Do I see that right? Isn't there a cliff off in the distance?' When Franz agrees, she asks him, 'Shouldn't you tell the helmsman?' When he does not answer, she quickly climbs down, leaps over to the helmsman and says: 'The pirate in the crow's nest has spotted a dangerous cliff. We need to change course quickly.' Once the course has been changed, the cat asks the helmsman: 'Shall I ask the pirate on the lookout if our new course is safe, or whether he has seen a dangerous whirlpool or hidden reefs?' When the helmsman orders the cat to tell the look-out pirate to watch carefully, she climbs quickly back up the mast and gives Franz the message. Now Franz changes his posture, he is no longer hunched up, but enters more clearly into his role and looks out carefully at the indicated ocean. However, in order that his withdrawn behaviour does not become reinforced because the therapist is there only for him, plays only with him, and the others become jealous of this special attention, she regularly climbs back down to the rest of the crew and hangs about with the pirates. Here, too, she repeatedly tries to include Franz in the group. For example, when all the pirates are eating chicken and drinking cola, she asks the captain, 'Shouldn't someone bring a chicken up to the sailor in the crow's nest? He can't leave his post; otherwise the ship might run into a reef.' When the captain gives her the order, she refuses: 'I can only hold the chicken in my mouth and drag it up there. But then the pirate surely wouldn't want to eat it anymore.' The captain then brings the chicken up himself. Later in the game, the cat asks Franz: 'Isn't that a tornado up ahead?' When Franz agrees, she says, 'We have to tell the captain right away.' Franz says that she should tell him, but the cat is reluctant: 'The captain won't believe that from a cat; the pirate from the crow's nest has to report it himself.' In this way, she manages once again to create a small interaction between Franz and the other children in the game. Finally, when the fight against the warship begins, the cat encourages Franz to join the fight: 'Every man is important now. There is a whole army hidden inside the Spanish warship. We need every pirate to fight; otherwise we will all be captured and put in chains.' Franz is then prepared to fight against the imaginary enemies; he pretends to stab several soldiers with his sword. The cat, who has hidden behind a barrel in fear, comments admiringly on the pirates' courage; she also emphasises the how bravely the pirate from the crow's nest is defending the ship against the superior strength of the attackers, defeating one soldier after another.

A further possibility for using a permanent double consists of assuming an auxiliary function with uncontrolled and aggressive children. This can help to strengthen their underdeveloped ego functions, foster appropriate aggressive and self-assertive behaviour and develop social skills.

Example

In a group of twelve-year old children, the boys are playing ninjas fighting against an American troop, which they have assigned the therapists to portray. Alex, an uncontrolled boy who has only a limited and rigid repertoire of roles, is unable to engage in the scenario with the other children: as ninjas, they want to sneak up on the Americans and set traps. Almost as soon as the Americans begin to approach, Alex immediately leaps out of the bushes and kills them with his ninja star. He then asks for new American troops to be sent into combat. The game plays out in a similar way once again: again, Alex overrides the other children's ideas for the scenario. The other children become increasingly annoyed. In the closing round they reproach him, saying it is not possible to play with him. He does not stick to the plan. Besides, they find it boring to simply mow down the enemies every time. In the next session, the boys want to play ninjas again. However, Alex says that today he is the Terminator and is going to fight against the ninjas. Since they can foresee that Alex wants to overpower the other boys in the play scenario and that aggressive conflicts are sure to arise, the therapists do not ask the children what roles they should play. Instead, the male therapist suggests that he should be a Vietnamese rice farmer who offers to help the Terminator by guiding him through impassable territory. The other boys agree to this on the condition that the female therapist comes to their camp, cooks for them and attends to their wounds. In the role of the rice farmer, the male therapist then attempts to support Alex and steer him toward other ideas besides constantly knocking down and destroying the others. As a subservient rice farmer, he warns the Terminator not to storm into the ninjas' camp immediately because the ninjas have built traps all around the camp. It is only possible to reach the camp by first crossing over steep mountains and dangerous ravines, helping each other to rappel down on ropes. After this, one has to cross a swampy area filled with highly poisonous snakes. Only then will they be able to sneak into the camp at night. In this way, the therapist attempts to increase the boy's low tolerance for frustration: up to now, he has scarcely been able to tolerate any tension in the play scenarios but has always ended the game quickly by shooting everyone down. As a permanent double, the therapist attempts to steer the boy's fantasies of omnipotence from a destructive course to a constructive one. For example, in the swamp area, he discovers that an American soldier has fallen in and no one wants to rescue him because all the other soldiers are afraid of the poisonous snakes. He quickly changes his role and plays that of the drowning soldier who is calling for help. As the Terminator, Alex can then risk his life to fight against the snakes and rescue the soldier. For this heroic act, he is rewarded by the general (again played by the therapist in a role change) with the highest medal of bravery. As the characters approach the ninja camp, the male therapist briefly interrupts the scenario as a play leader and proposes an alternative to the perpetrator/victim scenarios that the group has played up to now. He asks the boys if it could happen that the ninjas capture the rice farmer, who has fallen into a trap; then the Terminator could sneak into their camp at night and free the farmer. As they are escaping, however, a guard discovers them and a chase begins. The children agree to this scenario only if the ninjas can capture the two intruders. Alex is not able to accept this limitation on his omnipotence. The farmer should be captured, but he is able to reach a helicopter in the nick of time and fly off in a rain of bullets. Since the children have delayed the fight scene up to now out of fear that Alex will once again mow them all down with his machine gun, they agree to this idea. In this session, the children are able to play out their scenario to the end without constantly being disturbed by Alex's uncontrolled behaviour. For the first time, in the closing round, they say that they were able to play well with Alex today. Alex himself also states that the various adventures he had to go through in the role of the Terminator were exciting for him.

The permanent double method is also indicated in the case of children who have a limited capacity for play. Particularly preschool children from environments where they receive little support need one of the two therapists to act as a permanent double in order that their play does not become chaotic and out of hand or peter out into a rigid play structure. Thus, for example, in a group of boys who are playing jungle animals, the therapist can offer to play the role of a lion; then, as the lion, he can encourage the other predators to sneak up on a buffalo (represented with cloths), encircle it and at the signal of a hiss, attack it as a group and eat it.

3. Explorative doubling

We can use explorative doubling to enquire about the children's feelings, the content of their experiences or their intentions. If one of the therapists wonders aloud in his or her role—or the two therapists discuss with one another—why a child or the group is behaving in a particular way and what might be going on with him or her, they prompt the children to examine the phenomenon and perhaps say something in response. The therapists can also incorporate interpretations into these soliloquies or dialogues.

Example

Six-year-old Johannes has been accepted into the therapy group because he is very inhibited in relationships and stutters. According to his parents' account, in his first four years of life, he was a lively child—even rather wild. As the only child in his whole extended family, he received a great deal of admiration and attention. He reacted almost as if in shock to the birth of his brother (and his own accompanying dethronement) with the inhibition of all of his impulses— and he began to stutter. He became a dejected, docile child who clung closely to his mother. In the initial phase of the children's therapy group, which at first consists of only three boys, Johannes plays the role of an aggressive tiger who repeatedly attacks and injures the therapists (in the roles of animal researchers). Given that Johannes behaved in a very depressed manner in the preceding family meetings, the therapists are completely surprised by the liveliness of his play in the first sessions. However, when an additional boy joins the group in the third session and plays the role of a small, orphaned baby puma that needs to be cared for, Johannes has a severe reaction to the repetition of his own history. While the other children continue to play wild animals in the rain forest, Johannes changes his role. He decides to play a German shepherd that guards the animal research station. In this role, he remains lying in his kennel almost all the time, scarcely moving. Whereas he previously played the role of the tiger with glowing eyes and great physical commitment, he now becomes very depressed and tense. In the roles of the animal researchers, the therapists wonder aloud about the animals as they lie in their beds at night: 'Can you understand why Bello, who used to be so wild, has now suddenly become so tame? Ever since the little puma arrived at the animal station, it is as if he has been transformed. It is as if all of his power has been locked up. I can't explain how this could have happened.' The male researcher considers: 'It seems like Bello is paralysed. Could it be a sickness that is limiting his movement so much?' The female researcher expresses her doubts: 'Didn't you notice that Bello became so tame when the little puma appeared and we had to care for this little orphaned animal so much and couldn't spend as much time in the rainforest?' The male researcher answers: 'Do you mean that maybe Bello thinks we don't have time for him anymore—that we can't pay attention to him and care for him enough? Could it be that he now has to lie down in front of our door and doesn't let himself jump about and be wild because he thinks we wouldn't notice him otherwise?' The female researcher observes: 'Maybe he also thinks that we only like small, quiet animals and not the big and lively ones?' Johannes, who, like the other children has been listening to the therapists' dialogue with great interest, suddenly says that he is becoming very ill during the night. The researchers will notice it in the morning, and then they will not have so much time to study the other animals. They have to stay with him because he is dying. Since the other children also need the animal researchers' attention, the therapists split up. The male therapist goes into the rain forest, films the wild animals and admires their strength, beauty and agility; meanwhile, the female therapist takes care of Bello and expresses her worries about him aloud. She wonders whether they paid too little attention to Bello while they were working on films in the rainforest. Maybe they didn't care for him enough and this is why he became susceptible to illness. Johannes says she must stay by his sickbed all the time; otherwise he will immediately get much worse. When the other children notice the care Johannes is receiving in the role of Bello, suddenly all of the animals fall ill. All of them have to be brought into the animal hospital. The researchers hurry back and forth, caring for the sick animals and wonder whether the animals think that only small or sick animals will be cared for and large and strong animals will be left alone.

In addition to the possibility of enquiring about a child's behaviour from their transferred roles, the therapists may also assume an explorative role—for example, that of a doctor or a reporter—and address questions to the children in this role. Faith in the children's creativity constitutes the fundamental attitude of a psychodrama therapist (Krüger 2002, p. 293). Therefore, he or she has the important task of using the children's own creativity to find solutions and encouraging creative processes in search of those solutions.

Example

A mixed group of twelve-year-olds wants to play *Schwarzwaldklinik* [*The Black Forest Clinic*—a popular German television medical drama]. All of them are crazy patients and the therapists are assigned to be psychiatrists. During their rounds, the two doctors wonder aloud how the patients have come to be so crazy. When they examine Julius—playing the role of the 19-year-old patient Mike, who twitches and flails about—the doctors wonder how he lost control over his body; Mike says that he was poisoned as a baby. Unconsciously, Julius has provided a biographical explanation: his mother is an alcoholic. When Julius was 18 months old, he was brought to an orphanage in a state of total neglect; there, his extreme aggression attracted attention. As the doctors are considering a therapy for the character of Mike, Julius says that he needs sugar water; then he will become normal again. The therapists accept this suggestion for therapy, saying that after all the bitterness that Mike has experienced, he now needs a great deal of sweetness and attention from the doctors.

Anne—whose parents are completely focused on their business, leaving their accident-prone daughter to her own devices—plays the role of the 18-year-old patient Jane, who constantly falls out of her bed and seriously injures herself. When the doctors asked how this falling sickness could have come about, Anne answers that she fell off a table when she was a small child. She can only be healed if the doctors hold her hands, both left and right. The doctors then make the diagnosis that Jane received too little attention when she was small. Therefore it was no wonder that she injured herself. Apparently she had to grow up much too early. They prescribe a stay for her in the clinic, where she will be well cared for and watched over until she can really grow up. The doctors make similar observations with the other patients. Thus, at the symbolic level, each child can receive an explanation for his or her behavioural disorders in coded form—and at the same time, unconsciously gain access to solutions for her problems.

This explorative doubling can also be used when the dynamic in the group suddenly shifts and the therapists do not immediately know how to explain the change.

Example

A mixed group of seven-year-olds have been playing a farm scenario for the past several sessions. In the next session, when the female therapist is absent due to illness, the children—in the roles of pigs—become extremely hungry. The male therapist, in the role of the farmer, cannot satisfy the pigs' uncanny greed, even though he brings in enormous amounts of feed. He wonders why the animals cannot be satisfied. Could it be because the pigs miss the female farmer? Then the children say: 'During the night, we steal the farm wife's most beautiful clothes. But the farmer doesn't notice; he is fast asleep.' The leader asks how the farmer should react the next morning when he sees what has happened; the children answer he should scold them terribly. When the farmer then enters the barn early the next morning, he is horrified to see the pigs wearing his wife's clothes. He scolds them for taking such a liberty. Then he wonders, however: 'Could it be that with pigs it is the same way as with children—that when they miss their mother they need at least a scarf that smells like their mother?' At this, all the pigs cuddle up in the clothing and lie close together in the barn. After a while, they give the instruction: 'Now the farmer goes to sleep. And we steal the tractor and drive away on it; but we drive off a cliff and are taken to the hospital. You do not notice anything. But in the morning the police telephone and scold you because you were not paying attention.' The pigs have great fun driving the tractor around until they have the accident. Then the children bandage their heads, arms or legs, quickly build a hospital and lie down injured in the beds. When the children say: 'Now it is morning,' the farmer goes into the barn to feed the pigs. He is alarmed to see that the barn is empty and he becomes very worried. One child changes his role and telephones in the role of a police officer: he scolds the farmer and threatens him with prison. The farmer reproaches himself and anxiously hurries to the hospital. Now the children say that he should first scold them but then become kind when he sees them lying there injured.

In the next session, when the female therapist is back again, the children want to continue playing at the point where they had to stop. They want the farm woman to come to the hospital with her husband, be alarmed and reproach herself. The children clearly enjoy the farm woman's wailing and self-reproach. The two farmers then carry the injured pigs home and care for them. They quickly get well and suddenly transform themselves into vicious animals who attack the female farmer in particular; they bite her, poop in her bed and lay waste to the farmyard. In desperation, the farm woman calls the vet. She does not understand what has happened to her formerly well-behaved animals. The male therapist changes roles and arrives as the vet. He diagnoses the pigs with 'anger sickness' and asks: 'Have the pigs been left alone or neglected? Because that is often the cause of this illness.' When the farm woman guiltily admits that she left the animals alone, the vet prescribes plenty of attention and stroking, because this is the best medicine. The farm woman doubts the effectiveness of this prescription: the animals are so dangerous. Nevertheless, she then carefully strokes the animals' heads; they quietly extend their heads toward her and smile. At this, the vet says: 'So you see how good this affectionate stroking is for the pigs. This medicine works immediately.'

4. Ambivalent doubling

In adult therapy, two doubling individuals placed on the left and right behind the protagonist each represent one of the opposing tendencies, with the aim of bringing the protagonist out of an ambivalent state. In children's therapy, on the other hand, the therapists—in the roles that the children have assigned to them—conduct a dialogue in which each therapist represents one of the opposing tendencies.

Example

A group of twelve-year-olds are playing wild animals, such as panthers, jaguars and leopards. The therapists are assigned to play animal catchers who capture the animals and want to sell them to a zoo for a lot of money. Once the wild animals have been delivered to the zoo, they become sick. The children say that the male therapist should now play a vet. All of the vet's attempts to save the animals fail; the animals only become much sicker. At this, the vet wonders whether it is even possible for wild animals to get well in a zoo—in captivity. Perhaps they need to be able to run free in order to become well, but lose their vital life energy when they are in captivity. In response, the children give the vet the direction to scold the zookeeper. He reproaches the zookeeper (played by the female therapist), telling her how irresponsible it is to fence in and isolate such beautiful wild animals. It is no wonder that they are dying in captivity. He threatens the zookeeper with charges of animal abuse. The children are visibly enjoying these accusations, and give the therapist the direction to scold even more. They then escape from the zoo and once again become strong, wild animals when they can run free. The vet admires their strength, agility and natural grace from a distance. After a time, however, they return to the zoo, become ill again and need to be cared for. In the process, the children compete to see who can be sicker and require the most care. In a dialogue, the vet and the zookeeper represent the two opposing tendencies. The vet expresses the desire for freedom, independence and self-sufficiency, while the zookeeper verbalises the wish to continue being cared for and protected. They come to the conclusion that even wild animals must need both of these things.

With regressing children, the therapists can address the regressive and progressive tendencies through ambivalent doubling. Thus, for example, in the roles of a farm couple, they could lie in bed at night and share their thoughts about the little cat that is sleeping in its basket beside the farmers' bed. The farm woman speaks about how much care and protection the little cat still needs; her husband comments on how much its teeth and claws have already grown and that when it is ready, the little cat will certainly use them to catch the mice that are always sneaking into the larder and gnawing on the cheese and sausages.

4.2.8 Interpretive Interventions

According to Moreno (1973, p. 77), in psychodrama, insight takes place through action: psychodrama is the method 'which reveals the soul's truth through action'. Therefore, no interpretation can take place without preceding psychodramatic action.

By playing the roles that are transferred onto them—both directly and symbolically—and as objects of transference, paying attention to what they perceive and experience in themselves through concordant or complementary identification, the therapists can gather valuable material to help them understand and interpret the inner processes that are at work in the children. Their countertransference—through which they react to transference from individual children and from the group as a whole—will show them what an individual child or the group of children feels about them and how they behave toward them. If the therapists are able to control their own personal feelings and see through the children's play scenario, then they will have a strong basis for demonstrating their transference or their object relationship to the children in a clear and lively manner and making the children conscious of it. In this regard, the therapists' participation in the play is an act of interpretation. Nevertheless, there is an inherent danger—which Rubner and Rubner (1982, p. 22) rightly point out—that because of their own personal problems, fears and desires (ultimately, that is, due to uncontrolled countertransference), the therapists may lose their distance from the children and from themselves and thereby repeat the play scenario which the children have created and which they actually intended to free from the compulsion to repeat itself.

Example

Six-year-old children are playing a farm scenario during the initial phase. Due to another important appointment, the male therapist is unable to take part in the session, so the female therapist is alone in the role of the farm woman. The children are very young animals that still require a great deal of care. One girl, who is being raised by a single mother and has had to take care of herself from very early on, is playing the role of a cat. In the role of the farm woman, the female therapist rushes back and forth tending to the wishes of the little animals. Eventually it becomes too much for her. She then praises the cat: she is glad that the cat is able to take care of herself and catch mice, and that she doesn't need the farm woman's help. Without realising it, the therapist is reinforcing the behaviour of a child who also tries to unburden her mother at home. It is only in supervision that the therapist remembers that the cat was injured at the beginning of the play scenario and could have used the farm woman's care. At the same time, she recognises that she has treated the girl in the same way that the girl's mother treated her: the mother also always praised her daughter's self-sufficiency in order to unburden herself.

In addition to interpretation through action, it can be important to point out to children which roles they repeatedly assign to the therapists or to other children and which roles they choose for themselves. This can help children achieve immediate comprehension and an experience of insight.

Example

In a mixed group of eight-year-olds, it so happens that all three of the boys suffer from the same situation at home: all of them have younger sisters who monopolise their parents' attention. In the initial phase, the three girls in the group are playing little animals on a farm. The boys, on the other hand, want to be trappers out in the wilderness. At the request of the girls, the two therapists are to play the farmers. When asked, the boys agree to this transference of roles. At night, however, when the animals and the farmers are sleeping, the boys arrive in the roles of werewolves; they attack the animals and want to drink their blood. The farmers are only able to chase them away by force. In the next session, the boys repeat this scenario. Even though the therapists ask every time whether the boys really want to be alone while both therapists care for the animals in the roles of farmers, the boys confirm this choice of roles. After the scene is repeated for the third time, the therapists refuse to accept their roles. They address the fact that the boys always agree to the role assignments; however, it seems that they are quite annoyed that the girls take over so much of the therapists' attention. It is similar to the situation at home, the therapists point out, where the little sisters completely occupy the parents. Following this verbal interpretation, the boys are able to express their anger that the girls—like the little sisters at home—are drawing all of their parents' attention toward themselves. The boys then express the wish that the male therapist play the role of a trapper along with them. When the trappers sell furs at the farm and receive milk and bread in return, a connection is created between the boys' and the girls' play scenarios.

In children's psychodrama, interpretations most often take place during play, at the symbolic level, when one of the therapists makes observations in his or her role in a soliloquy—or the two therapists do so in a dialogue—questioning or trying to explain the behaviour of a child in his or her role or of the group as a whole. Thus, for example, the farmer (the therapist) wonders why Bello the dog (Franz) has become so vicious. Maybe he started biting because the farmers were so busy with their work that they didn't even notice him and haven't been taking care of him. This symbolic form of interpretation provokes less fear and resistance on the part of the children. It allows them to make the connection to their own selves at the point when they are ready to do so. Furthermore, they allow the highly expressive images created by the children's unconscious minds remain in place—images whose depth cannot be fathomed in words.

We rarely make genetic interpretations; more often, we make interpretations which improve the connection to reality and pertain to the current relationship. These interpretations must be tailored to the children's language as well as to their level of emotional and cognitive development. It is also important that we express them gently in order that the children do not develop a resistance to the play scenario. Children will also usually defend themselves when they are not ready to accept an interpretation. For example, they might say, 'You go to sleep now and don't talk anymore.' Or if the therapists have been captured, they simply bind up their mouths. Since the reality that we comment on in the interpretation is also what they are experiencing in the action of the game, it is often possible to observe its effect immediately in the further progress of the action.

Example

A mixed group of twelve-year-olds are playing a royal court scenario. The girls are playing princesses who get into an argument with the queen, played by the female therapist. Two boys play the roles of court huntsmen. René, whose mother treats him as a substitute partner—he sleeps in his mother's bed, is not allowed to grow up and is therefore failing miserably in school—chooses the role of the queen's valet. The male therapist is assigned to play the king. A fierce dispute arises between the princesses and the queen. When the queen faces increasingly vicious attacks and insults, she does not call the king to her defence; instead she calls the valet. Since there was a conflict between the two therapists shortly before the start of the session, and the female therapist is unable to control her anger at the male therapist during the play scenario, she stages a repetition of a domestic scene for René. She says to René: 'So that you can support me in difficult times, I hereby make you a knight.' At this, René cries out 'Oh no!' and falls 'unconscious'. The male therapist comes to the valet's aid and says aloud 'The queen's wish seems to be too much for the valet. He doesn't even seem to be able to defend himself against it. Maybe he is afraid that she will have a breakdown without him—or that he might be fired if he says no. Actually, it is the king's job to promote pages to knighthood.' When the valet regains consciousness, the king says to him, 'Valet, you don't have to worry about the queen anymore. I will support her in her disputes with our daughters. Now you can join in the tournament with the other pages and have adventures. Prepare yourself for the knighting ceremony. In one month, I will dub you and the other pages to knighthood.' René beams in response to this supportive doubling and joins the other boys.

In order to temper their interpretations—to make them less invasive and provoke less resistance—the therapists can also claim to have read the 'interpretation' in a book or heard it from someone else. They can also call imaginary experts and repeat their 'statements' out loud.

Example

A group of ten-year-old boys want to play ghosts. The therapists are assigned to play Ghostbusters. Uwe und Mark, who passively resist their very intrusive parents and are engaged in a power struggle with them, say that they are ghosts with negative energy who can knock the Ghostbusters unconscious with a touch. The other two boys are ghosts who can cover the Ghostbusters with slime and frighten them. When the Ghostbusters are called into a haunted castle, they attempt to capture the ghosts with their suction machines. However, the ghosts Mark and Uwe render them completely weak and powerless, so that they are no longer able to carry their machines. The ghosts take their weapons from them without a struggle. Terrified, the Ghostbusters retreat to their office. In the roles of the castle owners, the children call and say that the Ghostbusters must come back to the castle immediately. The same sequence of events repeats itself. When the children want to repeat the scenario once again, the Ghostbusters speak loudly with each other in their office: 'We don't have a chance. It is pointless to get into a fight with the ghosts again. Even though we are famous

Ghostbusters, we do not have enough power over these ghosts.' The children protest and say that the Ghostbusters should come back one more time. However, the Ghostbusters refuse, saying they must first consult a specialised manual to find out how to deal with ghosts like these. They then read the section of the book aloud: 'Ghosts with negative energy are the ghosts of people who were not allowed to say no; they were not allowed to defend themselves openly. One must not fight with ghosts like these, since that will simply recharge their negative energy. The only thing to do is to politely request that they stop haunting on their own.' The Ghostbusters then consider out loud how they could save face with their employers—who, after all, want them to get rid of the ghosts—and still avoid engaging in a futile power struggle with the ghosts. Maybe they could ask the ghosts to not haunt the castle in such a scary way so that they don't frighten the castle owners so much. When they present this request to the invisible ghosts at the castle, the ghosts are willing to comply only under the condition that the Ghostbusters acknowledge the ghosts' power. The Ghostbusters admit their helplessness: they have experienced the power of the ghosts and realised that despite their state-of-the art technology and long experience, they are helpless against them. At this, the ghosts promise to be less bothersome and frightening to the castle owners if the latter agree not to fight against them anymore.

Interpretations can also emphasise the interpersonal context of a given role; the therapists can speak about the function that a certain child's behaviour plays in the group's interaction. In this way, the child as well as the group as a whole can recognise that this child's behaviour also serves the needs of the group.

Example

In a mixed group of ten-year-olds, the three boys choose the roles of wolves; the two girls want to play St Bernard dogs. They assign the female therapist the role of an animal protectionist; the male therapist is given the role of a hunter. In the play scenario, the wolves vehemently attack the hunter. When the dogs begin to bite him as well, and all five animals set upon him—which is clearly too much for the therapist—a conflict arises. The wolves want to have the hunter all to themselves, and they chase the dogs away. In this conflict situation, Achim places himself in the service of the group. (Achim is a boy who is treated as a substitute partner at home and he always volunteers to help the teacher in school; in this group he wants to dominate, but he avoids the rivalry conflicts among the boys.) He says the hunter should capture him and train him. This role change defuses the conflict. Once Achim—in the role of the wolf—has been captured and trained, the other wolves attack him and fight with him. The dogs, played by the girls, can now attack the hunter undisturbed. The hunter, for his part, is somewhat unburdened and has more breathing room. In this situation, the animal protectionist comes to visit the hunter. She expresses her surprise that the wild wolf has given up his freedom and is now protecting the hunter— that he is taking on the fight with the wild wolves and thereby bringing an end to the fight between the dogs and the wolves. The hunter replies that the wolf-dog has many advantages in the situation: as a house dog, he is treated well. Here, he does not have to vie for his position in the pack with the other wolves. The animals, lying in their caves and kennels, hear this short exchange. In the following session, Achim no longer wants to be a dog: he chooses the role of a wolf along with the other boys and begins to compete with them in the play scenario.

Through their interpretations, the therapists can also make the children conscious of the *hic et nunc* processes that take place within the group—and through which they fend off their fears, aggressions, conflicts and desires.

Example

In the last session before the long school holidays, the female therapist informs a group of eight-year-olds about the holiday break. The children do not react to the news verbally; instead they continue with their play scenario from the previous session, in which they played the roles of children with the therapists as their parents. Nevertheless, the announcement of the break greatly alters the game. The children secretly build a ship, without their parents' noticing anything. During the night, they sail away and discover an island where there is an abundance of delicious food. When the parents wake up and discover the empty nursery, they wail and cry and are very worried about their children. In order to interpret the children's reversal of their fear of being abandoned and the anger that this triggers into its opposite in order to protect themselves, the male therapist (in the role of the father) calls the police and tells the mother about the conversation. The police say (he tells her) that it is no wonder that the children have disappeared: after all, the parents wanted to simply go away on holiday and leave the children uncared-for. This is neglect, and it is a punishable offence. At this interpretation, the children react with the playing direction that it is night again, and the parents should lie in their beds and sleep. Then the children secretly sail back home; they attack the parents, tie them up and throw them in jail. Here, the parents are smeared with eggs; they have to drink a brown broth full of stinky noodles which gives them a terrible stomach-ache.

Particularly in children's psychodrama, the therapists need to be aware of the danger of interacting with the children and simply playing along with their game. Their task is rather, as Lebovici (1971, p. 331) describes it, to play 'without playing the sick person's game'. This demands from the therapists that on the one hand, they identify completely with the children's wishes and fears; at the same time, they must remain sufficiently removed that they can recognise the children's defence mechanisms and at the right moment, refuse to follow along with the children and their acts of resistance. In particular, monotonous repetitions in the game, in which a state of idling sets in and the therapeutic process does not progress, are a signal that something has been misunderstood. The children remain like unredeemed spirits, repeating stereotypical sequences until they can find a solution and a release. To simply rely on the children's inherent capacity for spontaneous development and allow them to play their roles as often as they wish (Pruckner 2001, p. 85) neglects the fact that children also require psychological support in order to break out of deadlocked patterns of play.

Example

A mixed group of eleven-year-olds, all of whom come from families affected by divorce, play out the same scenario over the course of several sessions: the three boys are football stars who want to fly to Brazil for the World Cup. One girl, who helps her mother care for her younger siblings at home, plays a doctor; the other two girls are models who want to travel to an important fashion show. The male therapist is assigned to play a pilot; the female therapist plays a flight attendant. The football players become drunk during the flight. One of the plane's engines fails; the pilot is unable to handle the breakdown, and the aircraft crashes in the jungle. According to the children's directions, the pilot and the flight attendant are lying unconscious inside the plane. The football players stagger drunkenly through the jungle, and the two models are completely helpless. All alone, the doctor takes over the responsibility of caring for the accident victims. The children repeat this play scenario over and over. Only in supervision do the therapists understand that in this symbolic catastrophe scenario, the children are acting out the divorce situation: with their drunken state, the boys are illustrating their sense of disorientation, but also the fact that they are not to blame for the misfortune of the divorce. It is only when the therapists comprehend this situation that they are able to propose alternative scenes with possibilities for new adventures and experiences. In the next session, when the children repeat the scene yet again, they no longer play the roles of the unconscious pilot and the helpless flight attendant. Instead, the pilot assumes responsibility for the crash. He should have done a better job of caring for and maintaining the aircraft. The female therapist also changes her role; in the role of the flight attendant, she cares for the injured passengers. Together, the two of them also take on the task of leading the football stars, the models and the doctor out of the jungle. The fact that the pilot takes the blame for the accident and both the pilot and the flight attendant feel obliged cope with the consequences of the crash changes the game. Suddenly, the football players are no longer drunk; instead, they angrily berate the pilot for bringing on the catastrophe. The girls now also express their needs: suddenly they are all badly injured, so that the flight attendant and the pilot need to treat their wounds, care for them, and carry them out of the jungle.

It is important to introduce the interpretation that is being acted out so that the therapists do not place themselves in danger of abusing their power. Before they precipitate a different outcome to the play scenario than that which the children wished for or feared—or perhaps even interrupt the scene—they must first speak about the feelings and tendencies that they believe the children are harbouring in the background of the game in a soliloquy or a dialogue, in order to thereby confront the children with themselves. Thus, for example, in a scenario in which the children constantly overpower the therapists, they could wonder aloud (in the roles of researchers) whether the prehistoric people are compelled to behave so aggressively toward them because they are afraid of being rendered powerless and helpless themselves. If these interpretations in soliloquies or dialogues between the therapists do not lead to a change, the therapists can go one step further within their transferred roles and—through the interpolation of the children's resistance—defy the children's wishes bit by bit and present them with small doses of tolerable and workable frustration. Step by step, for example, they limit the children's exaggerated fantasies of omnipotence in which they always want to win—without entering into a power struggle themselves.

Example

Over the course of several sessions, a group of eleven-year-old boys, playing Jedi knights, fight against aliens (the therapists), whom they hopelessly slaughter each time. Given that a monotonous repetition of the same scenario has set in, the therapists—in the roles of the aliens—begin toning down their own helplessness and limiting the power of the Jedi knights. The aliens, they say, have developed a new type of armour which the Jedi knights' laser beams cannot break through. Only on their feet do they still have a weak point which the laser beams can penetrate.

Only when all of these interventions have failed to bring about a change can the therapists confront the children with the intervention of 'active interpretation' (Anzieu 1984, p. 139 f). They assume a different attitude in the game than the one desired by the children and maintain it consistently until the children change their own behaviour. Contrary to the children's expectations and the roles they have assigned them, the therapists vary the roles that they embody. They can maintain this to the point of revoking the corresponding role and refusing to continue playing in the assigned role configuration—provided always that the children can tolerate these interventions.

Example

For a period of several weeks, a group of ten-year-olds remain immersed in a state of narcissistic and megalomaniacal satisfaction, in which the therapists must subject themselves to the children's fantasies of omnipotence. The boys play the roles of wild cowboys; the female therapist is a saloon owner and the male therapist is the sheriff. Again and again, the wild gang of cowboys ride into town, smash up the saloon and beat up the sheriff when he tries to maintain order. They humiliate him in every possible way and render him powerless. They cut off his hair and make him take off his uniform and stand there naked. The gang make him dance, and shoot at his feet so that he has to hop and jump. They give him pee to drink when he is thirsty and poop to eat when he is hungry. After interpretations and attempts on the part of the therapists to fight against this powerless fail to make any difference, the sheriff consults with the saloon owner during the next session: 'I'm not going to go on being so stupid as to put my life at risk. I am constantly being shamed and humiliated. I am going to hang up my sheriff's star, quit my job and get out of town.' The saloon owner adopts the opposite standpoint in the conversation: 'You can't do that: then everyone in town will laugh at you and call you a coward.' The sheriff answers: 'I would rather let myself be laughed at than be killed.' The saloon owner agrees with him: 'Yes, I am also sick and tired of having to fix up my saloon all the time. I'm going to ride off with you and move to another town.' The two of them then ride away, telling the children that they have left the town unnoticed and are already far away. When one of the boys says that they have better horses and they will catch up with the sheriff and the saloon owner, the therapists refuse to play along: they say that they rode away during the night and are already over the hills and far away. Another boy says the sheriff's horse is lame and he will have to continue on foot. The sheriff disagrees: he says his horse is fine, and he is already in another town where he cannot be found. At this, the boys become angry and start to complain. After all, they say, they should be able to decide what the group will play: the leader assured them of this at the beginning. This is once again typical of adults, the children say: they never do what the children want—they only make empty promises. Now they don't feel like playing anymore. In the closing round, the therapists give feedback on the roles. In their roles, they felt that it was necessary to flee from a situation in which they were only being constantly humiliated and rendered powerless. The children must be familiar with this feeling. However, it will not help them to simply turn the tables here in the group. In the following session, the group begins to approach reality more closely. The children want to play pirates while the therapists are soldiers on a disguised merchant ship. Battles arise in which it is possible for the children to alternate between power and powerlessness.

Before the therapists step into the children's play scenario with such a major intervention, they must carefully determine whether they have allowed the children enough room to develop freely. For example, particularly in the case of aggressive children, fantasies of their own grandiosity are important for neutralising aggression. They open up possibilities for the children to cope with threatening aspects of their lives through the fantasy of omnipotence and to thereby overcome the fear of their suppressed feelings of helplessness, powerlessness and abandonment. It is only possible to gradually confront children with reality once they have been able to strengthen their own Selves. Therefore, we must permit these fantasies of omnipotence to exist for a long time, as counterparts to the children's own powerlessness, helplessness and fear. Only through a corrective relationship experience can these images of themselves gradually become more realistic. It is also important to help children not to live out their fantasies of omnipotence at the expense of others, but rather to act out their powerful ideals in such a way that they can be useful or helpful to others. Children require the help of the therapists in order to find hero figures or stories which do not simply contain the interaction models of victim/perpetrator or powerful character/powerless character. In the television series that the children tend to draw on for their play scenarios, for example, omnipotence is achieved exclusively through physical or armed force. In fairy tales and heroic myths, on the other hand, a character can achieve heroism through cleverness, tenacity, helpfulness, love or the capacity to learn.

4.2.9 Active Interpretation with Traumatised Children

In the case of traumatised children, we had to learn to change the children's roles—or the psychological aspect of their roles—through active interpretation. Traumatised children can continue to act out distressing violent or sexual content over a period of weeks or months or remain bogged down in the aggressive patterns of perpetrator/victim inversion without any visible signs of the 'healing power' of play—without processing anything or setting any development in motion. In role inversions, they play the roles of brutal offenders and assign the therapists the roles of helpless and defenceless victims who are exposed to violence. In these victim roles, the therapists experience feelings of total helplessness, victimisation and hopelessness, of desperation and waiting in vain for help. By verbalising these feelings in soliloquies or dialogues, they can express—through this act of mirroring—how it feels to be a victim, completely without hope that anyone will come and help them and bring the horror to an end, and that this situation is unbearable. With such soliloquies, they can at least communicate to the child that they understand his or her message within the play scenario and acknowledge the horrific experiences that the child has had to endure—often over a period of years—without receiving any help or protection.

Example

In the opening round, a group of ten-year-old boys who have experienced early childhood trauma propose playing the roles of mass murderers; the therapists should play a couple taking a hiking holiday in the mountains. While we are admiring the alpine meadows, the boys approach us in a friendly manner as mushroom-gatherers and invite us to join them for a picnic. We are enjoying their hospitality when suddenly, out of the clear blue sky, they attack us and beat us up. We cry about how terrible it is when a pleasant scene suddenly changes into its opposite and we—although we are completely blameless—have to helplessly endure all of this. The murderers laugh at this and simply say: 'Tough luck!'—and then throw us into an abyss. Then, as children, they give us the direction to enter the scene as a new couple who want to go camping in the alpine meadow. Once again, they approach us in a friendly way and tell us about a nearby cave where there are beautiful stones and minerals. Would we like them to show us this cave? When, according to their direction, we follow them—naïve and unsuspecting, looking forward to this amazing sight—we are once again attacked without warning and slowly chopped into pieces.

In the next session, the boys repeat the symbolic staging of their traumatic experiences. They assign the female therapist to play the role of a famous singer; the male therapist is given the role of her chauffeur. When (according to their directions) we get out of the car to admire the beautiful view, they secretly install a remote control system into our sports car so that they can now control the vehicle. As if controlled by magic, the car no longer drives the way the chauffeur intends; instead, it drives backward into a cave. Here, the murderers are already waiting for us. Before we are really able to comprehend the situation through all of our confusion, we are already being dragged out of the car and tortured. The boys egg each other on to see who can come up with a more violent idea. And unlike other children—for whom identification with the aggressor leads to an experience of overcoming fear and discovering a capacity for control, and who then become calmer—these boys become increasingly excited. The result is a heated play situation without any cathartic effect. We beg for mercy, wail and moan. Yet the more we express our helplessness and powerlessness, the more they ridicule us and the more brutally they treat us.

In the next session, when the boys want to continue playing this perpetrator/victim scenario, we ask them whether people have begun to talk about the mysterious disappearance of all of these tourists, and whether the police have begun to investigate. The boys agree: by now, they say, the mass murderers have been sentenced in absentia to death in the electric chair. However, the simple-minded police are fooled by the mass murderers' friendliness and do not recognise their deception. When we land in the alpine meadow in our helicopter, the murderers present themselves as peaceful mountain farmers who want to help the police track down the criminals. They lead us on the wrong track, and while we are collecting evidence, they suddenly attack us. They cut off the policewoman's breasts and vulva and the policeman's penis and sew each one's sexual organs back onto the other person. Once again, we verbalise the shame and total helplessness of having to endure all of these things and being unable to defend ourselves. It is unbearable, we say, and we lapse into unconsciousness. But the murderers revive us with electric shocks: they say we have to witness and endure all of the torture in a fully conscious state. Finally they use dynamite to blow us up.

Once again, the children let us relive their traumatic experiences, in which neither the child welfare office nor the courts were able to hold the offenders in check or bring an end to the abuse and neglect of the children.

In the next session, when the boys yet again wish to continue the game in which innocent tourists are murdered, we ask them whether it would be possible for someone to come to the aid of the helpless and innocent victims. The boys whisper to one another and then declare with a grin that they will now be a UN peacekeeping troop to whom the victims can flee. However, when, greatly relieved, we run to the peacekeepers in the hope that we have escaped the criminals and that the horrors will now be at an end, they take us prisoner and begin to torture us. When we protest and express our outrage, they retort that we are telling lies: we are probably the guilty ones. The male therapist protests and asks to speak to their superior. One boy switches to the role of the general. The therapist complains about the brutal treatment: a peacekeeping troop, he says, needs to protect the weak and should not commit any acts of violence. The general laughs at him, saying that they are the strong ones; they are always right and can therefore do whatever they wish. The general beats the therapist up, and we are slowly tortured to death. The more we verbalise our weakness and helplessness, the more extreme the destructive acts become. Again, in a dialogue, we express our deep disappointment that our hopes were shattered in this way, that we went out of the frying pan and into the fire.

Some of the boys had had the painful experience in their own lives that after their mothers separated from the violent father, they took a new partner who was also violent or was addicted to drugs or alcohol, and who took advantage of the child's desire for closeness by abusing him. Therefore, at the symbolic level, they were restaging their experience of being abused further under the guise of care.

The children were trying to protect themselves from being overwhelmed by powerlessness, as well as from object loss, not only through identification with the offender (if I behave the way he does), but also through offender introjection (if I also think and feel the way he does), and as a countermove, they massively disparaged the weaker characters. Therefore, in the next session, when the boys wanted to continue enacting the perpetrator/victim scenario, we resorted to the intervention of 'constructing a good introject' in order to lead them from identification with the perpetrator to identification with the rescuer. Dorothea Weinberg, who also conducted psychodramatic work with traumatised children, arrived at a similar point: 'Since the severely traumatised child cannot spontaneously produce any defensive reaction and cannot even express a plea for protection—and it is possible that some children cannot even perceive a need for protection—the intervention of "constructing good inner entities" begins at this void' (Weinberg 2006, 2.A., p. 206).

Example

In the opening round, we ask the children directly whether in this session they might play the bravest heroes in the world, whom the German Federal President has asked for help in freeing innocent victims from the grip of violent criminals and finally putting a stop to the mass murderers who have eluded capture for years. We, the two therapists, would take on the roles of the criminals, whom the heroes will overpower in a difficult fight. This heroic act would then be rewarded with the highest medal of bravery and broadcast in television reports all over the world. The boys accept this offer to play positive heroes. They decide to play the special unit IMF (Impossible Missions Force); the male therapist is assigned to play a mass murderer who has a secret hiding place in the sewer system. Here he carries out gruesome experiments with kidnapped children and sells their organs to a scientist, played by the female therapist. The scientist is aware of the atrocities, but she portrays herself in public as ignorant and blameless. The agents must then overcome many challenges (disabling alarm systems and explosive traps; crossing through a room filled with poisonous snakes) before they can rescue the injured children (hand puppets). According to the children's directions, we should attempt to flee in a sports car. However, the agents have secretly installed a computer inside the car ahead of time. When we already believe that we have escaped, the agents take terrible vengeance on us via remote control. We have to endure alternating baths—first freezing cold, then scorching heat—then we are deprived of air until we nearly suffocate; next we are crushed by extreme pressure. While we wail and cry, the agents call out to us over a loudspeaker: now we should get a feel for what we have done to the children. Finally, they bring us to a cell on death row where we are beheaded. Afterward, the male therapist switches into the role of the President of the United States (according to the children's direction) and presents the agents with the highest medal of bravery, which they receive with their chests swelling with pride. The international press (the female therapist) immediately broadcasts the scene around the world.

The children continue to play the roles of rescuing heroes in later sessions. Here, we cannot expect them to play humane rescuers. The decisive factor is that in the roles of positive heroes, they are allowed to play out their affect toward the perpetrators—they can act out all of their rage and desire for revenge cathartically in symbolic play. Bit by bit, they pay the offenders back for the suffering they have endured: this has nothing to do with sadism, since the children comply perfectly with the limitations of 'as if' play. The aim here is not to build social competence, but rather that through their identification with the benevolent heroes, the children permit themselves to experience care and empathy.

Thus, the intervention starts from the point of traumatised children's experience of receiving no help or protection and therefore being subjected to complete powerlessness. However, this method of constructing good introjects functions only through the identification with strong, invincible 'good heroes', and not through identification with the weak and helpless. Nevertheless, it is essential that the children take the position on the side of the helpless victims—even if they play the roles of brutal avengers—and not on the side of the violent perpetrators. And many therapy sessions will be necessary before it is also possible to integrate the weak and vulnerable side.

4.3 The Closing Phase

The conclusion of a session poses particular difficulties since, in the course of a symbolic play scenario, intense emotional processes are set in motion over a short period of time, and they now need to abate or be calmed down. The goal of the closing phase is to conclude the action—the play scenario—and allow for a brief look back at what has taken place. We bring the play phase to an end approximately ten minutes before the end of the session, by means of a closing ritual. For example, in a session where the children have played the roles of wild animals and the leaders were animal catchers we say: 'Unfortunately the time is up and we have to stop playing. Night is falling and the animals go to sleep in their lairs.' Accompanied by the trickling sound of the rain stick, the leaders continue: 'Now we are no longer the animal catchers; we are Ms. G. and Mr. A. again. And you are no longer the wild animals. You are no longer a tiger; you are Andi. You are no longer a crocodile; you are Hans', etc. When prompting the children to shed the roles they have assumed in the game—initiating the 'de-rolling' process—the therapists must behave very decisively. Particularly if the game was very exciting or they were fully immersed in their fantasies of omnipotence, the children will want to continue playing—to maintain their roles and not be confronted with reality. During the initial phase with the group, it is important to explain the closing phase emphatically so that the children realise that it is not something they can haggle over. Otherwise, in the later group phase, they will tend to want to eliminate this closing phase in favour of the play phase. In order to suspend the play situation and the symbolic level of action and to reinstate the level of reality, the leaders also let the children take off their costumes and dismantle the scenery far enough that there are sufficient cushions available for the discussion round. In the process, the leaders must repeatedly intervene to provide structure—pointing out, for example, that this cushion is no longer a horse; now we need to use it as a seat cushion for the closing discussion round.

The therapists then ask the children to sit together in a circle for a short discussion round. They are insistent that the children join the circle—and they go after a child and bring him or her into the circle if, for example, he wants to remain in his cave or stay seated high upon his throne. Just as in the opening round, they must firmly insist upon this structure and may not allow themselves to be drawn into a power struggle. Again and again, children defy this request and try to alter the closing phase to suit themselves. This might be because they were aggressive during the play phase and are now feeling guilty and fearful of repercussions. It may be because they do not want to step back out of their fantasies of omnipotence or because they wish to continue the theme that was enacted in the symbolic play— namely, rendering powerful figures powerless—in the real situation. The leaders can also address this resistance interpretively, saying, for example: 'In the game you were very powerful and strong. Now you are suddenly supposed to be a child again, who has to obey the adults. That is very difficult.' Or: 'In the game you were a wild and ferocious animal: maybe you are afraid that we will be angry at you for that now. But in the game you were very careful not to really hurt us.' Children who are so wound up that they cannot calm down—or refuse to do so—need the security provided by the leaders. Therefore, it can be important to take a child by the hand and ask him or her to sit down beside one of the therapists.

In comparison with adult therapy, the discussion phase is much shorter. We only request that the children give us general feedback. We ask them how they felt during the play scenario, what they liked and what they didn't like. Most often, the children simply say it was 'great', 'cool', 'dumb' or something similar.

Reflection during this discussion phase takes place primarily through the leaders. They give the children a brief feedback in which they highlight any new alternatives for action or behaviour that the children have tried out in a positive way in the hope of reinforcing them. Thus, for example, they acknowledge the usually aggressive Franz: 'You were a very wild and dangerous puma again. But today you were very careful not to hurt anyone. I like that.' To Jutta, a shy girl, they say: 'Today the mouse dared to steal the bacon from the farmers. The way you quickly snuck into the pantry without anyone noticing you—that was super.' They also address the conflict between the boys and the girls: 'Even though it wasn't easy at first to find a subject that everyone liked, during the game you found a lot of good ideas for how you could play together.'

The leaders do not demand that the children give a role feedback like that which is done in adult therapy. However, they speak briefly about how they themselves felt in their roles. If it seems appropriate and there is an opportunity to do so, they then ask the children whether they have also had similar experiences, thus inviting them to briefly share their feelings. For example, a leader might say: 'When I was playing the king and was so walled in and unable to move, then I realised what it is like when someone else is commanding you and you can't defend yourself. Maybe you also felt like that today when we told you that there will only be five more sessions with this group?' Or: 'When I came into the jungle as an animal catcher, I didn't know my way around and heard all sorts of threatening sounds, I became very afraid. Maybe you feel like that, too, if you have to enter into a group and don't know what is going to happen.' Sometimes the children pick up on the subjects which the leaders have addressed in the role feedback and give their own brief contribution. For example, when the leader speaks about how humiliating it was to be laughed at in the role of the sheriff, and asks whether the children also sometimes feel this way, one boy says: 'Yes—this morning the whole class was laughing when I gave a wrong answer in a lesson. I thought that was very mean.'

In this discussion phase, however, we do not interpret the children's play in the same way as it is done in analytical psychodrama. Nor are we concerned with the emotional and rational processing of the play sequence, as in adult psychodrama. Instead, the aim of the closing phase in children's psychodrama is to bring the action to a conclusion, to bring the emotional processes of the action phase into a state of calm and to make it possible to take a brief look back at what has taken place.

With very restless children, it has proven useful to leave the 'playing stage' and return to another room (the 'meeting stage') to conduct this closing round.

In the case of traumatised children with attachment disorders, for whom the end of every session feels threatening and triggers a high degree of stress, a consistent closing ritual can help alleviate this situation. Thus, for example, in his group work with severely traumatised children in residential care, Stefan Flegelskamp (verbal statement) developed a closing ritual in which the children lie on their bellies on mats and each of the therapists lays his or her hands on the backs of two children and gently massages them (provided the children wish them to); at the same time, one of the therapists retells the story that has just been acted out, emphasising the successful scenes and brave role choices.

We do not ask the children to tidy up in the group room; we do this ourselves, because we do not wish to end the session with a pedagogical measure. In the past, when we used to ask the children to tidy everything up afterwards, we experienced the great degree to which the clean-up at the end of the session provoked negative transference emotions that were associated with disciplinary struggles with their parents. We were then forced to battle with the children when they tried to flee from the room or created more of a mess in order to provoke us.

The Complete Group Process

5

Walter Holl

Abstract

In this chapter, we will place our focus on the group process. The optimum effect of a group therapy process can be achieved in 30–50 sessions, which corresponds to a time period of 1–1½ years. However, this does not preclude the possibility that with focussed work, results can be achieved over a period of fewer sessions.

We divide the overall process into three phases:

- The beginning phase, covering approximately 5–10 sessions,
- the middle phase
- and the concluding phase, consisting of approximately 10 sessions.

5.1   The Beginning Phase

With respect to the overall process, this is the 'warming-up' period. According to Petzold (1985), the purpose of this phase is to 'to foster the cohesion of the group, develop a "we" feeling and to reduce resistance. (…) however, the "warming-up" process applies not only to the group as a whole, but also to the individual participants and to the leader of the psychodrama' (p. 131). During this phase, the children develop their first group theme, into which each child can incorporate his or her own personal set of problems. In the case of six-year-olds, this often occurs as early as in the first two sessions; eleven-year-olds generally require more time for this.

© Springer Fachmedien Wiesbaden GmbH 2017   91
A. Aichinger and W. Holl, *Group Therapy with Children*,
DOI 10.1007/978-3-658-15813-2_5

We would like to describe the following goals of the beginning phase in more concrete terms:

- Reducing anxiety
- Discussing the contracts
- Introducing symbolic play
- Communicating rules and boundaries
- Bringing the group together as a unit.

Reducing anxiety

With five-year-old children, we repeatedly have the experience that they will only enter the group room together with their mother or father and that even then, they are not yet able to part from their parents. We allow the parents to be present for several sessions—and in some cases even allow them to join in the play—until the children are able to separate from them. If, however, we realise (for example) that a mother is unable to detach from her child, it is necessary to address this dynamic in our meetings with the parents. Older children are generally no longer so anxious: above all, they no longer show it, or they compensate for their fears through loud or boastful behaviour. Therefore, we may underestimate the anxiety which, even among twelve-year-olds, might be quite significant. It is the therapists' task to speak about the fact that feelings of unfamiliarity and insecurity are normal in this situation.

In the group situation, we allow ourselves enough time to pick up on the contact with each child which was formed in the preliminary meetings. If, in the first session, a child does not participate in the play despite our help, we help him or her to find a place as a spectator and occasionally offer suggestions for roles or actions without putting any pressure on her. At the end of the session, we then try to give the child some positive feedback—for example, that it was completely fine to give herself some time and simply watch the action; however, we also saw that she participated very attentively with her eyes and ears, and perhaps she will feel like participating more actively in the next session.

Discussing the contracts

During the beginning phase, we should once again broach the subject, within the group context, of why each individual child has joined the group—naturally, of course, in a positive manner. We need to use our intuition to get a sense of when this can take place, keeping in mind the cohesion of the group and the overall atmosphere. The fifth session, in which the children participate in the decision as to whether or not they will continue to participate, is usually a good opportunity for this. The way in which it can be done depends upon such factors as the children's age, stage of development, the set of symptoms and the place that each child has found in the group by this time. Under no circumstances should a child be made to feel ashamed by this. We must therefore carefully consider what causes and behaviours we can talk about—and above all, what we should not say. For example, we first ask the general question: 'Do you remember why you came into this group? Would you like to say something to the other children about it?' (Naturally, we would not ask in this way if a child had stolen something). If the child cannot think of something to say, we ask whether we may say something about it; we then choose something from among the child's multiple symptoms that will not hurt his or her feelings. The simplest way is to speak about reasons which are more or less a problem for every child in the group, for example: 'Peter is in the group because he keeps getting into arguments with other children in school and he wants to learn how to make friends.' Sibling rivalry is another subject can easily be talked about. Sometimes we have a number of children of divorce in the group. Then we can also talk about separation and divorce and about the sadness, anger and listlessness that accompany these events.

Particularly with older children, it is appropriate to make a point of taking them seriously as contractual partners; this strengthens their self-esteem. Furthermore, we are dependent upon their cooperation. This openness will allow us later, in a relevant situation, to discuss the fact that the child is in the group for a particular reason and that what is happening right now is the same kind of thing that happens, for example, at school. In this way, we can verbalise the child's feelings and show our understanding. We can explain why we are reacting this way to him or her in particular: 'Now you want to change your role so that you can dominate the other children; and then the same thing will happen here that happens at school—finally no one will want to play with you anymore. We don't want that to happen here as well!' We then continue with the question of what the child could do differently this time; perhaps he needs our help in finding another possibility.

It unburdens the children when we speak clearly about the fact that each of them is here for a particular reason and that the play—as much fun as it is—is not an end in itself.

Introducing symbolic play
This takes place after the leaders have once again introduced themselves with their surnames and each child has introduced him or herself with her first name. We explain the sequence of a group session in a brief discussion phase: 'We have one

hour for each session. We begin by sitting in a circle, like we are doing now, and thinking of a story. Each of you can tell us a story that you know, and together we can figure out which one we will play or which ideas we could combine together to make a story. After that, each of you can choose the role that he or she likes best. You can also help to decide who we should be in the story, because we will play with you. Ten minutes before the session is over we will sit down together so that you can tell us what you liked about the game. We can play with the things that are here in the room (point to the materials). Of course, we will have to imagine many things. For example, we can pretend that a pillow is a sack full of gold. We can play all kinds of great stories here: you simply have to take care that you don't hurt each other. So if someone is playing a ferocious lion, he or she is not allowed to really bite: he can just pretend to do so by grabbing firmly with his hand, for example. In order that you can see how this works, we have chosen a story for this first session which we will play together now.'

The further introduction of symbolic play then takes place very pragmatically, through our example, as we will describe in the following sections. Of course, this introduction is always adapted to the developmental stage of the children in question.

As Straub points out, however (Straub 1975), the therapists must not be afraid to adopt a directorial attitude in this beginning phase, since this helps to reduce the children's anxiety.

Rules and boundaries
We enforce the following rules and limits in situations in which they are overstepped:

- Play takes place only in the group space.
- Children may not bring any toys or props from home.
- Friends are not allowed to participate as guests.
- The requirement not to hurt one another also applies to severe insults.

We do not allow the children to address us by our first names. We have tried this out with various age groups and had the experience that it is also important for the children to address us more formally. This simplifies our transitions between the leader position and the symbolic roles, without breaking down the child/therapist structure. Furthermore, we believe it has a negative effect on the transference process when this boundary is blurred.

Bringing the group together as a unit

In addition to the diagnostic examination of whether or not the children are compatible with each other and whether every child can benefit from the group, the most important goal of the beginning phase is the experience of shared, lively and enjoyable play. The positive experiences in this phase form the basis for dealing with conflicts later on, as well as having a positive influence on the children's motivation to continue participating beyond the fifth session.

5.1.1 Structuring the First Group Session

We would now like to describe in detail how we attempt to achieve the above-mentioned goals in the first session. We will describe a beginning session with six- to eight-year-old children and by way of comparison, the first session with a group of ten-year-olds.

The first session with six-year-old children

We place just enough seat cushions in the circle that there are no extra cushions and that no indiscriminate gaps or distances are formed. We then bring the children in from the waiting room and greet each child in the group space by name. When everyone is seated, we introduce ourselves again and then speak in a general way about the fact that the children are here because they are having difficulties at home, with friends or in school. This is followed by a 'getting to know each other' game—one, for instance, that we explain more or less as follows.

'Now we are going to play a short game to get to know each other, so that it is easier for you to remember the names of the other children. (At the same time, one of the therapists places an extra seat next to his or her own). The game goes like this: "The seat on my left is free: I'll ask Peter to come sit by me!" Then Peter asks: "What should I come as?" We name an animal that lives on a farm and say, for example: "As a rabbit!" Then Peter pretends to be a rabbit and hops over to the seat next to mine. Then each child who has the empty seat on his or her left side can ask someone to come and sit next to her in the same way.'

This game reduces the children's anxiety since it is familiar to most of them, and the movement helps release tension. At the same time, it serves as a warm-up for the symbolic play—the theme of which we suggest in the first session, since the children first need to learn how they can play here. When each child has had approximately two turns, we conclude the game and continue: 'You really played these animals very well. Now we would like to act out a story together with you: it is called "Animals on the Farm". What are some animals that live on a farm?' We encourage the children's suggestions and add our own, so that a large number of animals are named. We then invite the children: 'Now each of you can think about which farm animal you would like to be. We will play along and be the husband and wife on the farm.' When each child selects an animal role, we ask him or her whether it is a young animal, what colour its fur is, and what it does on the farm.

Some children require the support of one of the therapists in order to develop their idea of a role verbally in such a way that both they and the other children have a vivid picture of it in their mind's eye. When helping in this way, however, we must take care not to overtax the children's verbal abilities for their age. In addition, we use this description to feed the children's narcissism. At the same time, they can see that we also accept them in such roles as a vicious sheepdog or a cheeky goose.

In this first session, we do not yet ask the children what roles we should play. Instead, we offer them positive transference roles in order to reduce their anxiety and provide them with support. In all of the subsequent sessions, the children can help decide what roles the two therapists should play and how they should play them, so that we can incorporate the children's projections and transference. This does not exclude the possibility that in order to intervene, we may modify our roles or choose a different role for ourselves—but we will say more about this later.

When all the children have chosen their animal roles, we show them where the farmyard, the pasture and the forest are located and ask them to decide where each one wants to have his or her nest, stable, etc. We also inform them that the animals can speak to one another and visit each other; and we help them to construct their spaces using cushions, pillows and cloths. This process of building, cushioning and decorating their spaces, which the therapists encourage the children to do, is an important part of each respective role and opens up play possibilities for the further course of the scenario. Furthermore, it is fun for the children, and helps them to become familiar with the room as well as making initial forms of cooperation possible. It is especially important that the 'dwellings' are set up along the walls rather than in the centre of the room, and that they do not occupy the entire space, so that there is enough room left over to create a garden, pond, pasture, etc. After all, this is the important space where the encounters will take place.

We introduce the transformation as follows: 'Now each of you should lie down in his or her sleeping place: close your eyes and imagine that it is night-time, when you will turn into animals. When the cock crows, you will wake up as animals, and life on the farm will begin!' As soon as the game is set in motion with the cock's crow, the 'farmers' begin to wake up and feed the animals; they take in the animals' reactions and develop the continuation of the play from there. This highly structured process helps the children to understand how the play functions and reduces their insecurity and anxiety. Since we attribute an important diagnostic and therapeutic significance to the symbolism of the roles and the way they are played out, we would like to make a few remarks on this as they relate to the beginning process we have described.

Widespread experience tells us that children in this age group can identify very easily with animals—that animal roles are very well suited to symbolising children's fantasies and their urge to express themselves holistically through their bodies. The wide variety of options animals provide lets each child select a role that best corresponds to his or her current intrapsychic situation. Thus, for example, a very fearful child might choose the role of a new-born kitten that is still blind. One boy once said: 'I am a tick: I am nearly invisible, but I could suck all your blood.' After a long hesitation, a seemingly very nondescript girl said: 'I am a brightly-coloured parrot that lives in a cage inside the farmhouse.' The symbolism of the chosen role, the way in which each child furnishes his or her pen, stall or cage and where he places it in the room is an indication of the way in which the children are trying to cope with this disconcerting beginning phase.

In their roles, the therapists present themselves as 'good parents'. It is very important, especially in the first session, that the therapists really are the farm couple during the play scenario: children can only take on their own roles well if they experience true role identification on the part of the therapists.

Once the five- to six-year-old children have settled into their roles, they sometimes identify with them so strongly that they do nothing but bark or bleat, for example. In this case, the children need to be given additional permission to speak in their animal roles.

In addition to the roles that are assumed, emphasis also needs to be placed on the description of the overall scene. Appropriately coloured cloths may be used to make a pond for the ducks, a front lawn and a vegetable garden recognisable. It must be clear to the children where the door to the farmhouse is located and how it may be opened and closed—which can normally only be done by the farmers. The same is true for the window and the door to the larder. The locations of such things as the stove and the bed must also be easy to recognise. It is necessary to point out this 'living environment' to the children once again before beginning the game—and sometimes to do so repeatedly in the course of the game, if the children no longer remember. The entire set-up provides a wide variety of possibilities for play, which can easily be forfeited if they are not created with the necessary care: this is particularly true for the first session, which serves as a template for all the sessions that follow.

Each child must be sure that his or her stable or lair cannot be simply knocked over, since the cushions are 'real walls'. It gives them a sense of protection from invasion to be assured that no other child may enter without their permission. For the 'ferocious sheepdog', the safety of his kennel is important, among other things, because it means that his aggressive impulses will not be triggered so quickly; and the little cat will more likely dare to participate in the game when she knows that she can retreat back to the security of her basket at any time and be well protected there. The certainty with which the therapists communicate these boundaries and rules is no less important for an anxious child than it is for an aggressive one.

Approximately five to ten minutes before the end of the session, we bring the play at the symbolic level to an end: 'Unfortunately, we have to interrupt our game now! If you want to, we can continue playing this same story next week, or you can make up a new story. Now you are not animals anymore. Hans, you are not a dog anymore; Isolde, you are not a horse; etc. And we are no longer the farmers. Now we will sit down together in a circle again, and everyone can say what he or she liked about the game. You don't need to tidy up; we will do that.'

The discussion phase that then follows should help the children to emerge from their roles and return from their fantasies into reality. To this end, it is helpful to ask each child the question: 'What did you like about the game?' By speaking about themselves, the other children and the play scenario, they begin to detach themselves from the symbolic sphere. Many six-year-olds are scarcely able to say anything yet in the beginning phase; nevertheless, we use the discussion round to give positive feedback, which is especially important after the first session. We reaffirm for each child what a beautiful, skilful, clever and brave animal he or she was. We express our happiness that the children were all able to play so well together even though they didn't know each other. We let them know that we enjoyed playing with them and that we are looking forward to the next session, eager to see what story the group will invent.

Over the years, we have experimented with numerous alternative introduction scenarios and determined that 'Animals on the Farm' is very suitable for five- to seven-year-old children. Through his or her choice of a role and a place, each child can bring his individual experience to expression in this session and despite any anxiety or unfamiliarity, is made to feel secure in the overall setting of the farm with the two farmers. The themes of 'Animals in the Forest'—or, alternatively, 'Animals in the Safari Park'—lend themselves well to groups of seven- to eight-year-old children. The roles available in these scenarios, such as adder, fox, wolf, eagle, etc. (or in the jungle, poisonous snake, cheetah, tiger, elephant, monkey, etc.) allow them to cope with anxiety through strength and aggression and stimulate correspondingly adventurous fantasies which might be too threatening for younger children. If we offer the children one of these scenarios, we give ourselves the roles of gamekeepers with a veterinary clinic for injured animals or lost baby animals, etc.

The goals of the first session and its structural format remain the same as that described above. This also applies to another variation which is well suited to groups of eight- to ten-year-old children: 'The Adventure Journey!'—be it an expedition into the mountains, to an island of hidden treasure or to a temple in the jungle. The children can then play such roles as doctor, researcher, navigator, armed escort or some other specialist. In order to fulfil their objectives in the first session, the therapists should assume the roles of captain and helmsman or expedition leaders in these scenarios.

Which story is ultimately chosen will depend upon the composition and developmental level of the group. What is important for every initial scenario that is offered, however, is that it contains images and roles which allow the dynamics of the current beginning situation to be expressed.

For the ten- to thirteen-year-old age group, we prefer to employ a more open format in the beginning. However, following a brief greeting and introduction round, we speak even more directly about the purpose of the group work and the participants' individual responsibility: 'We are glad that you have come here. We have already met each of you and your families and spoken about the reasons why you are joining the group. One reason is that each one of you sometimes has difficulty getting along with other people your own age. Here you will be able to find out why this happens and try out ways that you could change it. Who would like to start and say something else about this?'

Sometimes an open discussion develops. However, it can also happen that the children remain very quiet and keep a low profile. Then we do not push them; we simply continue with our introduction: 'As we agreed, we will start out by meeting five times as a group so that you can get to know each other and get an idea of how we want to help you to make a change. At the end of the fifth session, each of you can decide whether he or she wants to continue to take part. As you know, we want to act out stories that we make up together, and each one of you can play a role that is fun for you to play. We want to start doing this now. Take a moment to think about it and tell us what stories you come up with. Then we will decide together which story we want to play—or which parts we can put together to create a new story.' Alternatively, we offer them a story to play in which six children meet at a camp and have an adventure together.

With this age group, it no longer seems necessary to us to present ourselves as 'good parents' in order to dispel anxiety; rather, we emphasise the children's age-appropriate autonomy.

Once the group has found a shared story, we help each child with the selection and elaboration of his or her role; then we explain our own readiness to play along in the scenario—in roles that the children assign to us or in roles that we choose ourselves.

To our surprise, in a group of four twelve-year-old boys, the beginning of the session following our introduction proceeded as follows.

Florian (immediately very animated): 'I know lots of stories!'—And after naming a few: 'But the best one is "Moby Dick", the battle with the whale!' Uwe, a precocious boy without friends, considered our question for a while and said: 'I can't think of anything!' In response, an obese, restless boy named Jakob interjected: 'I like "The Robber Hotzenplotz" [a popular German children's storybook]!' The quiet boy, Sven, agreed with this idea: 'I don't have any ideas, but Hotzenplotz isn't bad.' We were rather baffled at the idea of this story for very young children. The boys then discussed the various Hotzenplotz stories and agreed to play the story in which Hotzenplotz steals the Grandmother's coffee pot and the Policeman and Kasper retrieve it. In the course of discussing how this story could be played and who would assume which role, the boys created an age-appropriate gangster story.

'Moby Dick' illustrated the threatening aspect of the situation. Resistance was expressed through the boys' statements that they 'couldn't think of anything'. By means of the regressive intermediate level of the Robber Hotzenplotz fantasies, they ultimately found their way back to an age-appropriate level. The long discussion helped determine where they stood in terms of the group dynamics and helped clarify their limitations with respect to the two adults.

In addition, it is always astonishing to observe the degree to which—alongside their critical and rational mental alertness—childlike experiences and behaviour are still possible with children of this age group. These near-adolescents can permit themselves to regress as soon as they are certain that they will not be shamed or become objects of diagnostic observation. We have even witnessed 13-year-olds who played the roles of dogs, crawling around on all fours and barking.

With this age group, the discussion round at the end of the first session is an opportunity to communicate to the children that regression during the symbolic play—and/or the staging of their fantasies of omnipotence—are possible and acceptable here. Needless to say, every type of validation does the children—even the 'big ones'—good, and has its place in the closing round.

5.1.2 The Situation of the Therapists in the First Group Session

The therapists also need to get warmed up, since it is not only the children who are anxious and nervous in the first session. This is understandable, since unlike the situation in individual therapy, we are confronted with a very complex dynamic from the very beginning. Even if we already know the individual children, the 'mixture' in the group can provoke completely unexpected behaviours in the children. Here are a few highlights to illustrate what we mean.

For example, it is our intention to act as 'good parents' for the group. However, when a seven-year-old says: 'Playing animals—what a bunch of crap!' it is not easy to stomach this, and our affect makes it difficult for us to be 'good parents'.

Furthermore, we want to divide our attention fairly: every child should have the feeling that he or she is important to us. Yet when six-year-old Maria very firmly demands: 'I am a little lamb, and you (the female therapist) are a sheep. You have to be the little lamb's Mama!' How should we react?

Another aim of the first session and the beginning phase is to bring the group together as a whole. In the first quarter of an hour, however, ten-year-old Kevin denigrates 'the bitches' with expletives and sexual remarks, causing the female therapist to feel a rush of adrenalin. Already we are confronted with a problematic situation with which we had not yet reckoned at this point in time.

We want to set up the first session in a well-structured way, so that the boundaries provide the children with a sense of security. But now, seven-year-old Peter has already started to rock back and forth on the cushions and tip them over. In the midst of the ensuing laughter, the children's tension is released, and in no time the other four children are also rocking and tumbling from their seats to general merriment. None of them listen to our request to sit back down and listen. Our feelings of helplessness and annoyance do not make it easy for us to restore structure to the situation.

We could go on and on with such anecdotes. But what we can observe from these few examples is that the children's means of defence against anxiety are widely varied, but also similar, and they can morph into group resistance. Then it is a question of whether we allow our own behaviour to be determined by our defences against anxiety.

For example, we might be tempted to react in an authoritarian manner in order to gain control of the group—albeit with good intentions; or we could deny the attacks and insults and evade the situation through feigned understanding; or, in the case of the denigration of the girls, we could put up with the splitting for tactical reasons and rationalise it by convincing ourselves that the cohesion of the group will work itself out over time.

The act of being 'good parents' in the first session means to consciously take notice of our own fears and then, as much as we sympathise with the children, to firmly maintain the boundaries. With regard to the examples we have described, this could mean, among other things:

- that for Kevin s protection as well, it would be appropriate to explain to him immediately and clearly that even though he might be feeling insecure, his coarse insults toward the girls are not acceptable;
- that out of awareness of the group dynamics, the female therapist helps Maria to play the role of a little lamb without participating in her symbiotic anxiety-deflecting mechanism and allowing herself to be assigned the role of a sheep. Instead, the therapist can play the role of the farm woman, who will be able to provide Maria with sufficient protection;
- and that one of the therapists could bring the child who started rocking the cushions over to sit beside him or her, and even hold the child in her arms if he continues inciting the other children to go on with this activity.

If this strategy is not effective, we can try to pick up on the children's actions and funnel them into symbolic play: 'You are just like energetic animals—what kind of animals are you?' We can then develop a story with the children based on these roles. We can communicate the structure and the rules in the further course of the session.

For a pair of therapists who are not yet familiar with one another from co-therapy, it can be helpful to agree upon a division of functions in order to manage as well as possible in such situations, especially in the beginning phase.

5.1.3 Developing a Group Theme

Here, we define a group theme not only as the central play idea with its corresponding roles—such as 'Robin Hood', for example—but above all, as the psychodynamic focus of the group, which serves as a primary common denominator for each of the individual children's sets of problems. Like an initial dream, this focus may become visible in the beginning phase and form the core of the work for a long period of time, but it may also disappear temporarily. All in all, it is subject to a process of change which corresponds to the internal development of the group. However, it can also happen that the theme which was supposedly understood to be the focus during the beginning phase disappears completely. The group theme and its development—as well as resistance in the form of stagnated repetitions—can best be comprehended by keeping careful logs of the sessions. We then have the possibility to read back through our notes and follow the step-by-step differentiation over the course of many sessions. In our experience, this works even better with written notes than it does with video recordings. It is easier to gain an overview of briefly notated process descriptions from numerous group sessions than it is to view hours and hours of video recordings. (Nevertheless, video recordings are a good means of understanding the effect of interventions, transference processes and therapeutic interactions and developing them further).

In the following section, we will describe how the theme took shape in the beginning phase with a group of six-year-olds and with a group of twelve-year-olds.

Developing the theme with a group of six-year-old children
The children and their role choices for the 'Farm Animals' scenario in the first session:

Sabine	An adopted, only child who was enrolled in the group because of her aggression toward her adoptive parents and other children. She wanted to be a calico house cat
Vanessa	The second child of a single mother suffered from neurodermatitis and emotional outbursts and exhibited strong regressive tendencies. She decided to be a turtle in a lake, with a stuffed turtle as her baby
Nina	An only child, displayed psychosocial underdevelopment; she did not eat any solid food and was extremely inhibited in relation to her peers. She wanted to be the big brown and white horse called 'Fury'
Max	The fifth of six children, he did not speak outside of his family and was very inhibited. He wanted to be a white mouse
Michael	The only child of a single mother, he was restless, aggressive and lacked age-appropriate emotional control. He wanted to be a black sheepdog

The therapists played the male and female farmers.

The first four group sessions
In the first 20 minutes, all of the animals allowed themselves to be cared for and fed. The cat (Sabine) and the turtle (Vanessa) demanded a great deal to eat. The mouse (Max) quickly disappeared back into his nest as soon as he had received

some cheese. Correspondent to their symptoms, the children had arrived at an orally-focused group theme. The sheepdog (Michael) temporarily switched to the role of a fox who stole a goose. This orally aggressive role let him express his neediness; at the same time, it was a way for him to react to the frustration of not having the 'group parents' all to himself. In this way, Michael also expressed an impulse of the group as a whole and experienced the way in which the two therapists reacted to the oral aggression. The therapists' reaction: 'Maybe the fox thinks that if he doesn't fetch any food for himself he won't get anything. He is such a clever fox that we can't catch him!'

Our intention with this intervention was to reduce the fear of retribution. Encouraged in this way, in the further progress of the game, the cat (Sabine), the horse (Nina) and the sheepdog (Michael) dared to hiss at the male farmer, to scratch him, bark at him, snap at him and kick at him with her hooves (Nina) until he fled into the house in fear. The female farmer remained in the role of the caretaking 'good mother'.

The children had set up a splitting situation with a good and a bad object: this allowed them to direct their own aggressions toward one of the therapists.

The turtle (Vanessa) sought out a place for herself in the farmhouse and was strongly attached to the female farmer: in keeping with her set of problems, she created a symbiotic constellation that complemented the aggressive dynamic of the group.

In the second session, the children 'transformed' themselves into the same animals again—with the exception of Michael, who also wanted to be a cat like Sabine. Together, the two of them built a shared cats' nest. In this way, Michael once again avoided putting himself into an exposed aggressive position. The therapists were again assigned to play the two farmers.

After each child had built his or her nest or stable and the therapists had constructed their house, the game began again with 'caring for and feeding the animals'. The oral expectations quickly escalated to open greed, accompanied by increasingly aggressive behaviour. The longer each individual child wanted to be fed, the larger the amounts of food he or she demanded, the greater the inevitably resulting frustration became for the animals that were still waiting. They began to cry louder and louder and to snap at the two farmers. Their anger at their rivals was shifted onto the therapists, leading to a stronger alliance between the children. They developed anger toward the therapists—both of them were now 'bad parents'. The animals became increasingly aggressive, forcing the farmers to flee into the house.

Since this degree of aggression no longer corresponded to the children's roles, the therapists interrupted the play for the following intervention: 'You have become so wild that one might think you are large animals, like the animals in the jungle. The cats were as fierce as lions or tigers!' The children seized on this idea and selected new roles: the two cats (Michael and Sabine) played the roles of tigers; the horse (Nina) became a black unicorn; the mouse (Max) became a wild jungle mouse and Vanessa remained in the role of the turtle. In the roles of animal catchers, the therapists were directed to attempt to catch the animals with a net: this was the wish of the children, who said: '... but you won't be able to catch us!'

The game of being chased was very enjoyable for the children. Near the end of the session they also occasionally allowed themselves to be caught, having specified ahead of time that they would be able to escape from the cage after a short period of time.

In this session, orally aggressive behaviour became the group theme, triggering a fear of reprisal which gradually became lessened. Apparently the children could not yet tolerate having the therapists be defeated.

At the beginning of the third group session, the children wanted to play 'Farm in the Jungle' again; however, the play evolved back into a farmyard scenario. Again, Max wanted to play the role of a white mouse who had his nest directly beside the farmhouse. He didn't want to hear anything about how wild he had been in the previous session. This was also the tendency among the other children. Michael and Nina wanted to be tame, white unicorns; Vanessa chose to be a cat who had her place inside the farmhouse; Sabine was a dog who guarded the farm.

Here, the way in which the children stimulated each other to broaden their range of roles becomes very apparent. The animals let the two farmers feed them, brush their fur or shoe their hooves; they helped with ploughing and harvesting. In addition to oral expectations, the wish for acknowledgement of their autonomous, age-appropriate abilities had also become a theme in the form of their participation in work.

In the fourth session, the animals had secret treasures which a robber (the male therapist) wanted to steal. However, the animals were on the alert and helped the farm woman (the female therapist) fend off the intruder. The children had secured a good object for themselves and projected their own greed onto the male therapist.

The psychodynamic focus which became apparent in the beginning phase may be described as an orally-based set of problems with reactive anger and the associated fear of repercussions. As the group progressed further, other themes also took shape; however, the children repeatedly returned to the farm scenario and to processing the oral theme.

Developing the theme with a group of twelve-year-old children
Separation and divorce were part of the psychogenesis for all the children in this group. Claudia and Martin also displayed substantial irritation with their gender identities. In the discussion round, Claudia declared in a silly, flippant manner: 'Today I am going to play the Emperor of China!' From this starting point, a theme developed with the following roles:

Claudia	Emperor of China
Tanja	King Leopold
Martin	Princess of China
Johannes	Police officer
Foundling child	A shabby and tattered cloth doll
Female therapist	Servant
Male therapist	Cook

The 'lords and ladies' let themselves be cooked for, waited on and told stories. They were very strict with their employees if tasks were not performed quickly enough or according to their wishes. The theme of separation and abandonment had already taken shape in this first session with the symbol of the foundling child.

The scenario was continued in the second session. However, rivalries arose to an increasing degree as the emperor, the princess or King Leopold alternately 'fainted' and thereby demanded special care and attention from the servants.

At the beginning of the third session, the children spent a long time arguing over the seat cushions and pillows with which they wanted to furnish their royal rooms. They then assumed their previous roles, with the exception of Johannes: this time he chose to be a knight instead of a police officer. Pairs of children formed subgroups who once again argued with each other.

When the therapists described one such argument as a 'marital dispute', Martin picked up on this idea and said: 'The emperor and empress are going to get divorced!' The other children agreed to this with interest; the group staged a divorce—which, however, was followed soon afterward by a wedding: the marital row was quickly over. Next, the children wanted to build a shared house, but they soon disagreed with each other again and the harmony rapidly came to an end. Now the parents' separation had clearly moved into central focus as a group theme.

Both Martin and the female therapist were absent from the fourth session. The children were disconcerted and only found their way back into the scenario from the previous session after a long time.

The absence of the female therapist corresponded to the children's experiences of parental separation. Their anger was revealed in the subsequent session.

The children constantly bossed the female therapist around, calling her a poor and unreliable servant; ultimately, they threw her into the dungeon.

These two examples should suffice to demonstrate how a group's theme can develop during the beginning phase. The roles of the two therapists allowed the children to stage their early childhood desires for care and control, their experiences with separation and their desires for union. Connected to this was an emotional release which led to the children's unburdening.

5.1.4 The Fifth Session

The fifth group session marks a turning point—the end of the trial period. As agreed upon in the contract, we ask each child (at the appropriate verbal level), how he or she has liked the group sessions so far and whether he would now like to continue participating in the group for one year in order to find out how he can get along better with himself and other children. In this fifth session, we also discuss with the group any critical statements that the children make, to the extent that they are related to the group. In addition, we give each child feedback about our experiences with him or her in the group, primarily emphasising the positive aspects. With older children, however, we also speak about specific modes of behaviour in relation to the contract in order to address the goal of the children's participation once again. Observations and experiences related to the particular individual situation of each child and his or her family are only discussed privately with the parents and the child. Particularly for older children, it is important for them to understand that their participation in the group is their own decision. In this way, they feel that their age-appropriate autonomy and responsibility is being acknowledged and addressed, which in turn reduces resistance.

Fortunately, it quite seldom happens that we must face the difficult decision of removing a child because he or she does not fit into this particular group. If, however, this decision is unavoidable and we can already recognise the fact by this time, we speak with the child and her parents prior to the fifth session and ask the child if she would like to come to a parting session.

For a group, the removal of a child—even when it happens as early as the fifth session—is an unsettling event. We have had the experience that at the end of a group therapy cycle—even after more than 1½ years—the children spontaneously remembered a child who left the group long ago, and even remembered his or her roles. Sometimes it is only possible to make this decision at a later point in time, and then it is even more difficult.

5.2   The Middle Phase

Over the past years we have got to know many groups. In comparative longitudinal studies of our logs, we investigated whether it was possible to identify any regularity in the development of the groups. As could be expected, in group therapy—as in individual therapy—the healing processes did not proceed in a linear fashion. Oral, anal and oedipal themes overlap with one another and occur in every possible order. Progression and regression can alternate within a single session as well as in the overall process. While certain processes and themes are described which can be found in the majority of the groups, they do not appear in the same recurring sequences. For example, we observed that in one group, an oral theme was staged during the first fifteen sessions; in another group, it appeared only in the last four sessions. Understanding the children's scenarios as expressions of their intrapsychic and interpsychic conflicts and working through them in repetitions is the goal of the middle phase. We have described possible therapeutic reactions to the themes and group processes in detail in the other chapters. In this section, therefore, we will simply draw attention to a number of general structural and group dynamic processes.

Organisational and structural factors
The children should always be made aware of upcoming school holidays and break periods several sessions ahead of time—particularly the long break during the summer holidays. For the children, it means a great deal to hear that the therapists are looking forward to continuing the sessions after the holidays.

It occasionally happens that one of the therapists is not able to participate for one session—or is perhaps absent for several sessions due to illness. If possible, this should be announced to the children ahead of time. In all of these cases, it is important to carefully register the group's reaction—and as far as the individual children are concerned—both in the session in which one of the therapists is absent as well as in the following session. The children generally have a reaction to this, and it provides a good opportunity to broach the subject of various biographical references—for example, separation from a mother due to illness, a father's return following a separation or divorce, etc.

The intensification of transference
Whereas with 'the little ones', strongly affect-based transferences often take place as early as the second or third session, with older children—in accordance with their ego development—this occurs several sessions later and intensifies with their increased feelings of trust within the group.

Fastest to develop are the transference relationships between the children—for example, sibling relationships and rivalries with classmates—which repeat themselves in the group dynamics in the form of striving for dominance, arguments, withdrawal, etc. If a child is then frequently absent, it is important to determine whether he or she is unable to cope with the rivalries within the group (for example, the formation of excluding pairs in a group of five children) or whether his negative situation with his siblings is being repeated in the group and triggering his resigned withdrawal.

Sometimes the confrontations take place primarily in the waiting room or on the way home and are not visible to their fullest extent during the session.

Strongly negative transferences or oedipal courtship do not usually begin to appear until the middle phase. Then these instances of transference are not only limited to the symbolic scenarios; they also clearly have an effect in the discussion rounds—for example, when choosing places for the opening round, where the 'little ones' openly seek closeness while the 'big kids' demonstrate such wishes by deliberately creating distances.

'Getting stuck'—whether it takes the form of recurring symptomatic behaviour in the case of individual children or a constant return to the group theme—calls for interventions, which we will describe further down.

Changes in group dynamics
In all of the groups, after a certain amount of time, the children seek out confrontation with the therapists at the real level, by overstepping boundaries or disobeying rules. Whereas in the beginning phase, it is appropriate to circumvent such provocations by steering them into a scenario at the symbolic level through skilful intervention, in the middle phase it is advisable to face the confrontation at the level of reality. Especially given the current uncertainty that exists among parents and childcare workers as to when and with what consequences values and limitations should be upheld, children need to have a different experience. They need to have the experience that the therapist stands firm in his or her position and does not allow herself to be enticed into manipulative reactions or become entangled in a power struggle. The children must realise that while the group only functions as an 'interaction' with each other, this nevertheless depends upon certain conditions and limitations. This act of standing one's ground corresponds to the 'holding function' that Winnicott describes as a fundamental prerequisite to development in the mother-child relationship (Winnicott 1974).

In the case of prepubescent children, we occasionally observe that they require a great deal of time to get around to constructing a symbolic scenario. This may have to do with their tendencies to avoid certain subjects—for example, sexuality. However, it may also be related to a special transference situation—for example, refusal to cooperate with teachers and/or parents, and the attempt to embroil these figures in a power struggle. Sometimes, however, it is simply due to the children's desire for verbal debate, which can be just as important to them at this age as the play.

One special phenomenon is the repetition of the same 'story'. Among the most common reasons for this kind of stagnation are:

- One child is dominating the group with his or her subject matter.
- Rivalries between the children cannot yet be accepted.
- The division between boys and girls is being maintained, contributing to the resistance to certain themes.
- Particularly in groups consisting only of boys, the children are fending off oedipal themes or oral desires for care and closeness for example, through repeated fighting games.

It is only possible to determine with some certainty whether or not it is actually a case of repetition as a form of resistance by comparing the situation with the previous sessions: sometimes changes take place in nearly imperceptible steps, even with ostensibly similar choices of roles and scenarios. In fact, when the children have found a story into which each one of them can incorporate his or her individual theme, they tend to repeat it in order to deal with these themes over the course of numerous sessions. Starting from the initially symptomatic repetition, they are able to work through their intrapsychic problems with the aid of the setting and the therapists' interventions.

Parental influences
Sometimes the change takes place too rapidly for the parents, and it may be different from what they expected. For example, their well-behaved child suddenly fights back not only at school, but also cheekily at home—or he detaches himself from his mother more quickly than she can tolerate. Children can usually sense their parents' ambivalence or uneasiness. The result can be that at home they may declare that they don't feel like taking part in the group anymore—which usually in no way corresponds to their active and enthusiastic participation during the group session. These children find themselves in a difficult conflict situation which can only be resolved in consultation with the parents or the family.

It can also happen that the parents expect the symptoms to be eliminated more quickly and are disappointed when this is not the case: they may then demotivate the child as far as his or her participation in the group is concerned. Here it might be the case, among other things, that the effects, goal and methods of the therapy have not been discussed thoroughly and carefully enough in the contract—including the necessity for cooperation and assistance from all the parties involved.

Occasionally however, we also fail to recognise, for example, that the dynamics in the classroom or the rigidity of the family system are stronger than the child's wish to make a change.

If, for example, a child is drawing attention away from a marital conflict by being a 'troublemaker', then the accompanying work with the parents is especially important. In this case, the aim of the group therapy corresponds to the parents' wishes; however, the couple's resistance is standing in the way of it. They are therefore unable to perceive the changes; they continue to complain about the symptoms and question the effectiveness of our work. For the child, this is a 'double-bind' situation. It can happen that a child with this systemic function appears relatively normal to us in the group, while at home, he or she remains the person who is identified as a patient. The conclusion cannot be to remove the child from the group, since access to the long and tedious process of addressing the conflict in the partnership might be made possible via the child. It can sometimes take a long time for the parents to develop the necessary trust to engage with their own set of problems.

If a child waxes enthusiastic about the group and idealises the therapists, this could potentially trigger feelings of rivalry in the parents, which may be expressed through criticism or devaluation of our work. Such parents urgently require our acknowledgement for coping with their many difficult day-to-day situations, and it is important that we give them credit for any positive changes so that we can possibly avert any negative reactions.

If the parents separate during a group therapy process, we must be especially careful that we do not allow one side to use us against the other in the conflict. In targeted separation counselling, we should try to insure that the child can remain in the group—since transference onto the two therapists can provide a good opportunity for him or her to address her painful experiences in relation to the separation.

5.3 The Concluding Phase

The therapists generally define the number of group sessions, and consequently the end of the group process, to cover a period of one year. The children's co-decision in the fifth session in favour of their continued participation also essentially includes the conclusion of the therapy (the same is true for extensions of the process, which are agreed upon together with the parents and the child). Nevertheless, most children experience the end of the group work as an arbitrary decision on the part of the adults. In our experience, almost all children would like to continue participating in the group—with the exception of the 14-year-olds: we will say more about that further down. There are several reasons for this; some of these are:

- The symbolic forms of emotional release are safe, disencumbering and enjoyable.
- These opportunities to spontaneously create their unconscious worlds and to be seen and understood in this process aid the children in their development and help increase their spontaneity, creativity and autonomy.
- Each child has his or her place in the group and is connected to the other children and the therapists in a network of relationships.

We see, therefore, that with the conclusion of the group, the children lose an environment for creative play, and numerous relationships are dissolved. This event corresponds to all of the children's various experiences with separation. Many of the children have been affected by their parents' separation or divorce and are still suffering from this experience. It is often associated with a change of residence and/or schools and the loss of friends and relatives—to name only the most existential separation experiences that children undergo. These and other experiences of separation are reawakened through the conclusion of the group work, and they can set in motion a wide variety of coping strategies on the part of individual children as well as of the group as a whole. In our experience, the group as a whole tends to deny the approaching end of the work together. Therefore we have made it our duty, beginning approximately with the tenth-to-last session, to remind the children at the beginning or the end of each session that, for example, six group sessions remain before the conclusion of the group. Whereas the 'little ones' generally protest, the age groups twelve years old and above frequently react with such dismissive remarks as: 'I have better things to do anyway!'

The ongoing 'count-down' is an intervention which normally results in the approaching end of the group and the associated parting becoming a theme which is addressed in the play scenarios.

Here are a few examples of this, along with further possibilities for intervention.

Example

A group of eight-year-olds, three girls and two boys, staged the following story during the concluding phase:

The therapists were assigned to be a farm couple; the children all wanted to be cute little kittens that the farmers would care for. The concept and choice of roles corresponded to a series of scenarios played during the beginning phase.

Intervention: 'Now, since the group work is drawing to a close—we only have three more group sessions left—think about what it was like at the beginning. You were still very little at that time; now you are much older and more independent.' The children responded to this, remembering how they built their nest in the beginning phase. 'Let's not talk anymore now—I want to play!' one boy reacted after a short time; the other children agreed. They once again constructed their kitten nests in the places that they remembered, and at first they simply demanded to be fed, stroked and praised for the mice that they had caught.

Intervention (female therapist): 'You are really quite big cats now; you catch mice, so I notice that you don't need as much food anymore.' The cats cried out for milk more than ever. Then they began to run away and hide: they wanted the farmers to search for them and find them. One of the cats became injured; all the other cats then picked up on this idea and wanted to be bandaged and cared for as well. Little by little, however, they became more defiant and naughty and began stealing from the larder.

Interventions: The two therapists reacted by verbalising opposing developmental impulses. The male farmer became angry and suspected the now-larger cats of sneaking into the larder. The female farmer didn't want to believe that her little kittens had become so cheeky and clever—and anyway, she already had some warm milk waiting for them in the kitchen.

Not long afterward, the children explained: 'We are cats who are going to go out into the big wide world: we are wandering cats. We robbed the larder and took everything with us; but we live in America—you can't come there!' They then used all of the building elements to construct a house together; there were none of the usual disputes over cloths and cushions.

The farmers remained behind, completely destitute. Intervention: In a dialogue, the farmers wondered aloud how the cats were faring in America. They alternatively expressed concern and confidence, ending the conversation with the observation: 'Now we know what it is like to be left behind. You feel sad and angry. Maybe the cats wanted to show us what it is like when the farmers wish they would grow up, start catching mice and no longer need us to take care of them?' Every now and then, one of the cats would return from 'America' and tell the farmers how good and pleasant their life was there. But the farmers were not allowed to follow their trail to America. Christian said, for example: 'You look for us and find my paw prints, but then I spread a new layer of asphalt on the path (he lays down a black blanket) and you can't find us again!' The children directed us to make several attempts to find the way to America, but they always made sure that we failed. The story was like the Grimms' fairy tale 'Foundling Bird', in which new obstacles constantly appear by magic in the path of the pursuing witch.

The following example describes the kind of reactions which can arise from a mistaken intervention.

Example

A group of ten-year-old children decided to stage the scenario 'Expedition to Africa' as their concluding game. Their chosen roles: the twenty-year-old children of wealthy parents, English aristocrats. The story: the parents were opposed to the children making this journey, but since the parents were not at home, the children would seize the opportunity and sail off on the yacht. The therapists, in the roles of the servants James and Jenny, would try unsuccessfully to prevent the children from leaving.

James and Jenny expressed their fears that the Duke and Duchess would hold them responsible if they did not prevent the children from making this dangerous journey. 'We don't give a damn!' responded the young aristocrats; they made fun of the two fearful and foolish old people. A short time later, after the ship had set sail, the male therapist said: 'Now we have some time off from work: we could go on a journey too—to London, for example...' This remark apparently had a negative effect on the children and gave rise to attachment behaviour. They explained: 'We only pretended to sail away; now we are coming back in disguise to see what you are up to!' This was followed by a series of machinating and aggressive actions, through which the children prevented James and Jenny from going on their outing. Finally, the servants were put in prison because they supposedly wanted to run off with the family jewels.

The male therapist had clearly resisted the separation experience by taking action. Therefore, with his intervention, he apparently did not take into account the children's wish that the 'parents' would mourn their parting.

If the theme of separation does not arise in the play scenarios, it is advisable for the therapists to introduce the subject and help the children to connect it with their play choices. A further example illustrates this.

Example

A group of six 11-year-old boys had played an ongoing space adventure story over a period of several sessions. Even though we had drawn their attention to the approaching end of the group process, as described above, they denied this fact and continued to play one episodic story after another.

Intervention in the final session: 'Even though today is our last session, you want to keep on playing as if you could continue with another space adventure next week. But today is the last session, and there won't be any continuation. We would like to give you a suggestion about how you could build the end of the group work into your play idea—is that all right?' You were all here in this group because each of you had some problems; now you are able to deal with them much better. Therefore we would like to suggest the following: that with your spaceships—which have been damaged on a dangerous journey—you land at our repair workshop so that we can put everything in order for your future adventures into space. For example, to refuel, to replace the nuclear engines, to adjust the weapons, repair the computers, etc. Afterwards, you can head off for your research in faraway galaxies. This would be your life in the future with your families and in school, where you will also have a lot of adventures.' The boys agreed to this. Nevertheless, as in the previous sessions, they wanted to fly together in pairs.

The therapists constructed a repair dock on their space station, where the space flyers recounted their adventures. During the repairs, the flyers also chipped in and supervised the work of the technician (the male therapist), who once again had no idea of what he was doing and could not get over his amazement at the spaceships' state-of-the-art technology. When the stars were well aligned, all of the flyers started off again. For each machine, the technicians went through a checklist, giving the therapists the opportunity to address any child's particular problems at the symbolic level. For example, with a boy who still lost control of his emotions easily, they could check the fuses on the electrical system so that short circuits and disruptive explosions could be avoided. In the case of an inhibited boy, they made sure that he had also double-checked his weapons system and reviewed the ways he could defend himself against alien attacks. They assured him that he had become very resourceful and that there were many ideas displayed on his computer as to how he could defend himself.

The boys understood these hints about their everyday life situations very well, and in instances where the therapists were uncertain, the boys themselves became more precise. The two therapists also spoke about what a shame they felt it was that these space adventurers were taking off again: they admired their courage and hoped that they would overcome all the dangers they faced.

Not long after the six astronauts disappeared into the depths of space, they declared: 'Now a meteor shower arrives and destroys your space station!' They flung all the pillows they could find at the therapists; then they stormed the station, knocking everything over and then running away again. It was only with difficulty that the therapists could hold the boys back for a closing round. The boys themselves did not want to say anything.

Female therapist: 'You have just shown us again how well you have learned to communicate with each other and play together. And at the end you let us feel that maybe you are angry and sad because your time together here at the counselling centre is coming to an end, and that is really a shame. We will see you again when you come with your parents for a final meeting in a few weeks, because we want to know how you are doing. But the group will not meet anymore; so today you have to say good-bye to one another.'

After that, the boys did their very best to remain cool and nonchalant as they said good-bye.

Since it happens again and again that the therapists need to offer the children a separation story in the final sessions, here are a few more ideas: the theme of 'Animal Medical Station' is appropriate if, for example, the group have played 'Animals on the Farm' or 'Animals in the Jungle' during the beginning phase and are still able to identify with animals in the concluding phase.

Intervention: 'What would you think about playing a story in the last session where you are jungle animals at a veterinary clinic? At the beginning you would still be injured or sick; then you would gradually get well and want to return to the wild. The animal veterinary clinic is like the group that you joined because things were not going well for you. And now that you feel healthy and stronger again, you don't need the group anymore—sort of like the healthy animals who don't want to stay at the veterinary clinic any longer.'

If the children agree, we let them choose their roles and then ask them what illness or injury they have that has brought them to the veterinary clinic. We try to relate their ideas to their emotional or psychosocial situation at the beginning of the therapy and to the process of development that they have gone through in the meantime. Alternatively, we can offer them appropriate images ourselves; for example, in the case of an aggressive boy: 'You used to charge into every fight and you often got hurt. Now the doctors have treated your wounds and healed your rabies, so you can think ahead of time about whether you want to fight or whether it is enough to simply show your claws and be menacing. Would you like that?'

Or for a child who had no friends: 'Maybe you could be a little puma who always hid when the other animals came around because you weren't sure if it would go well. But here you got food to make you stronger and you have started to play with the other animals and go hunting with them. Would you like to play that?'

Or a child who has experienced separations: 'Maybe you lost your herd and stayed at the veterinary clinic for a while so that you would be safe until you got so big and strong that you are scarcely afraid at all to back into the wild, because you will get along very well there now.'

If the children accept these ideas, the therapists can then double the children's ambivalencies in their roles during the play scenario—for example: 'I think he can go hunting by himself now/I'm afraid he might hurt himself', etc.

Whenever it is possible—either in their roles or as leaders in the closing discussion round—the therapists should express their own feelings: for example, that they are happy that the animals have become so healthy, beautiful and strong, and how sad it will be for them to no longer have the animals with them at the clinic. It is important for the children to hear that the therapists are also 'losing something'—if (hopefully!) that is the case.

Other variations are:

'Damsel (or girl knight) and (boy) Knight', who have survived adventures and injuries and are now being honoured by the king and queen with special rewards. In relation to the children's individual problems, these might be: a special coat of mail for the cautious prince; an amulet for the princess to keep her from becoming angry so quickly; a talking raven for the wild warrior, to warn him from attacking recklessly; a spirited horse for the girl knight, to help her feel how much strength she has. Afterwards, the monarchs bid them good-bye, since they will now head out into the world for further adventures.

'Ghostbusters'—specialists who have extraordinary abilities and equipment for capturing scary ghosts such as: The Slimer, who makes a mess of everything; the Greedy Monster, who eats everything up; the Shocker, who frightens everyone terribly. Armed with diplomas, the Ghostbusters go forward to free other castles and mansions from dangerous ghosts. The background for this story is a film which is familiar to many older children and which can be easily modified. Here again, the prerequisite for this scenario would be that the children have used the theme of 'Ghosts and Monsters' in their past scenarios.

Special Interventions for Individual Children

6

Walter Holl

Abstract

For the sake of presentation, Chapters 5 and 6 will be divided between disorder-specific interventions aimed at the development of a specific child and those which are directed toward the entire group—in the full knowledge that every intervention aimed at an individual child will have an effect on the dynamics of the group as a whole, and vice versa.

The reasons for enrolling a child in group therapy can be roughly classified as follows: over-adapted, inhibited, anxious and depressive behaviour or dominant, disruptive or aggressive behaviour—be it within the family, in nursery or at school.

It is well known that girls respond to damaging events and trauma with different coping attempts and symptoms than boys do. The reasons behind this lie in collective, handed-down patterns and biographical experiences. Girls more often react through adaptation, reaction formation or depressed withdrawal, extending as far as psychosomatic symptoms—in other words, their symptoms tend to be more inconspicuous at first. Boys are more likely to react with disruptive behaviours—for example, with refusal to perform, increased aggression or even delinquency. For this reason, interventions with girls often employ different images and roles than those used with boys. In some cases, this can mean that male and female therapists need to supplement their existing repertoire of characters and stories with images related to the opposite gender. For example, the male therapist must learn to navigate through secret intrigues between princesses or stage a fashion show. Similarly, the female therapist will need to become familiar with the operation of laser weapons during outer space battles.

In selecting the following examples of interventions, we used this symptomatic polarisation as a guideline—even though this distribution cannot do justice to the

© Springer Fachmedien Wiesbaden GmbH 2017
A. Aichinger and W. Holl, *Group Therapy with Children*,
DOI 10.1007/978-3-658-15813-2_6

countless mixed forms which can exist in reality. From a structural point of view, we make a distinction between interventions during the play phase and those in the warm-up and concluding phases, which we always conduct from the leader position—for example: an interpretation of the group's resistance when choosing a theme in the opening round; verbalising a particular child's emotional state during the closing round; setting boundaries at the end of the session, etc. During the symbolic play scenario, interventions can take place either from the leader position or in the context of a role.

Interventions should be based on a diagnostic understanding of the child's problems and take the current group-dynamic situation into account. We need to be aware that any intervention can become a manipulation if it is not carried out with the necessary respect for the child's autonomy.

6.1   Interventions with Inhibited or Anxious Children

6.1.1   Psychodynamics

Over-adapted, inhibited, anxious behaviour and depressive moods can have a variety of meanings, which we need to be able to understand in order to intervene appropriately. The following sketches describe some of these psychodynamic factors and themes.

Such behaviour can be a way of warding off liveliness and aggression due to the assumption or experience that the parents cannot tolerate such behaviour well—for example, because the mother was ill; or because a severely ill or disabled child placed extreme demands on the parents' energy; or the parents are in the midst of a separation or divorce process. Inhibited or anxious behaviour can also be a way for a child to stave off his or her desires for autonomy. For example, the child does not seek out contact with her peers because the mother cannot be alone at home and finds meaningful occupation in the child. The mother herself might be fending off a depressive reaction in this way. Through over-adaption at home or in school, some children attempt to gain the attention and acknowledgement that is usually directed toward a younger sibling.

This expressive behaviour may also sometimes mask a depressive mood, brought on by the child's belief that he or she is not lovable enough—for example, because the father has separated from the rest of the family and is no longer interested in his children.

Feelings of inferiority and corresponding anxious, inhibited behaviour can also be the result of a specific learning disability which has led to repeated experiences of failure in school and criticism from the parents.

This list could go on and on. We can see that over-adapted, inhibited, anxious behaviour can serve as a defence against aggressive fantasies and desires for autonomy, or it may primarily be the expression of low self-esteem.

If there is a need to ease and process resistance, the child requires our help in finding forms of expression for his or her wildly proliferating fantasies, so that her emotions can gradually be permitted to express themselves and be differentiated through symbolic representation.

If, however, a feeling of inferiority is the child's primary problem, then it is above all the 'sparkle in the eyes' of the therapists, their differentiated perception of the child and their acknowledgement of his or her statements and expressions which will strengthen her feelings of self-worth. For many children, there is a double aspect to this behaviour: it expresses their feelings of inferiority at the same time that it serves as a defence against repressed aggression.

6.1.2 Leader Interventions

In the first session, a six-year-old child cannot enter the group space without the accompaniment of his or her mother or father. We intervene in stages: first we ask the child if he is able to sit with the other children in the circle if his mother takes a seat in the corner. If the child is not able to accept this, then we allow his mother to sit with him in the circle. Nevertheless, we always speak to the child as the participant in the play, and not the mother. If the child can only manage to sit on the side-lines with his mother and watch the session, we allow him to do this. We ask the mother/father not to put pressure on the child to participate more actively. During the scenery-building phase, we ask the child whether he would also like to build something for himself.

We sometimes combine this question with the offer of a role—for example, like this: 'You are watching so attentively, like a cat. In the game, could you pretend to be a cat that just sits and watches?' Whether this child would feel even safer in the role of a bird that sits on a branch out of reach, for example, depends upon the other children's choices of roles.

In the closing discussion round, we try to communicate to the child that we understand and accept his reticence. We say, for example: 'You paid attention well and you saw everything. Now you understand how we play here, and next time you can build yourself a nest or a house again and watch from there—or maybe then you will also feel like playing along!'.

Normally, we phone the parents later in order to hear what the child said about the session afterwards and to help the parents with their insecurity. If the child still displays the same fearful and resistant behaviour in the third and fourth sessions, we should carefully consider whether or not this child should continue in the group therapy. In any event, we take care that the resistant child is not attracting too much concern. He should not achieve any symptomatic gain from his behaviour or provoke any negative effects on the group dynamics.

It sometimes happens that other children react quite negatively toward an inhibited child. In this case, it is important to prevent him or her from being laughed at; at the same time, we should not give the other children the impression that the inhibited child is more important than they are.

Example

Robin, an inhibited boy, was part of a mixed group of seven-year-olds. The other children had already decided to play the roles of a bear family. Robin attempted to attach himself to the female therapist by responding (after long hesitation) to the question of which role he would like to play with 'I don't know!' He looked so troubled that the leaders began to consider roles for him, trying to make a wide variety of roles appealing to him. Robin responded to every suggestion with 'I don't know!' The female therapist recognised the attachment and remembered that Robin's inhibited behaviour had started following the birth of his younger sister. She therefore made the following suggestion: 'Maybe you want to think about it for a while—and if you want to later on, you can be the baby bear who is just being born!' Robin was able to accept this. This intervention succeeded in picking up on Robin's regressive wishes and helping him to find a place among the other children.

This form of 'mothering' deprived him of the nurturing that his symptomatic behaviour demanded; however, he received a form of attention which helped him to enter into the play with the other children.

In addition to anxiety in reaction to the unusual and unfamiliar situation of the beginning phase, we also observe other anxiety reactions in children. For example, there are some children whose fear is primarily related to their function in the family system—such as when a child's anxiety triggers extra care and solicitude on the part of the parents and thereby suppresses the latent conflict in their partnership; or because a mother cannot detach from her child and the latter identifies with the anxious mother and/or fends off his or her anger at the attention through anxiety. In such cases, we work intensively with the family—if possible, before the start of the group therapy, or as an accompaniment to it.

If, for example, a child plays well in the group but does not speak, this is especially noticeable in the opening and closing discussion rounds. If the child's refusal to speak is also the reason for his or her enrolment in the group, then she has usually already been exposed to a wide range of attempts to make her do so, and she will expect the same treatment from the therapists. Independently of our diagnostic assessment, we interpret such behaviour as a 'decision' on the part of the child, and we respect that decision. We try to clarify with the child through what nonverbal means she is able to communicate things to us—for example, her play choices. Again, in the case of a child who refuses to speak, it is also important to remember that while she requires special attention and perhaps a certain amount of protection, she should not experience a symptomatic gain. Thus, for example, the beginning of the play session should not be held back by the fact that it is so difficult to figure out what role the non-speaking child would like to play. We then encourage this child to construct the scenery along with the other children and in the process, try to determine what roles we can suggest to her. Here, we must also be careful not to create any suggestive pressure.

Similar considerations apply in the case of a motorically inhibited child, who can easily tempt us to move cushions around for him or her and build his lair for him, rather than simply supporting him in doing so. Nevertheless, the way in which we help such a child will also depend upon whether the inhibited child comes from a situation of being spoiled or whether he comes from a cold, achievement-oriented and overly demanding family situation. In the former case, with every action, we express our admiration for what the child is able to do by himself; in the latter, it can sometimes be better to provide active support and share in his delight at his beautiful lair.

In some cases, an inhibited child will attach him or herself to a lively child, frequently choosing the same roles and generally identifying strongly with the other child. In such cases, we pay attention to whether the stronger child accepts this situation or whether he or she reacts negatively. We then verbalise the situation for both parties so that the children can find arrangements that are tolerable for them. Here are two examples of this from group practice.

Example

Peter, aged eight, decided to play the role of a 'black panther' in the first session and was indignant when, after long hesitation, Kevin finally said: 'I'm a black panther, too!' It was clear to see that he experienced Kevin's choice as competition. Female therapist to Kevin: 'Did you choose the same role to show Peter that you would like to play together with him? But now Peter is annoyed: he probably has the impression that you are taking his idea away from him.' To Peter: 'Could you play with Kevin if he didn't choose the same animal—for example, if he played the role of a jaguar?' Kevin needed the therapist's help in order to find another role. He finally agreed to play a puma. Peter, on the other hand, needed support in defining his boundaries. He was therefore able to accept that we helped Kevin construct his puma's cave, since in this way we supported Peter's own wish for demarcation.

The following example deals with two nine-year-old girls who mutually stabilised each other in their symptomatic behaviour. The therapeutic interventions needed to apply to both of them.

Example

Maria was articulate and dominant, Sybille anxious. Maria not only allowed Sybille to choose the same role that she did; in fact, she sometimes almost forced her to do so. Here, it is important to understand that Maria's parents were very focused on her two significantly younger siblings and that Maria felt neglected. Despite all the attention we paid to her, we considered it appropriate to repeatedly address her fear of relationship loss and deprivation, which she fended off through her pursuit of dominance. This is illustrated in the following excerpt from a session in which Maria played the owner of a grocery shop and Sybille played her assistant:

Male therapist (in the role of a customer) to Maria (the shop owner): 'Your shop is so well-run; everything is of excellent quality. How do you do it?' During the entire long period that the customer was shopping, Maria pushed Sybille completely into the background. From her role as another customer, the female therapist tried to let Sybille know that she was also being seen, even in her subordinate position, by saying to Maria: 'Your assistant is very helpful. As an owner, you must be very pleased to have such a good employee. She has even offered to help us carry all our things home—if you as the boss could spare her for a short time.'

Maria: 'Yes, that would be all right—no, wait! I think maybe I will do that myself!' Male therapist (from the leader position): 'You can hardly stand it when Sybille gets some attention. Do you feel as though people don't like you anymore? I think maybe you sometimes feel that way at home?' Maria responds: 'Ok—then let her go!' Sybille then accompanies the female therapist home with her shopping. The male therapist remains in the shop with Maria and continues to buy several more things. While it was appropriate to offer Maria understanding and limitations in response to her neurotic desire for dominance, Sybille required support and acknowledgement for every small step she made toward greater autonomy. We therefore initially defined her subordination to Maria as a wish and a capacity for humility, since she was still very reliant on Maria during this phase.

In a later session, however, we said to Sybille (from the leader position): 'Imagine you had your own shop. You would certainly be a good business-woman. But for now you would rather work together with Maria. Maybe you are unsure of whether Maria would be able to tolerate the competition, and you wouldn't want to lose her as a friend in the group.'

6.1.3   Interventions from Within a Role

In the following examples, we will describe how the therapists can help children through supportive doubling.

Example

In the beginning phase of a group, seven-year-old Annika had chosen the role of a rabbit and remained in her hutch most of the time. The therapists were playing the roles of a farm couple.

Male farmer: 'If the rabbit doesn't want to come out of her hutch, she must have her reasons. After all, with her ears she can hear everything, and she certainly must be thinking about it.' (Ego-supporting double).

Female farmer: I will lay a turnip down in front of the hutch. I'm sure she will come and get it if she wants to eat it. She is a very quick rabbit: the turnip will probably disappear without us seeing anything!' (Ego-supporting double, stimulus to action).

Annika picked up on this stimulus and always retrieved the 'turnip' when the farmers were not paying attention. The farmers, in turn, were surprised every time when the turnip had disappeared again.

Example

For the third time, 'Robbery' was the theme in a group of boys, all of them nine years old. The female therapist was the owner of a jewellery shop which was robbed; the male therapist was assigned to play the police officer pursuing the robbers.

Peter was a boy who was strongly attached to his mother. Under pressure from the other boys, he initially agreed to play along with the robbery scenario. When questioned by the police, the jeweller said: 'And there was one robber in the gang who didn't seem so dangerous to me. I thought I would be able to hold onto him when the gang was trying to run away with the stolen goods. But then he gave me such a fierce look that I got frightened.' (Ego-supporting combined with reinterpretation).

The group played several other continuing stories. Peter was more and more readily convinced to play along, and he repeatedly structured the situation spontaneously in such a way that he could threaten the female therapist in her respective role with his ferocious glance—so that she was 'frozen with fear' (an antitype to his busy mother).

In further sessions of the Robbery series, the group discussed the differentiated roles, including each robber's special skills. The other boys were an excellent marksman, a ninja fighter, an explosives specialist and a safe cracker/computer hacker. Peter could not come up with an idea. The female therapist then asked him if he would like to be someone who specialises in escapes and rescues. This idea appealed to him, and with great dedication, he drew up plans of the sewer system which would serve as the escape route from the bank when it was surrounded by police.

After the female therapist made this suggestion from the position of a leader, the male therapist supported it from his role as the officer-in-charge: 'Message to Scotland Yard: We have surrounded the bank, but the gang has brought their escape and rescue specialist along. Even under the most difficult conditions, he has managed to help the gang escape. But this time we are the clever ones! We have posted officers outside the air and elevator shafts on the roof. They won't get away from us this time!'.

These interventions were designed to stimulate the children's imaginations during the play scenario and above all, to stabilise Peter's position in the group. Through his transference onto the female therapist, he already found the courage to test his first attempts at detaching and setting boundaries by threatening her at the symbolic level with his fierce glances and escaping from her grasp. At that point, more active and aggressive confrontations were not possible for him.

Doubling ambivalencies can be another aid to a child's development. Here is an example of this from a group of six-year-old children who played 'Animals on the Farm' from the beginning phase up until the eighth session.

Example

The group consisted of three girls and three boys. Jana was a gloomy and anxious child who up to now had always sought out a strong connection with the female therapist.

In the seventh session, the children wanted the female therapist to play the role of the good farm woman; the male therapist should play a chicken thief. Similar to the 'Bremen Town Musicians', the animals wanted to help the farm woman. Jana suddenly declared: 'This time I'm not going to be a cat. I will be a little goat who hides inside the clock, and the robber takes the clock with him. But during the night, I will escape back to the rest of you.' Since the fairy tale fantasy with the clock was difficult to play, Jana agreed to hide inside the chicken thief's sack.

The female therapist supported this progressive impulse, saying to the other animals: 'The little kid is not as frightened as she used to be; maybe she can help us?'.

The robber was quite surprised to find not only chickens inside his sack, but also the little kid. But the next morning, the kid had disappeared. 'What a shame,' he said, 'it might be a lot of fun if the little kid would visit me again. But maybe she thinks that then the farm woman (female therapist) would be sad.'

Jana's father had separated from the family almost one year earlier. Jana was still unsure of whether she could show and tell her mother how much she missed her father and would like to visit him.

Depending on the child's age, the contract and the group-dynamic situation, in the subsequent discussion round, we might be able to connect the kind of doubling described above with the psychogenetic interpretation. This is especially likely to work well if there are other children in the group whose parents are separated or divorced. In this case, for example, we could have said in the closing round: 'When parents have separated, some children feel like the little goat did in the play scenario. They want to be with their mothers, but they are also curious about what the father's apartment looks like.' Of course, it is important not to overload these moments with too much meaning.

In inhibited or anxious children, their psychological situation affects all of their expressive behaviour, extending as far as physical rigidity. The psychodramatic play in the group setting encourages children's desire for movement and via the body, usually initiates a loosening of tension. A 'Circus' scenario provides many opportunities to support and encourage a child in his or her expressive behaviour by means of mirroring and doubling. Here is one example of this.

Example

Jonas, an anxious, overweight and clumsy boy, was part of a group of ten-year-old children. His mother had pampered him as 'my little boy' for too long, while his father criticised and rejected him to an increasing degree. Conflicts arose repeatedly between him and the other children due to his awkward manner. This was also initially the case in an opening discussion round, where the children decided to play a circus scenario. The other children wanted to be tightrope walkers, acrobats and wild animals—but Jonas could not come up with an idea. With the help of the therapists, he then settled on the role of 'Zampano the Strongman', who picked up boulders and defeated the strongest man in Europe (the male therapist) in a tug-of-war.

Circus director (the female therapist): '…and now, ladies and gentlemen, watch how Zampano's muscles tense up—and now he is actually lifting this enormously heavy boulder into the air! It is unbelievable how much strength is hidden inside the good-natured Zampano!' (Mirroring) 'And now comes the thrilling tug-of-war. The Spanish Bull [the male therapist] versus Zampano! … The battle is not over yet!'

Male therapist (thinking out loud): 'Blast it, this Zampano is tough. I thought it would be easy to beat him, but I underestimated him!' (Supportive doubling) Circus director: 'Hoorah! Zampano wins! Sound the trumpets!'.

In this scenario, Jonas's relationship with the male therapist was particularly important. However, it was also important for the therapist to appear as his 'opponent'. One of the boys from the group would not have been able to concede defeat to Jonas due to his own feelings of envy and competition. And even if any boy had been prepared to do so, he would not have been able to respond to Jonas's physical strength in such a differentiated way as the therapist could. Through his reactions, the therapist was able to encourage the boy's self-confidence and with it, his physical development as well.

Two girls in the group, both of them insecure and anxious, played the roles of trapeze artists in this scenario. It was important to them that their acrobat act really take place at an elevated height, and not on a rope that was laid on the floor. We therefore stood several cushion elements on end so that the girls could perform their act on a wobbly 1.2-metre-high surface. The girls faced a real physical challenge, and the therapists' commentaries corresponded positively to their immediate experience of height and instability. (The male therapist remained close by the entire time.) The circus director commented as follows: 'Ladies and gentlemen, now turn your attention to the wire stretched high up underneath the roof of the circus tent! It takes great courage to walk along a wire at this breath-taking height. This is one of the greatest attractions in all of Europe. And now, ladies and gentlemen, watch how gracefully, nimbly and confidently these tightrope artists move …!' This was once again followed by applause and fanfare

6.2 Interventions with Aggressive Children

Children can behave aggressively for a wide variety of reasons; here is an incomplete list:

- Quite often, their parents are authoritarian or aggressive.
- Another cause is emotional neglect.
- An inability to find stability in a situation where they are spoiled or indulged can trigger aggressive behaviour in some children.
- For many children, excessive demands to perform can be another reason.
- Some children react aggressively because they don't know how to get along in a group and they quickly feel threatened by the other children.
- There are also some children who have been labelled in their classroom or in the family as aggressive or as having a behaviour disorder; the system perpetuates this dynamic, causing the children to become trapped in their positions.
- Specific deficits such as mild spasms, processing disorders, or biographical situations of extreme stress can give rise to aggressive behaviour.
- In addition, there are children for whom it is difficult to cope in complex social situations. They feel troubled and oppressed by the lack of clarity and behave aggressively as a preventive measure. The aggressive behaviour leads to a different quality in the child's emotional state: the agitation is not fearful, but rather, angry or very decisive. As a result, the fear and insecurity lessen and a pleasant state sets in; thus, aggression leads to a perceived (emotional) release and This establishes a self-regulation model, which gradually increases the aggressive behaviour (Petermann and Petermann 1987, p. 218).

Frequently, by the time we meet them, aggressive and dominant children have already had a rather long career as 'behaviourally disturbed' children behind them, which has contributed to their symptoms becoming entrenched. Thus, for example, an emotionally neglected child may have initially received attention in nursery school thanks to his or her conspicuous behaviour. However, the conflicts which result from it bring the child further and further into the position of an outsider, and

increase his aggressive tension. Later, when he enters school, if he cannot compensate with good performance, the dynamics repeat themselves. Performance
failure and a lack of friends then lead to increased aggression or depressed withdrawal. If, for example, these difficulties contribute to preventing his
performance-oriented father from an intended separation from the family, a problematic symptomatic gain is added to the mix. In many children, the persistence of
their symptoms can be explained by such developments and repeated determination,
and we are faced with the question of: What can still be done to help?

Therefore, we must carefully consider what issues we can work on with the
child in the group, which aspects need to be addressed in family counselling, and
what can happen in the wider environment.

Strong feelings of inferiority and aggressive behaviour go hand in hand all too
often. One first step toward breaking down this reciprocal effect is the symbolic
staging of fantasies of omnipotence. Thus, for example, the role of 'Robin Hood'
allows for aggression in the service of the poor and downtrodden, followed by
recognition and admiration. The roles used to embody fantasies of omnipotence
vary according to gender. Girls transform themselves into such figures as: a
beautiful but mischievous cat, the fastest and most elegant horse, a witch, a doctor, a
princess, a millionaire or a karate fighter. Boys choose roles such as: a sheepdog, a
cunning magician, a strong knight, a robot or a doctor. Such figures are associated
with the children's ideal selves. Given shape in a scenario, they help the children to
compensate for negative experiences—for example: failure, lack of ability, inferiority, devaluation or shaming. They serve as self-regulating mechanisms: inwardly,
with respect to their own impulses, affects and moods; and outwardly in the formation of their relationships with the other children and the therapists.

In their most negative form, we encounter fantasies of omnipotence as destructive
fantasies of absolute power—for example, such as 'wicked witch' or 'indestructible
Terminator'.

Through these omnipotent roles, children defend themselves—in a process of
splitting—against emotions and negative self-images which can usually be traced
back to serious traumatisation. These figures are characterised by their brutality and
the compulsion to repeat their actions. In such roles—in which they identify with the
aggressor—children attempt this time to force 'the other person' into the role of
someone who is abandoned, injured, helpless, etc. 'Narcissistic anger enslaves the
ego and permits it to act only as a tool or a rationaliser. Aggression, on the other
hand, is under the ego's control, and the ego regulates the degree of neutralisation in
accordance with the goals toward which it is applied' (Heinemann et al. 1992, p. 28).

In our groups, we witness countless role variations which occupy a position in
between fantasies of omnipotence and destructive fantasies of absolute power.

These images are antitypes to the children's inferior self-images. As important as it is to allow children's aggressive fantasies to be expressed, it is equally necessary to ensure that these fantasies are not simply acted out. We must assist these children in differentiating and limiting these sadistic impulses so they can find their way to better self-control and compromise-ready behaviour.

The following examples of intervention can therefore only function as suggestions; they cannot claim to cover the entire spectrum of this problem situation.

6.2.1 Leader Interventions

If a child is frequently 'dropped off' a long time before the group session begins, this has an unfavourable effect; this is particularly true with aggressive children. In these cases, the child usually already comes into conflict with the other children in the waiting room. In addition, the child's dissatisfaction with his or her mother, who has dropped him off so early in order to have more time to herself, can have an effect on his relationship with the therapists in the form of negative transference—for example, in a rejecting attitude toward the female therapist. In such cases, it is important to work with the parents so that they can adjust their behaviour.

Even in the beginning phase, it can be useful to explain to an aggressive and restless child why he or she is sometimes treated differently. Why, for example, during the discussion round, the female therapist takes the place next to him in the role of an auxiliary and if necessary, uses physical contact in order to control the child's excitement (auxiliary). In doing so, it is important not to shame the child in question.

If a child is particularly tense and restless in the beginning phase, one can even go so far as to say to him or her: 'You are already so excited that you can hardly even think about what role you want to choose. Come over here in this corner with me, so you won't be so distracted. We can think about it together, and then afterwards it will be easier for you to decide.' This will help both the child and the group.

After he or she chooses a role, we ask the aggressive child, for example: 'If you are going to play a lion (or a gladiator or Rambo or a robber, etc.) what do you want to pay attention to so that you don't really hurt the other children—so that they will continue wanting to play with you?'.

This is an intervention which increases the child's awareness of his or her aggressive impulses and fosters the self-control that he needs.

Whereas we might be able to allow one child to construct a sword out of Baufix elements, we might only be able to allow another child to use a soft pillow as a weapon. Here is an example of what we mean:

Example

In the case of seven-year-old Till, for example, we were certain that when he laid down Baufix blocks as 'bombs', these would be sufficient to satisfy his fantasy. With Sven, also aged seven, we needed to set limits from the very beginning, since it was clear to us after just a few sessions that he could not restrain himself sufficiently in the heat of the battle. Here, we set the rules in the following way: 'You think it's even more fun when you throw the bombs, but you also know how hard you just threw them, don't you? If someone got hit by one of those it would really hurt. So we need to put your wooden blocks back into the basket and think about how we can play the scene with the bombs in this game.' After a great deal of discussion, Sven agreed to use only small pillows as bombs for the time being and to see whether he could manage without throwing them.

Naturally, unequal treatment leads to protest and conflict. It is therefore important for the therapists to explain why distinctions are being made. For children who have a very difficult time controlling themselves, this can serve as a motivation to pay more attention to boundaries.

In the following example, we describe the way we set limits on a child's ostensible attempts at dominance.

Example

The participants in this group were nine years old, two girls and three boys. Christian, a late-born second child, was emotionally neglected due to his father's severe illness and his mother's professional stress. In school, he constantly provoked his teacher in order to gain her attention.

In the beginning phase of the group, Christian immediately assumed the role of the assistant therapist and rigidly reinforced the rules with the other children. It was necessary for us to counter him in a friendly but firm manner: 'You want to help us and show us that you want to abide by all the rules here—but enforcing the rules and boundaries, that is our job.'

In one session, when the children had chosen their roles for an animal scenario—the girls wanted to play dogs, the boys wolves—Christian declared: 'I am a dinosaur'. We did not think it made sense at this stage of the group's development to uphold the principle of a free choice of roles for Christian. We were convinced that it would not be helpful for him to obtain a special role once again, and we told him: 'Think about whether you can come up with a role that fits in better with the others, so that you won't be alone again!'

Christian (after some consideration): 'All right, then I will be a wolf, too!' The children decided that the female therapist should play an animal lover; the male therapist was assigned the role of a threatening hunter.

After a little while, Christian allowed himself to be captured by the hunter and then declared: 'Now I will become tame and be the hunter's wolf-dog. I will live together with the hunter!'

Male therapist: 'For me as a hunter, it is very good to have a wolf-dog like this, but the wolf-dog might lose his friendship with the other wolves if I keep him here with me.'

Nevertheless, Christian wanted to hazard the consequences in this session. We allowed him to do so, since here he was expressing his wish for attention, and a desire for domination as a replacement and defence against his longing for a relationship was not at the forefront. Naturally, this had consequences for the dynamics of the group. In the following session, the other boys declared: 'We are going to let the hunter train us!' At this, Christian retreated in disappointment, since he would no longer be able to have the male therapist all to himself. Only after several more sessions was Christian better able to tolerate not having one of the therapists for himself alone.

Limiting fantasies of absolute power
We encounter children who attempt to act out their fantasies of absolute power in every scenario. Therefore we are unable to avoid placing limits on them even in their choice of roles and/or in the formation of their roles. If we did not do so, they would be rejected by the group more and more, and in the end they would have exactly the same experience that they have always had in school or in free play situations. Generally, their destructive fantasies of omnipotence mask strong feelings of inferiority. If we can be aware of this, it becomes easier for us to help these children and to remain consistent in setting boundaries.

For example, we might say to a child: 'If you want to be a wizard, then we have to think about what magical things you can do. And we also need to find out which of the other children will allow you to put a spell on him or her.' Through negotiations with the wizard and the other children, we are usually able to agree that one child or another will allow herself to be put under a certain spell for a certain length of time. This is a corrective experience for the child with the fantasies of absolute power. Frequently, the therapists need to be prepared to submit to a magic spell, since children generally do not allow themselves to be enchanted as often or for as long a period of time as the witch or wizard would like. In this helpless position—transformed into a stone or a frog—we as the antagonists can experience very vividly what kind of experiences have led to these children's need for fantasies of omnipotence; in spoken soliloquies, we can verbalise this knowledge for the children. Another possibility for limiting fantasies of absolute power can begin if we, in our position as leaders, point out the problems involved with the child's role choice and then draw a connection to the group. If the child defines his or her role as an 'invincible alien', then we present him with the possibility that the other children might also wish to be invincible. We then ask the other children how they can imagine a shared play scenario. In most cases, they are not prepared to participate in a polarised scenario of an invincible perpetrator and vulnerable victims.

Children who have fantasies of absolute power often attempt to circumvent our limitations with clever evasion tactics in order to maintain their omnipotence. For example, they may switch roles frequently or reproach the therapists: 'But you said that I am allowed to choose my role myself!'

Clear and definitive limitations are therefore already necessary in the opening discussion phase—because once the children are acting out their fantasies, it is much more difficult to reach them and to agree on limits. If they then have the experience that playing with the other children is still satisfying despite the limitations, in the course of the therapy they will learn to limit themselves. Here is another example of this from our practice.

Example

A group of seven-year-old children, two girls and two boys, were playing a fairyland scenario. Tobias: 'I am a soldier and I have a tank!' Female therapist: 'A tank won't work here. Let's think about what kind of soldier you could be in this fairy tale. Could you imagine being a knight with silver armour, a powerful sword and a spirited steed who owns the castle in this fairy tale land?'

Simply setting a limit or saying 'no' is not enough. Due to their emotional state—and often strongly influenced by computer games and their perpetrator/victim models—these children's creativity is limited and they scarcely have any alternatives at their disposal. These children require an impulse or suggestion from one of the therapists which will help them to break away from their own ideas. Often they have already been focusing intensively on their fantasies during the drive to the session or in the waiting room, so that it then becomes very difficult for them to adapt to a different role.

Playing directions for maintaining an arc of tension

In general, children between the ages of four and seven have difficulty maintaining the suspense in a scene. This is all the more true of impulsive, aggressive children, who can destroy a game in no time at all if we do not keep a tight rein on them.

Example

Five six-year-old children were playing the roles of dwarves. The female therapist was a fairy and the male therapist an evil giant.

Female therapist to six-year-old Kevin: 'No, you cannot attack the giant right away again. All of the dwarves sneak up very slowly, and you must stay in the group of dwarves—right beside me, because I need someone strong to protect me against this dangerous giant.' This verbal bond can be reinforced by physical contact, and even by occasional holding. After the scene, we can then praise the child for his patience and skill in sneaking up on the giant. Such positive experiences with self-control will gradually increase his tolerance for frustration.

In this scene, an intervention from within the role of the fairy would also have been a potential option; however, it was not possible to communicate with Kevin in this form.

In the following example, we describe an unsuccessful attempt at setting limits in the discussion round. This is the summary of a video recording from a supervision session.

Example

A group of ten-year-old children consisted of two girls and three boys; it was the 23rd session. Joachim, an only child, had been enrolled in the group because of his aggressive striving for dominance. He was very verbal and occupied a central position in the group in the majority of sessions. In the 21st and 22nd sessions, Joachim was ill; in these sessions, the other four children played a 'Wild West' scenario with horses and horse thieves (the therapists). The development of the story and the dramatic play were relatively conflict-free. The children as well as the therapists were evidently happy that the difficult boy, Joachim, was absent.

Discussion phase in the 23rd session:

Even in the waiting room, Joachim was showing off quite a bit. Martina: 'We want to continue the story we played the last time.'

Joachim: 'What a bunch of crap! Horse trading, horse manure! You stupid girls don't know anything about the Wild West anyway!' The other two boys also said they would like to continue the story, but without any particular emphasis.

Joachim: 'That's horse piss! Girls can cook and wash up, or shag …!' Male therapist: 'Now you have been absent twice and you need to get adjusted back into the group—what would you like to play?'

Joachim: 'Definitely not that kind of crap. Southern States versus Northern States—that would be good. We (indicating the boys) are the Northern States and defeat the Southern States—that's you (the therapists).'

Female therapist: 'And the girls—what could they play in the story?' Joachim: 'They can cook, maybe take care of the wounded soldiers or something like that. I can be the general!'

The two other boys, who were initially uncertain, no longer want to go along with Joachim's idea and take orders from him. Joachim: 'You stupid wankers—you suggest something then!' However, the two boys were not able to return to their original wish—to continue with the Wild West scenario—on their own initiative; instead, they indirectly validated Joachim in his dominance. The steadily escalating exchange of verbal blows ultimately prevented any shared play scenario from taking place in this session.

Let us examine the remarks made by the two therapists, which can be understood as verbal interventions at the leadership level.

The male therapist said: 'You were absent from the group twice and now you want to come back in—what would you like to play?'

With the first half of his sentence, he addresses Joachim's problem. He could have elaborated on this remark by making reference to the feeling of being excluded and Joachim's uncertainty about finding his way back into the group. Joachim might not have admitted to this feeling; however, it would have corresponded to his day-to-day experience and to the general mood in the group.

A decisive factor, however, was the fact that the therapist accepted Joachim's disparagement of the entire group—including the female therapist—without commentary. In this way, he unintentionally supported Joachim's form of over-coming his fears with the help of fantasies of omnipotence. In this situation, Joachim not only needed understanding; he also needed the security and demar-cation of boundaries provided by an auxiliary in order not to continue repeating the strategies he had used up to now. For example, the therapist could have explained that he would not accept these insults; rather, he had experienced the last two play scenarios as fun and exciting, and he would be happy to help Joachim find a role in this scenario. It should also have been pointed out to Joachim that up to now he had only elicited rejection with this manner of behaving, and that he was in the group for this very reason. Furthermore, one of the therapists should have said: 'I would like you to first listen to the story; then you can decide whether you would like to watch or to play along!' This suggestion would also have rectified the insult toward the other children.

We have noticed repeatedly that therapists shy away from confronting children in the group so decisively. Many of them believe this would be overly pedagogical and are afraid that such action would humiliate the child in question in front of the others. At the root of this, however, is usually the uncertainty provoked by their own anger at a boy who behaves like this.

By asking Joachim: 'What would you like to play?' the therapist accepted, or even confirmed, the boy's disparagement of the game played in the two previous sessions and repressed his anger at Joachim through reaction formation. (During supervision, the therapist became aware that aggressive dominance on the part of other people triggers feelings of both fear and admiration in him, and that this ambivalence had prevented him from reacting appropriately.)

The female therapist's contribution: she asked: 'And the girls—what could they play in the story?' With this reaction, she 'sacrificed' the girls in order to help Joachim. One could see from the girls' faces that they felt betrayed by their 'mother'.

(In supervision, the female therapist remembered that as a child, she had accepted almost every kind of treatment in order to be allowed to play with her older brothers and their friends.)

Even though both therapists made a verbal effort to help Joachim integrate into the group, their nonverbal signals were anything but friendly. This inconsistency could not have been helpful.

When children behave the way Joachim did, it is difficult for us to keep in mind how threatened they are feeling, how alone they are, and how strenuous these battles are. In such situations, it is not easy to understand our own affect and countertransference and to regain a grip on our therapeutic competence.

6.2.2 Interventions from Within a Role

As auxiliaries within our roles, we can help an aggressive child to restrain him or herself and control her impulses without intervening as leaders and provoking negative transference or resistance from the child. Here are a few examples of this:

Example

In the role of a maidservant to a very domineering ten-year-old girl who is playing the role of the most beautiful and powerful princess, the female therapist expresses her thoughts out loud: 'Why is my most gracious lady, the noble and high-born princess screaming like this once again? After all, she is very clever, and she could simply explain what it is she wants.' (Supportive doubling).

Or: Playing the role of a page to knight (a nine-year-old boy) shortly before the tournament: 'My noble lord is behaving like a drunkard—how embarrassing. The other knights might think that he is afraid of the tournament. But after all, my master has fought successfully in many battles, and he might also achieve the prize this time. What shall I do so that the others do not laugh at him?'.

Eight-year-old Julian often played with uncontrolled aggression; in this scene he was playing a 'Tyrannosaurus Rex'. The therapists, who were playing the roles of prehistoric humans in this scenario, spoke about Julian in symbolic form.

Male therapist: 'I have heard that this dinosaur gets irritated easily. Maybe in his anger he will fall into our trap!'

Female therapist: 'But other people say he is also very clever, and he can lie very still for a long time, so that people might think he is not always dangerous.' (Supportive doubling).

Male therapist: 'But he is very strong. Imagine—with his strength, if he would help us to move the huge boulder away from the entrance to our cave.' (An attempt to suggest a positive focus for the aggression).

The following is the outline of a sample case for limiting aggressive fantasies of omnipotence. Interventions from within roles were alternated with those carried out from the leadership position.

Example

Michael, aged eight, frequently provoked arguments in the classroom with his extreme reactions; he had become a scapegoat there. The therapy group consisted of one other boy and two girls. They had been playing a cowboy scenario for several sessions. The two girls were playing ranch owners; the other boy was a shopkeeper. The male therapist played a farmer and the female therapist was a tradeswoman.

In every session, Michael wanted to play the role of the sheriff. And in every session, he interfered and attempted to provoke the other children to the point that a shootout would take place. He could not really comprehend the actual meaning of his role as the sheriff or the tasks that are associated with it. His desire to release emotion—particularly through exchanges of fire with the male therapist—was the most important thing for him. His trigger-happy tendencies made it nearly impossible for him to play his role in such a way that one could recognise him as a sheriff. However, he did not want to play the role of a bandit.

In one session, when Michael once again wanted to stage the usual gun battles between himself and the male therapist, the latter refused to accept his assigned role. Instead, he decided to be a cowboy who wanted to take lessons from the sheriff, who was known far and wide for his shooting abilities. (Resistance to play) This worked quite well for a while: the cowboy admired the sheriff as an excellent marksman, and he never succeeded in shooting as accurately as the sheriff could. (Mirroring in order to support damaged self-esteem) After a time, the sheriff (Michael) attempted to provoke the cowboy into a duel. However, the therapist did not want to be manoeuvred into the victim position once again; he intervened through active interpretation in the following way:

- Male therapist: 'No, I will not compete against you, sheriff, the world-famous marksman!'
- Michael: 'You scaredy-cat—draw your Colt already!'
- The therapist verbalised the issue that Michael was trying to ward off: 'No, then I will be wounded again for several weeks and I will be in pain. I don't want that anymore!'
- Michael: 'But you have to play! You think that you will defeat me!'

At this point, the therapist switched from the symbolic level to the leadership level and said: 'No, I won't play that. If I do, it will be like it is for you in your class, when you argue with the other children and hit them. In the end, you are the loser, just like the cowboy would be here. And in school you are also really concerned with how you can make friends.'

Michael temporarily retreated in disappointment; after a few minutes he returned with the question: 'All right, then you tell me how the story should go on!'

Male therapist: 'I would like to think together with you about how the story could continue—and in such a way that it fits in with the other children's game.'

In a subsequent session, the male therapist played the role of a farmer who obtains a firearms licence from the sheriff, buys a gun and takes instruction in shooting, but only goes hunting. Once again, Michael came up with many different ways of trying to provoke a duel. Since he did not know what else he should do in his role as a sheriff, he was in urgent need of support from the therapists. The farmer (the male therapist), therefore went to visit the sheriff and asked him to adjust his gun because he was never able to hit his mark while hunting. (A supportive permanent double provides a creative means of dealing with aggression.) In addition, he allowed the sheriff to accompany him on the hunt and shoot a stag for him, since he was not such a good shot. He bought a parcel of land and entered into a contract, once again calling on the sheriff for help: the sheriff affixed his seal and attested to the legality of the contract.

The female therapist also called on the sheriff for help in finding a lost horse, since the sheriff was a better tracker, etc.

The goal of all of these interventions was to differentiate Michael's idea of his role and to break down the perpetrator/victim constellation.

After approximately eight sessions, the girls became bored with the Wild West storylines. The therapist addressed their displeasure and put it to the children to invent a new story. The group decided to play an adventure story loosely based on the 'Famous Five' children's book series. In this story, the female therapist was assigned to be a countess and the male therapist a robber. The children wanted to play the roles of four friends who take the robber into custody. In this story, too, Michael required help in developing ideas for how to play along without immediately reaching for a gun.

In the following session, the story was called 'Mountain Expedition'.

Once again, Michael immediately armed himself to the teeth. The male therapist played Michael's porter (supportive permanent double) so that he could again suggest play ideas to Michael that would fit in with the group's fantasy scenario: e.g., hunting for game, chopping wood and building a fire so that the explorers could cook something to eat in the evening; killing a dangerous bear (stuffed toy) that threatened the expedition; breaking a snow slab loose with a well-aimed gunshot so that the group could cross the slope.

It was impossible to ignore the fact that Michael's creative ability to develop ideas for play and adapt them to the group's fantasy scenario was significantly less than that of the other children. This was a determining cause of his difficulties in playing with them. The rebuffs that resulted from this led to aggressive reactions, which he then played out in stereotypical roles.

Michael's diagnostically elusive inability to develop fantasies of his own that could be adapted to fit in with the group's fantasies only became evident in its full extent during the course of the group therapy. The hypothesis which seemed most obvious from his biography—that his behavioural problems were primarily neurotic—needed to be corrected.

In the group therapy, we made some first steps toward helping Michael; time and again, however, he will be reliant on support and mediation from adults in order to get along with other children.

In his account of the therapy of a six-year-old boy, Aichinger (2007) demonstrates how difficult group work with aggressive children can be, how changes can only be achieved in small steps, and how the therapy needs to function multi-modally through complex interventions in order to activate the resources of the children, the parents and the school.

Group Process Oriented Interventions

7

Alfons Aichinger

Abstract

In this chapter, we will explore interventions which apply to the group and to the group process. One explanation for why so little group therapy work is carried out with children may have to do with the fact that chaos and destructive interactions can arise so quickly in groups of children, and therapists often find themselves helpless in the face of them. Unlike adults, over the course of the group therapy, children begin to rebel against the predetermined structure of the sessions. Within the safety of the group, they try to revolt against the leaders and leave them hanging with their play directions. Aggravating the leaders becomes the game of choice. When this happens, the safety of the symbolic play—the 'as if'—is lost. When the leaders join in, the game becomes deadly serious. The children manage to provoke the leaders into helpless anger and must then remain in their position of power—if only out of fear of retribution.

Most publications on group therapy work with children recount such difficulties in dealing with aggression and destructive behaviour. Lebovici, for example, describes how, in his first therapy groups, the children screamed, hit one another, threw furniture and even smashed windows (cf. Anzieu 1984, p. 84). Anzieu also describes similar experiences: that chairs were used as projectiles, that his glasses were shattered, etc. (Anzieu 1984, p. 95). These experiences led both authors to introduce the rule of simulation and to establish more structure. The situation was also similar for Ilse Seglow: 'Every group meeting in this first phase evolved into fighting and chaos among the children within the course of five minutes. They taunted and mocked one another, argued constantly and injured the weaker children' (Seglow 1969, p. 784).

© Springer Fachmedien Wiesbaden GmbH 2017
A. Aichinger and W. Holl, *Group Therapy with Children*,
DOI 10.1007/978-3-658-15813-2_7

We still have vivid memories of our first experiences—for example, in a group of aggressive boys: as if they had planned it ahead of time, one boy ran out the door while two others jumped out of the two ground-floor windows and made their escape. We ran after them, and the scene turned into a wild chase on the street. We became increasingly enraged—especially when we then ran into the parents, who were visibly amused by our helpless actions. Nor have we forgotten a provocation at the real level, when a boy held a burning cigarette lighter up to the cushions in the group room. When we tried to take the lighter away from him, he quickly threw it to the other children, who then began a game of 'Keep Away'. Or we remember children who threw the cloths and Baufix elements around the room, becoming increasingly wilder when we tried to intervene. We can also remember children who did not want to leave the group room at the end of the session: we had to carry them out of the room, but they returned immediately. The more we attempted to exert our authority as leaders, the more they enjoyed making us helpless and powerless. We made many attempts to initiate a creative process out of the chaos. It was only when we ceased to react to these provocations solely from the position of leaders, insisting on a rigid structure, but instead transferred the conflict precipitated by the children onto the symbolic level and intervened from within our roles, that we were able to work through these disagreements. The symbolic level provided both the children and the leaders with the possibility of approaching the conflicts cheerfully and creatively within a protected framework.

7.1 Interventions in Conflicts Between Children and Leaders

Thanks to the sense of security that the group can convey to individual children and to its reinforcing effect, children project all of their negative images of evil, controlling adults onto the therapists much more quickly than they do in individual therapy—and they react with increasing aggression.

Particularly in groups of prepubescent children, the therapists are often disparaged in nascent attitudes of protest, endowed with negative transferred feelings and approached with extreme anger as real representatives of the adult world. If this attitude of protest increases over the course of the therapy and becomes condensed into a rebellion, the children will not limit the expression of their negative transferred emotions to the play scenarios. They begin to openly fight back and rebel against the leaders' instructions—refusing, for example, to take part in the opening discussion round. Then they often enter the group space with wild shouting and raging; they throw pillows and cushions at the leaders or block them from entering the room. With this wild activity, the children are attempting to establish a role relationship between themselves and the leaders in which the leaders are stripped of their power and the children take control. If the leaders attempt to resist this interaction—to maintain the structure of the session through pressure and to forcefully assert their authority as leaders—they will sink into a disastrously spiralling power struggle. They can avoid this trap if they enter into the scenario that the children offer them, recognise and comprehend the children's unspoken offers of roles through complementary identification, assume the countertransference roles, and thereby engage with the interactive relationship that the children intended. They integrate themselves into the status structure that fits with the children's expectations. From the position which they allow the group to assign to them, they can then carry out their therapeutic function in the appropriate roles. Thus, they must not insist on remaining in the power position of real adults. Rather, from the position of a powerful role in which they could nevertheless be overcome, they must protest against the children's actions. For example, if the children secretly sneak into the group room before the beginning of the session and hold the door shut so that the leaders cannot enter, the leaders can assume the roles of a king and queen and indignantly demand to enter their castle. They can identify the gloating children as rebellious subjects and order them to surrender unconditionally or face imprisonment in the dungeon. Or they might appear as police officers who, speaking through a megaphone, order the criminals occupying a house to leave immediately before the police attack them with tear gas. If the children run screaming through the room, jostle each other and toss the cushions around, the male leader can identify them as a lawless gang and confront them in the role of a sheriff who is responsible for peace and order in the city. He will not allow a horde of bandits to cause instability in the town, ransack the saloon or frighten the citizens. He wants to put the gang behind bars as soon as possible. Alternatively, the female leader can play the role of a distinguished lady who calls the police because bikers are wreaking havoc on her property and demolishing everything in sight. She demands that the police move in immediately with their patrol car and water guns. If the children are younger, we can identify them as rabid animals that we must quickly capture and lock up in a kennel. If the children throw pillows at the leaders, they can quickly take cover, call for help, and report that they have been ambushed and shot at by gangsters. With children who refuse to stop talking amongst themselves, the female leader can appear in the role of a teacher, order them to be quiet because she wants to begin the lesson, and threaten to call the headmaster for help. Or in the role of the caretaker in a high-rise building, the male leader can shout down from an upper floor that the rowdy neighbour children should finally be quiet and respect the house rules, get off the grass and do their schoolwork. We can identify children who resist passively—sitting with crossed arms and refusing to speak—as obstructionists at a missile station to whom the military police give an ultimatum to clear the street for a missile transport. Children who want to run out of the room can be made into convicts attempting an escape who must be stopped by the prison guards. If the children provoke the leaders by pretending to be tired, the female therapist—in the role of a nurse at a convalescent home—can prescribe a two-hour nap in absolute silence.

If the children react to the therapists' play with curiosity—if they accept the suggested roles and the play scenario appeals to them, the leaders then briefly interrupt the story in order to construct the appropriate setting (e.g., the saloon or the prison) or allow the children to put on costumes.

However, the children will only accept this type of play suggestion at the symbolic level if the symbolic level offers them more possibilities for expressing themselves than the real level does. It also makes a crucial difference whether, in the symbolic play, the therapists adhere to the children's unconscious role suggestions or whether they use the play as a trick in order to regain power over the children and control over the play situation. The images that the therapists propose here should be related to the themes which the children have employed in play up to now and should take their developmental state into account.

Example

In the preceding sessions, a mixed group of twelve-year-olds had played the roles of teenagers who sneak out of their parents' house at night, go to the disco, hang about with girls or boys and get into arguments with their parents. This game gradually shifted from the symbolic level to the real one in the sense that the children not only got into arguments with the therapists in their roles as parents, but also as the leaders in the opening and closing discussion rounds. At the beginning of this session, the children provoke the therapists with their behaviour: they insult us using obscene expressions and throw pillows at us. Since it is not possible to conduct an opening discussion, the female leader assumes the role of a fine lady and becomes indignant. As the wife of the Lord Mayor, she will not put up with being molested by these bikers. It is appalling, what foul language comes out of the mouths of today's young people; it turns her red with shame. She then hurriedly calls the police and tells them she is being harassed by bikers, who are even throwing beer cans at her. However, the children do not pick up on this role suggestion. They continue to throw cushions and insult us on the real level. Now the male leader, in the role of the chief of police, sounds an alarm and gives the order for a large-scale operation to put an end to the bikers' rioting. He says they are going on a rampage, demolishing cars, breaking shop windows and molesting law-abiding citizens. He then drives up in his police car with sirens and flashing lights and through his megaphone, orders the bikers to clear the streets or else they will be put in jail. It is only with this threatening gesture from the chief of police who powerfully asserts his authority that the children spring into action. They use the cushions to build a barricade. The police give the bikers an ultimatum: they must stop their destructive rampage; otherwise the police will retaliate with nightsticks and tear gas. The teenagers simply laugh. At this, the male leader temporarily steps out of his role and asks the children whether the police should now move in with water guns and break up the blockade. The children counter that the police should use their water guns, but they will not have a chance. The bikers will throw stones and Molotov cocktails at them. After a brief pause to construct the scenery, a street battle takes place in which the children push themselves to their physical limits and inundate the police (both therapists)—who have been advancing slowly, hiding behind shields—with a shower of stones. The bikers then overpower the police, strip their clothes off, and make them jump naked over the jets of the captured water guns while the bikers laugh and jeer at them. Since the children have been able to express their anger physically, and we are able to withstand their force, they now seem completely relaxed in the closing discussion round. Thus, it is even possible to speak briefly about how it feels to be rendered powerless.

If the children do not yet dare to engage in an aggressive confrontation with the leaders, but instead tend to withdraw in a depressed manner and hang about passively and listlessly in the opening round, then it is appropriate for one of the two leaders—preferably the one to whom less of the children's anger is directed— to assume the role of an accuser in the children's place. In order to find the correct role, however, the leader must first have comprehended the reason for the children's reaction: for example, that one of the leaders was absent from the last session; or that one of them responded too little or too strongly to the children's play. Then—in the role of a doctor, for example—he or she can wonder out loud what has happened to the lively children; what has been done to them that they are so low-spirited? Or—if the children have previously played animals—she can arrive in the role of a vet and be appalled at what has happened to the wild animals; who is responsible for the fact that they are lying around as if they were half dead? Or she may play an employee of the child protection agency or the youth welfare office who is checking to see if everything is all right. There has been a call from the neighbours saying that parents were mistreating, neglecting or even abusing their children. She can then initiate an investigation and verbalise her suspicions until the children pick up on this play suggestion.

In the previous session, a group of ten-year-old boys provoked the male therapist at the end of the play period by not wanting to bring their game to an end. They simply continued to play the roles of a group of gangsters, knocked over the cushions that the leaders had set up for the closing round, and shouted over every attempt the male leader made to give his feedback on the session. The leader became more and more annoyed, until he finally let out a cry of rage. Now, in the following session, the children sprawl around completely passively on the cushions and say that they don't feel like playing today. After unsuccessful efforts, the female leader assumes the role of the saloon owner, which she played in the last session, and calls the marshal from the next town. She suspects that the sheriff is operating outside the law. A gang who have always led a jovial lifestyle up to now—drinking a lot in her saloon, and sometimes ransacking it—are now sitting around apathetically at her bar. She suspects that in his last operation, the sheriff dealt too harshly with the gang—perhaps he even mistreated them. At this, one boy becomes very animated and says she should report that the sheriff tortured them with electric shocks. The saloon owner passes this information on to the imaginary marshal on the telephone. She then repeats the marshal's response out loud: he will come into town immediately and start an investigation. When the children begin to come alive at this news, the female leader asks whether they would like to act out this trial. The children agree. One boy wants to play the role of the marshal; one will play the judge, and the other three will be the gang members, who will display their wounds as evidence. Once the scenery is quickly set up—with a jail, courtroom and gallows—the marshal rides into town and arrests the sheriff. A trial takes place in which the bandits and the saloon owner testify against the sheriff. He initially denies everything, saying he has always abided by the law. Recently, however, he must have lost his temper: he handled the gang somewhat more roughly. It seemed appropriate with such tough criminals. At this, the gang cries out that the sheriff tortured them in jail: they show their scars to the judge and the marshal. The two of them depose the sheriff and strip him of his sheriff's star. As punishment, he is dragged over cacti and finally hanged.

However, the leaders can only find the appropriate countertransference roles if they reflect on their feelings of countertransference and thereby grasp the nature of the tension that is dominating the group.

Example

A group of eight-year-olds have snuck into the group room and hidden behind the cushions. When the leaders come to fetch them from the waiting room, there are no children to be found. Now the leaders are faced with a question: Do the children want to stage a wish fulfilment fantasy in which the 'worried parents' search for their children—or do they want to punish their 'bad parents' by running away? In order to understand which scene the children are playing in which group fantasy, the leaders examine the feelings that are triggered within them. They feel guilty and ask themselves what happened in the previous session. They recall that they were both overworked and had therefore lacked commitment and attention in their play. Starting from this realisation, they assume the roles of guilty parents. They enter the group room and wonder aloud why their children have run away. They blame themselves, saying that they have recently been bad parents and have not paid enough attention to their children. It is no wonder that the children have taken off. They cry and promise that if the children ever come back, they will take better care of them. From their hiding places behind the cushions, the children listen to the therapists' self-reproaches and they giggle. One child says that the parents should find a letter stating that their children have immigrated to America, and that they should then cry bitterly. When the parents find the letter, they are horrified; they cry and wail: perhaps they will never see their beloved children again. They remember the happy times they had with their children, how sweet and nice they were, and how empty and hollow everything seems now. Now the children whisper together: from their hiding places behind the cushions, they give the direction that the parents should accuse and blame one another. The parents then reproach one another for all the things that each of them has done wrong—when they were too strict, too careless, gave the children too little attention. Finally, they vow to do everything better if the children should ever come back. The leaders then ask the children if the parents should go looking for them. The children say yes, the parents should search all across America, but they will not find the children and will return home with heavy hearts. The parents then wander all over America, tearfully searching for their children. When they then return home, desperate and sad, the children are lying asleep in their beds. The parents must then be overjoyed that their children have come back to them, and they sit by their bedsides all night long.

7.2   Oedipal Conflict in the Group

The children's oedipal conflicts and the various forms that they take repeatedly present the two leaders with difficult situations. The dual-gender therapist team in particular places the children in a triangular oedipal constellation and encourages the resurgence of oedipal fantasies and conflicts and the revival of emotions such as love, hate, envy and rivalry. The children analyse the perceived relationship between the two therapists in sexual terms; primal themes and fantasies emerge; and their relationships to the therapists of their respective genders are marked by rivalry. In this way, conflicts arise between the children and the therapist pair. The children attempt to invade the pair's dyadic relationship, giving such directions as 'Now you get undressed!', 'Now you have to kiss each other!', 'Now you are having sex and we will secretly watch through the window.' In supervision sessions, we have repeatedly seen how such directions unsettle the two therapists.

However, even when the children remind them that they promised to play everything the children instruct them to, in this case the therapists actually should not give into the children's pressure to finally play what they want. They must not play along with the children's game; rather, they have to frustrate the children's wishes. Through active interpretation, they set generational boundaries for the children and make it clear to them that there are aspects of adult life from which they will remain excluded. For example, in the roles of parents, they can retreat into their bedroom and say that they are closing the door so that the children won't know what they are doing. In order to master the oedipal situation, it is necessary for the children to be guided into their age- and gender-appropriate places and to recognise these differences.

Example

In a mixed group of eight-year-olds, the three girls are playing the roles of beautiful princesses; the two boys are robber barons. The male therapist is assigned to play the king; the female therapist is the queen. While the queen has to deck out and admire her daughters, the king fights with the marauding knights and expresses his amazement at their strength in combat. During a lull in the fighting, the princesses want to celebrate with a banquet. They make themselves fine and set up a festive table. They then sit down between the queen and the king. When the king admires the princesses' beauty and elegance, Judith—a girl who competes intensely with her mother at home and disparages her as a woman—suddenly says that the queen is dead and lives in a castle in Paradise. The female leader should now play a servant and wait on them. The other girls agree enthusiastically. In the role of the king, the male therapist insists that his wife, the queen, is in the best of health and is sitting next to him at the table. At this, the princesses become enraged and vehemently banish the king from the castle. They then drive the queen away as well. They call the robber barons into the castle, barricade the gate and ridicule the royal couple, who energetically demand to be let back into their home. The children shower the king and queen with faeces and pitch, and then laugh at them because they are so ugly and smelly. They call them names like 'asshole' and 'filthy pig', stick out their tongues and give them the finger. The children have enormous fun at the expense of the outraged monarchs. In the next session, when the leaders want to fetch the children from the waiting room, the children quickly run ahead and hold the door to the group room shut. However, the leaders do not respond to this invitation to a power struggle at the real level. Instead, they translate it into a symbolic action and assume the roles that the children have unconsciously assigned to them. As a king and queen, they demand indignantly to be allowed into their castle. They identify the giggling children behind the door as rebellious princesses and knights and order them to lower the drawbridge or face imprisonment in the dungeon. They urgently need to enter the castle, they say: they are freezing cold, and the queen needs to have a warm bath with rose petals. The children remain laughing in the therapy room and shout out that the king and queen can freeze to death for all they care. Once the children are sufficiently warmed up for this scenario at the symbolic level, the male therapist briefly steps out of his role as the king and tells the children (from the leader position) that they can only continue to play this scenario—in which the king and queen are standing helplessly outside the locked gate—inside the group room. They cannot continue to play outside in the corridor, because it will disturb other people who have come for counselling sessions. The children agree to this. However, they say that the royal couple may only enter the room after the children have constructed the castle wall and the throne. A short time later, they open the door for us and then adorn themselves with beautiful cloths. We also put on costumes as the king and queen, and the male leader quickly constructs a large sword for himself. After this brief interruption, the game continues. The king and queen must stand outside the gate shivering. The princesses and princes stand on the castle wall and continue to taunt them. Then the two knights attack the king and engage in a sword fight with him. Andy, an inhibited boy, says that he has the second-best sword next to that of the king; he challenges the latter to a duel. The male therapist reinforces his impulse through supportive doubling. He admires the knight's courage in challenging an experienced fighter like the king. He reinterprets the knight's tentative movements with the sword as powerful, dangerous strokes which he is scarcely able to parry, and asks in amazement where this knight has learned the high art of swordplay. Andy spontaneously answers: 'From you!' After the boys have inflicted many wounds on the king and the girls have showered the queen with pitch, faeces and urine, the children say that they will now allow the royal couple to enter the castle. When the monarchs move in and triumphantly remark that the princesses and princes have finally recognised who the rulers are, the children say that they have prepared a nice bath for the king and queen. When the royal couple happily allow themselves to be led to the bathroom, they find themselves in the dungeon instead, where they receive only faeces and urine to eat and drink. For themselves, the princesses prepare a sumptuous meal. In an act of explorative doubling, the queen and king wonder out loud why they have been treated so badly—they have actually been a good king and queen. The children cry out indignantly that the parents have always told them what to do and treated them badly. The princesses then put on the queen's dresses, adorn themselves with her jewellery and parade provocatively past the king. The boys stand guard in front of the prison, their chests swelled with pride, holding the large swords they have constructed for themselves. In a dialogue, the king and queen acknowledge with admiration how beautiful the princesses have become—it is a joy to look at them. And they marvel at how strong and manly the knights have grown to be. The children enjoy this admiring mirroring to the full. However, when the king and queen recall that in their youth, the queen was also so beautiful and the king so muscular, the children become angry. Tobias, who competes strongly with his father at home, cuts a hole in the king's trousers so that his penis can be seen. The princesses tear the queen's clothes off: now everyone can see her drooping breasts and her pee hole. They shave the heads of both the king and queen. When the couple hide themselves in shame and lament that they cannot let their subjects see them like this, the princesses and knights are triumphant. They summon all the people, and in the roles of the subjects, they laugh gleefully at the royal pair. Andy, who wets himself, also puts a wet diaper on the king and shouts at him that he should be ashamed of himself, a king who still needs to wear diapers. The children then put the king in chains and lead him across the marketplace, forcing him to bark on command. In a soliloquy, the king speaks about how terrible it is to be so humiliated and to have to endure it helplessly. Together, the children then climb onto the throne and savour their triumph. The girls give the direction that the queen no longer likes the king and that he should become their servant. At this, the boys say that the female therapist should come to them in the role of a servant as well. Since almost all the children come from families affected by divorce or in which there are problems in the marriage and are being treated as partner substitutes by one of their parents, the therapists do not participate in the children's oedipal scenario. In an active interpretation, they establish a generational boundary and adopt a different attitude from that which the children wished. They refuse to separate as a couple and hold each other in their arms. Filled with anger, the princesses and knights demand that they separate immediately. When they refuse, the princesses throw the king back into the dungeon. Julia, who reacts very jealously to her one-year-old sister, attacks the king and says that she is going to bite off his penis so that there won't be any more princesses. Tobias, who sides with his mother against his father, also cuts off the king's penis with his sword and laughs triumphantly, saying that now he is no longer the king. The princesses pour faeces and urine over the queen, pull out her teeth, and then say that she now looks so hideous that the king will be horrified at the sight of her. Tobias threatens to cut off her head if she continues to call for the king.

For such oedipal confrontations, the children require a stable relationship between the two leaders. They need to experience the two of them as a pair who do not mutually destroy each other or allow themselves to be destroyed. Before acting out their oedipal fantasies, a group of twelve-year-old children expressed this in the following way: In the roles of American Indians, they attacked the two therapists—who were assigned to play a bandit couple who had argued with one another—took them prisoner and attached magnets to their penis and vagina, respectively, so that they were forced to stay very close together and could never separate. The more fragile and difficult the relationship is between the two leaders, the easier it is for the children to deny their primal fantasies in the oedipal phase of group development and to remain stuck in a dyadic relationship. Any disturbance in the relationship between the two therapists will have a detrimental effect on the group. The children will react to the tension with great sensitivity. They act out the things that they perceive as tension and rivalry between the therapists and attempt to come between them.

Example

In a mixed group of twelve-year-olds, the girls—in the roles of princesses—court the male therapist in his role as the king, while they treat the female therapist (playing the queen) very disparagingly and contemptuously. As the king, the therapist enjoys his situation of being wooed; he pays no attention to the queen, but instead sets out on a hunt with the princesses. The female therapist, who lives in a similar constellation at home, becomes increasingly angry at the male therapist. After the session, she reproaches him. In the next session, when the male therapist is away at a conference, the children pick up on the conflict between the two therapists, even though they were not aware of their confrontation. The girls report that King Lionheart has gone off to the Crusades because the queen had argued with him so often. They scold the queen, saying that she has driven the king away with her endless quarrelling and bickering. Jurek, who has assumed the role of his mother's comforter at home, comes to the aid of the queen: he chases the mean princesses away and sits down on the throne next to the queen. While the princesses run away from the wicked witch of a queen and live alone in the forest, the boys behave very chivalrously toward her. They stage a knight's tournament for her entertainment and let her admire them. The female therapist savours this treatment from the boys during this session. Just like the male therapist in the previous session, she does not set a generational boundary.

In the preliminary discussion before the next session, the leaders are able to recognise their actions and resolve their conflict. In this session, the children then act out the king's return. Jurek sits down at the king's place again. When the king returns from the Crusades, the princesses greet him rapturously, while the princes behave with great reserve. Jurek holds a knife concealed behind his back, which he draws when the king is not looking. In an intervention, the royal couple retreat into their bedchamber for a discussion and then announce to the princesses and princes that they have reconciled. The king thanks Jurek—who is still sitting on his throne—for the fact that he and the other knights protected the queen so well while the king was away and abstained from going on any adventures of their own. At this, Jurek beams from ear to ear. Then the king reproaches himself: it is actually his job to take care of the queen. He regrets that the knights had to take on a task which was not their own. From now on, he and the queen will resolve their disputes themselves and no longer draw the knights into their conflicts. Whereas the tensions among the boys are eased in response to this intervention, the princesses become angry. They say they are going to another kingdom to look for handsome princes. They haven't been happy at the castle for some time; it is much too boring for them; they ride away in contempt. After this, Jurek changes his role: he decides to be an enemy knight—the Black Knight—who challenges the king to a duel and gravely wounds him. A fierce battle ensues, during which the king acknowledges the bravery and courage of the foreign knight with admiration. Jurek then changes his role again: he is now one of the king's knights again and comes to his aid. He defeats the imaginary Black Knight and brings the seriously injured king into the castle, where the worried queen nurses him back to health. While the queen sits at her wounded husband's bedside and cares for him, the knights ride off on a hunt and fight against bears and wild boars.

Only when the relationship between the two therapists is stable can the children also enter into loyal subrelationships with one of the two therapists. If this precondition is missing, the subrelationships will inevitably turn to betrayal. The triangle of male therapist/female therapist/child breaks down into dyads that compete with one another and constantly threaten the third party with exclusion. Particularly children who are locked in a conflict of loyalties between their parents at home—or those who have only experienced a dyad—need to have a corrective experience in the group in order that they do not feel threatened by the presence of a 'third party' in their peer group as well. Therefore it is important, for example, that the male therapist in the role of the king finds it good that the princes treat the queen with so much chivalry and attentiveness—even though they are otherwise such rough and tough fighters—and that they accompanied her as bodyguards on her journey to the French court. Or that the female therapist, in the role of the queen, is pleased when the king is proud of his beautiful and charming daughters and is happy to accompany them to the ball.

In order that the children can be exposed to alternative scenarios, thereby making resocialisation possible, the therapists must not only be able to tolerate the sexual desires and competitive rivalry of the oedipal children, but they must also acknowledge their developmental progress—all the way to age-appropriate autonomy—with joy and pride. For example, in the roles of the king and queen, they could retreat together and conduct a dialogue in which they express their happiness at their children's development: 'Have you noticed what beautiful and clever princesses our daughters have grown up to be? How tastefully they dress and adorn themselves, how gracefully they move?' The king replies: 'Yes, it is truly a joy to look at them; and they are clever and brave as well'.

We often have children in our groups who have been made into partner substitutes and narcissistically/incestuously allied to one of their parents—to the disparaging exclusion of the third party. Since either one or both parents are engaged in a bitter fight over the child and by means of manipulation, are forcing him or her to take sides and form coalitions, these children are drawn into a conflict of loyalties. The results are associated defence mechanisms such as object splitting. The children also act out this relationship pattern in symbolic scenarios. In order to maintain the narcissistic illusion and the fantasy of uniqueness and grandiosity which such children have had to construct early on in order to combat the devastating experience of being powerless and unloved, they devalue or deny the sexual relationship between the pair. Like the father, the male therapist is thought to be impotent, the female therapist (like the mother), uninterested in sex. Thus, the depotentiated father or mother are not serious rivals who could cast doubt upon the child's phallic grandiosity and his or her wishes for an exclusive dyadic relationship. The child then feels like his mother's/her father's better lover and he or she fantasizes the triumph of oedipal victory. If children re-enact these family scenarios and play out their fantasies of omnipotence, the therapists must not grant this wish for fusion into a dyad. They must re-establish the irreconcilable difference in the triadic relationship and repeal this erroneous development through active interpretation.

Example

In a mixed group of 13-year-olds the children have been playing a family scenario for several sessions. They are playing the roles of adolescent children; the therapists are their parents. The three boys, all of whom come from families of divorce, and whose mothers have overburdened them by casting them as narcissistic objects—and in some cases, overstimulated them as partner substitutes—and who have little or no contact with their fathers, assume the roles of teenagers who build a gigantic racing car with 100,000 hp. In the next race, they will be able to leave drivers like Schumacher and Hill far behind. The three girls take on the roles of cheeky, rebellious daughters who get into arguments with their parents. They dress provocatively, put on garish makeup and insult the mother, calling her an old-fashioned cow. Since they are not allowed to go out, they sneak out the window at night and do not come home.

In the roles of the parents, the two therapists express their thoughts about the daughters out loud on the following morning. In a dialogue in which they split up the ambivalent feelings, the mother expresses more of her worries about what might happen to the girls; the father is more optimistic that the daughters will look out for themselves. Next, the girls say that on the next night the parents should catch them lying in bed with boys. Then there should be an argument. The father should get very upset and reproach the mother that she did not do a better job of raising her daughters. At first, the therapists follow these directions; but then they change the scenario. As parents, they realise that they must not argue with each other in this difficult situation; they need to stick together. The boys—who up to now have been following the confrontation with great interest from their workshop—intervene at this point. They accuse the father of having no right to talk: they say that he is also unfaithful—the old bastard. At this, the mother insecurely takes her husband to task. He claims that the sons are simply trying to drive a wedge between them with this slander.

However, the boys persist in their accusations and they produce evidence. They show the mother pictures of the father engaged in foreplay, having an orgasm and after intercourse. The mother is incensed. The boys advise her to get divorced, saying that the father is impotent with her and there is nothing going on sexually between them. The boys say that they will always stay with her; they will take much better care of her. Hans, whose mother behaves very seductively toward him, strikes a pose and says that he is much more virile than the old wanker. It would be better if she married him; then she would not be as unhappy as she is with that old sod. In order not to play along with this narcissistic/incestuous alliance with its disparaging exclusion of the third party, but instead to re-establish the triadic relationship with generational boundaries, the female therapist intervenes. She refuses to participate in the scenario proposed by the boys, who want to be the mother's better lovers and dream of an oedipal victory. She moves back in with her husband and says that she wants to resolve this conflict with him alone. The two adults then whisper together briefly; then they come back and announce that they have settled their conflict. As parents, they can cope with their problems on their own. It is not the children's business to get involved. The boys react to this boundary-setting intervention with great frustration and aggression. They insult the parents— particularly the mother—with obscene expressions. Filled with anger, they then join together with the girls and run away from home, with the aim of enjoying life in Paris. The parents are somewhat sad that their children have flown the nest so early and are going out into the world; however, they also make it clear that they will be able to cope as a couple alone and to enjoy their life together.

Resisting the children's oedipal desires, however, does not mean that the therapists may never separate as a couple in the symbolic scenario. Children who are suffering from their parents' constant arguing might give the therapists the direction: 'Now you will have a terrible argument and say that you are going to get divorced.' If the therapists follow this direction, they must take care to reconcile with one another again after the argument and verbally express their thoughts about how threatening this argument must seem to the children—that perhaps they are afraid that the parents really will separate and what will happen to the children then? In this dialogue, they mirror the feelings that the children have at home when their parents argue.

If children from families of divorce wish to express at the symbolic level how they feel after the divorce—their conflicts of loyalty, their longing for the absent parent, their anger at their parents' inability to overcome their conflicts—then the therapists can also assume the roles of a couple who have separated.

A mixed group of ten-year-olds acted out a circus scenario over the course of several sessions, allowing themselves to be extensively admired by the therapists, who played the roles of the circus director and the animal trainer. In this session, the children—all of whom come from divorced families and live with their mothers—give the direction that the couple should get divorced and that the animals will stay in the circus with the director (female therapist). The animal trainer will look for a new circus to join. Only Jenny no longer wants to play the role of an animal; she wants to be Pippi Longstocking and live alone in the Villa Villekulla. During the play scenario, the children act out their reactions to the parents' separation. The two Arabian horses (Julia and Heike) become very ill and lie motionless in the hay. The lion and the tiger (Hans and Kilian) become vicious and rage about in their cage. The monkey (Michael) screeches constantly and refuses to eat. The circus director becomes very worried about whether she can care for all of these sick animals by herself. Meanwhile, the animal trainer passes by the Villa Villekulla and is amazed that a child lives there without any parents. In a soliloquy, he expresses the fear, sadness and loneliness which Jenny is denying in the grandiose counter-image of Pippi. If he were still a child, he would be sad and full of fear if he were so alone and without parents. How does Pippi manage to be so fearless and strong? Is she simply pushing away her worries and sadness? Pippi responds that she does not need any parents; she can do everything by herself. Besides, she has still has her monkey, Mr. Nilsson, and her horse. Since the situation with the animals is becoming worse and worse, the circus director calls the vet in desperation. In the exploring double role of a doctor, the male therapist comes and examines the animals. He worriedly shares the results with the circus director: 'It is no wonder that the animals have changed so much. You and the animal trainer raised these animals together; therefore the animals are attached to both of you, and they need both of you. Out of worry, sorrow and anger, they have become ill. Even if you are no longer living with the animal trainer, you must see to it that both of you continue to care for the animals. Following the examination, the director calls the animal trainer and shares the doctor's advice with him. When he then comes over and begins grooming the horses, the girls beam with happiness. The wildcats, on the other hand, attack him when he tries to bring some meat to their cage. He calls the vet and repeats aloud what the imaginary doctor says: 'Do you really think that I cannot expect the animals to greet me in a friendly way after I have caused them such pain? You think the animals have a right to be angry at me because I left them alone? I have to tolerate their anger, and I mustn't retreat in disappointment?' Through this dialogue, the therapists verbalise the children's hidden thoughts and feelings and serve as mirrors to provide them with information about themselves.

7.3 Interventions in Relationship Conflicts Between the Children

'Just as children can become stuck in the family crisis—that is, in terms of their operative structures, lack the additional qualifications needed to overcome the conflict—their operative structures can also become locked in during the phase of relationships with their peers' (Krappmann 1982, p. 453).

Erikson (1974) places feelings of inferiority in contrast to industry and thereby points to the consequences of unsuccessful participation in social processes within the peer group. Depending upon their previous experiences and social position, the result can be a withdrawal from all relationships, an outsider role and aggression if children give up their attempts at cooperation—or social unreliability or rigid organisational strategies if they cannot maintain relationships with their peers. However, clinical psychology and children's therapy rarely place the blame for disorders on social relationships among peers. Problems are primarily attributed to the parent/child relationship. Addressing the problems and conflicts that arise in social relationships among peers and helping children increase their qualifications for action is an important issue in children's psychodrama.

Psychodrama is an invitation to interaction; it aims to foster relationships between human beings—which also need to be worked through by addressing conflicts and arguments. As a form of group therapy, it allows the disrupted balance between the individual and society to be restored through a new experience of solidarity with others and through the development of empathy, understanding for one another and consideration for each other, to counteract the 'ego epidemic'—the 'ego-thyosaurus' (Moreno 1925). Time after time, it is moving to witness the way children come to each other's aid in the symbolic play scenarios and act as 'therapeutic agents' for each other.

Example

A group of eight-year-old children are playing a 'Safari Park' scenario. Jo, an aggressive boy with an attachment disorder, wants to play the role of a cheetah. Alex, who has also been enrolled in the group because of his aggressive outbursts, wants to play a lion. An inhibited girl, Marie, wants to play a little wildcat; Corinna, who has joined the group because of her fears of separation, chooses the role of a baby monkey. We, the two therapists, are assigned to play a good gamekeeper (male therapist) and an animal caretaker (female therapist). At first we care for the animals attentively: we feed the baby monkey and the wildcat bottles of milk and toss large pieces of meat to the big cats. Following a peaceful phase of feeding and preening, Jo gives the direction that the animal caretaker cannot really handle the predatory cats, and she should secretly lock up the cheetah and whip him. (Traumatic early-childhood memories often arise when the therapists portray caring and supportive roles like those that the children would have needed for their early development.) The other children agree to this; however, they want to rescue the cheetah quickly. But Jo insists that he should be so well hidden that he can only be discovered after months of abuse have taken place. While the female therapist whips the cheetah according to Jo's direction (she has to beat a cushion placed next to him with a rope), the male therapist, filled with concern, sets out with the other animals to search for the missing cheetah. When Jo gives his permission, the lion sniffs out his location. We find him in a concealed shed, severely injured and completely emaciated. The lion places a thick bone (a Baufix stick) that he had been carrying in his mouth into the mouth of the lifeless cheetah, who immediately bites into the wet stick. The monkey and the wildcat stroke his fur gently; the therapist carefully applies a healing salve on his wounds. In a mutual effort, we gently carry the cheetah to the animal medical station, where we care for him attentively until he regains his strength. Here, the male therapist angrily asks who has committed this act of animal abuse: the animals need to be protected from this person. Together, the animals track down the caretaker, who has been hiding, and attack her, biting and scratching (pretended). When she complains, the male therapist tells her that now she can experience for herself what it was like for the precious cheetah. When the animals ask why she did this terrible thing, she answers that she doesn't have any experience with wild animals—only with house pets—and she tried to tame the cheetah with force because she was afraid. Emboldened by the male therapist's supportive doubling, the animals throw the caretaker into jail for 100 years, lying down in front of the prison so that she cannot escape.

In the next session, the children want to continue the scenario, but they change their roles. Corinna is a little rabbit, Marie is a little cat, Alex is a wild boar and Jo is a wolf. Jo tells us we should be good gamekeepers again, but we should be afraid that the wolf might kill the little animals, so we want to drive him away. During play, however, the wolf shows himself in a completely different light: he protects the little animals, brings them food and hides them in his lair. When, at Corinna's suggestion, a wildfire breaks out—having been started by an evil animal catcher—she allows herself to be rescued not by us, but by the wolf. Wounded, she lies on his back and allows him to carry her to the animal medical station and care for her. In order to verbally mirror the animals in a quiet setting, we decide that night should fall. The animals snuggle together in the wolf's lair; we lie in bed and speak aloud about the animals. It is not true at all, we say, what others have reported about the wolf. This wolf does not harm the little animals; on the contrary, he protects them and helps them. We definitely should not chase him away; instead, we must be very glad to have such a strong animal as our helper in the forest. At this dialogue, a smile flashes over Jo's face.

Jo continues with his theme in the sixth session as well, when the children are playing an animal clinic scenario. The two girls play wild rabbits who are sick; Jo is a wolf and Alex is a sabre-tooth tiger. Once again, the wolf is very caring and attentive. He hisses at us when, in the roles of vets, we try to give the animals injections; he will only allow us to treat them very gently. He lies down in front of their lair and protects them during the night.

The group is not only a place where the family, its subsystems and its environment are reproduced. It is also a learning environment where children can develop their social competence and performance.

We understand social skills as the ability 'to adequately apprehend and structure social situations. Social performance comprises the acts of appropriate interaction and cooperation' (Petzold 1980, p. 241). The goal of therapy, therefore, is not only to help the individual child in the group to develop possibilities for experience and behaviour which are bound up by unconscious conflicts, but also the improvement of his or her ability to form relationships and function in a community.

Psychodramatic symbolic play is always also social interaction, and it can succeed through creative cooperation and co-construction. In a continuous process of coordination between the participating partners in the interaction; in ongoing negotiation; in a shared interpretation of reality and the creation of mutual, shared interpretations; in a mutually agreed-upon plan of action; in the reciprocal adjustment and alignment of roles into role dynamics—it is possible to relate the Self to others and lay the groundwork for creating new, appropriate roles and possibilities for relationships. It is precisely in this way that psychodramatic play differs from children's normal play. 'The necessity of respecting the dramatic sequence forces the children to reciprocally adjust their roles to one another and to discipline their behaviour in order to guarantee a shared storyline. The dramatic sequence of events is the guideline for their shared co-improvisation' (Widlöcher 1974, p. 61). Since the improvisation in psychodramatic play is, by necessity, always co-improvisation, it can be a means of solidifying processes of socialisation. For the children, tasks which arise in the group include dealing with closeness and boundaries, asserting their wishes and adjusting to others, regulating their needs, experiencing a feeling of mutual support, building respect and empathy and learning to find consensus and compromises. The group should also foster the ability tolerate conflicts and disagreements—since particularly in our postmodern world with all of its uncertainties, children require a high tolerance for ambiguity.

Since the group processes are essential for the development of successful interactions, the leaders must be able to recognise the group processes, their disruption through group conflicts and the re-enactment of individual pathologies atmospherically and understand and explain them dramatically. Furthermore, they must be able to intercept uncontrolled and dangerous actions within the group and prevent a developmentally supportive group process from flipping over into a destructive process by intervening either as play leaders or in their assigned or self-chosen roles. In this way, children can be trained and empowered to develop new reactions to old situations and appropriate reactions to new situations—and to implement them through action.

Particularly in the beginning phase, strengthening group cohesion and creating a sense of 'we' is of central importance. Yalom (2001, p. 69) considers it essential 'in order that other factors in group therapy can become effective'.

7.3.1 Interventions at the Verbal Level

If the conflicts between the children intensify to such a degree that the children cannot decide upon a subject for play, but simply provoke, insult or attack one another, it is not advisable to force through the normal process of the session.

Instead, the leaders can sum up the ongoing group process in an image that can potentially inspire the children to create a play scenario and which provides a symbolic background for the action. Thus, for example, a leader can describe the tussles between twelve-year-old children as follows: 'It seems to me as if a gang war were raging here—where different gangster families are fighting to become the bosses in Chicago. The enemy gangs are ransacking the businesses of their rival gangs, blowing up their cars and burning down warehouses.' If the children pick up on this image, we divide up the roles and build the scenery. Then a play scenario can begin in which the children can act out their struggles for power and influence in the 'as if' structure of symbolic play. In order that the children will accept these scenarios that we describe, they must be age-appropriate and if at all possible, tie in with scenarios they have already played.

7.3.2 Interventions at the Action Level

More compelling and effective for children than verbal interventions are interventions at the level of action. The leaders can influence the group process if, based on therapeutic considerations, they take a certain position from which they can operate therapeutically in an appropriate role (cf. Heigl-Evers and Heigl 1972).

(a) At the beginning of a developing group conflict, from the standpoint of a participating observer role, the therapists support the emergence and development of solutions which are being blocked by defensive mechanisms. By taking the removed position of an observer, reporter or commentator who remarks on and interprets the situation and intervening in the role of a newspaper, radio or television reporter, one of the therapists can guide the group conflict at the symbolic level. In order to find an appropriate image for this purpose, however, he or she must first have understood the reason for the conflict. If, for example, the children are showing off and putting one another down, the therapist, in the role of a reporter, can give a live report from a sumo wrestling match. If they are fighting over cushions, he can assume the role of a television reporter and secretly make a film about rival gangsters fighting over a transport of smuggled weapons or diamonds. If they are insulting each other or threatening one another with blows, he can emerge as a tabloid reporter writing about a fight between biker gangs. If girls are disparaging each other, the female therapist can take the role of a fashion magazine journalist and report on behind-the-scenes rivalries at casting sessions for *America's Next Top Model*. From the role of a participating observer, one of the therapists can follow the intense, emotional group processes, describe them and comment on them out loud so that the children are confronted with their conflict-resolving process. In this way, he or she also establishes a certain degree of safety. The children have the experience that in the role of an observer, the therapist takes on an orientation function within the group; he makes an effort to recognise and understand the group process and point out where the group stands and where it is going.

Example

After rivalries had been increasing greatly in the previous sessions with a group of nine-year-old boys, each one wants to push through his suggestion for a play scenario; as a result, they reject all of each other's suggestions as 'crappy'. When the female leader addresses the rivalry, they do not respond to her, but boast all the more about their purported strengths, strike poses, put each other down and increasingly insult one another with obscene expressions. When the male leader steps between them, this also has no effect. The boys become enraged and want to brawl with each other. At this point, the male leader assumes the role of a television reporter who is announcing the live broadcast of a wrestling match: 'Ladies and gentlemen at home, listen to the way the contenders are rudely insulting one another and putting each other down even before the match. Observe how they are making threatening gestures and can hardly be held back. We are very excited to see the matches, which will begin in just a moment.' Bewildered, the boys pause in their arguing. The leader then asks whether they would like to continue fighting in the roles of wrestlers. The boys immediately accept this suggestion—which also represents safety—particularly because some of them are terrified of the escalating rage. After the children have chosen their roles, along with fitting names, and paired off as partners, they assign the female therapist to be the referee. The male therapist retains his role as a television reporter. The group then constructs a fighting ring. Within the protected space of the symbolic play scenario, they can show off their imaginary strength, insult one another without really hurting each other and act out their anger without using violence. At the same time, they negotiate solutions for ways to divide up victories and defeats so that each boy can register one win and one loss. In his broadcast, the television reporter admiringly points out each fighter's abilities and he empathetically verbalises how much the blows must hurt them and how difficult it must be not to let their pain, fear or disappointment show.

(b) Since the group is led by a pair of therapists, the group situation can bring sibling rivalries to the surface. The children fight for the therapists' attention and compete with one another. This reawakens such emotions as hate, envy, aggression and fear. Particularly in the beginning phase, these affects place a heavy strain on the group, given that the children's abilities to control themselves are limited. If these conflicts increase to the point that the group cohesion is endangered and the group is at risk of breaking apart due to escalating hostilities, the leaders can introduce an imaginary external enemy upon whom the group's aggression can be diverted.

Example

In the previous session, a group of ten-year-old boys played Wild West heroes who created instability in the town, threatened the sheriff (the male therapist) and plundered the bank, which was run by the female therapist. In this session, they cannot get around to playing the scenario because each boy wants to be the leader of the gang. Now the female therapist, in the role of the bank director, runs to the squabbling boys crying for help: 'Help, the Sioux are coming! They will burn down our town and take our scalps! We're doomed! And the gunslingers who could be protecting us right now are fighting amongst themselves and don't even notice the danger that is approaching!'

If such interventions are not sufficient to strengthen the group cohesion and help the group to overcome the disturbance, one of the therapists can personally assume the antagonist position. He or she purposely takes on a role in which she can divert the children's aggression onto herself and at the same time draw it away from the group. A threat from an external enemy binds the children together. Group solidarity increases and the tension within the group is reduced. Constructive interactions can be set in motion even if they initially only came into being because of the external threat.

Example

In a group of ten-year-olds, intense conflicts arise quickly in the beginning phase because each of the boys wants to be the most omnipotent. Based on ideas from the media, each one chooses a powerful role for himself, wanting to be Hercules, Batman, He-Man or Rambo. Whereas in the previous sessions, confrontations over power and influence only arose during the play scenario, this time the children already bring fierce conflicts in with them from the waiting room. They put each other down, becoming increasingly unruly and insulting, and the leaders are unable to stop them. An opening round is unthinkable. As the children become more and more aggressive and attempt to knock each other off their chairs, the leaders confer with one another briefly. The female therapist then runs into the circle of chairs and shouts: 'Help, help, King Kong is coming!' The male therapist, who has covered himself with a brown cloth, stomps in slowly in the role of King Kong; he knocks over chairs, which he identifies as houses or cars, and tries to grab one of the boys. The children immediately desist from their argument and attack King Kong. As soon as they are well warmed up for the symbolic scenario, the female leader interrupts and says: 'Can we quickly set up the scene? Who are you? What role should I play? Where is the battle taking place?' The boys choose the roles of supermen and assign the female therapist the role of a beautiful woman that King Kong has kidnapped, but the superheroes will rescue her. Then they quickly construct the skyscrapers of New York City. Now the game can continue. King Kong must kidnap the beautiful woman—who has now become the wife of the U.S. President—from the White House. The President—played by the male leader in a quick role swap—calls the bravest fighters from all over the world together to rescue his wife. He offers an enormous monetary reward. The heroes then join together to attack King Kong, who is hiding behind a sky-scraper. A mighty battle ensues, in which King Kong throws cars at the approaching heroes. Together, they defeat King Kong using their various powers—muscle strength, the ability to fly, laser cannons and karate—and after a hard physical struggle, they capture him and place him in chains.

If, in the initial phase of a session, the children agree on a mutual play scenario, and group conflicts begin to be expressed only in the course of the play phase, making it impossible to continue playing, the leaders can introduce an imaginary external enemy. If, however, the conflicts are so intense that the children require a real external enemy in order to channel their aggressions against one another, one of the leaders must shed the role he or she has played up to now and assume a role in which he can become a threat.

Example

A group of nine-year-olds have agreed to play the roles of knights. They assign the leaders to be their servants. The knights want to hold a tournament. However, fierce conflicts quickly arise as to who is the strongest knight in the tournament. Each boy wants to emerge as the winner. The boys become increasingly angry, knocking over each other's horses (cushions) and accusing one another of being spoilsports. As they start coming to blows, the male leader—in the role of a stable hand—runs into the castle courtyard and cries out: 'The Huns are attacking! They have already burned down the village and they are riding toward the castle. We need to quickly barricade the gates, heat up pitch and prepare the catapults.' The boys immediately stop their tussle and heroically throw themselves into the battle against the imagined enemies. However, since each knight wants to be the strongest and bravest, they now begin to argue about who has killed the most Huns and who deserves credit for defeating the enemy. As this new dispute arises, the therapists, after conferring briefly, discard their roles as servants. They tell the boys that they will now play the commanders of the Huns who attack the castle and avenge the defeat of the advance guard. As the Hun rulers, they loudly tell each other that they will be able to make quick work of the feuding and quarrelling knights; they will storm the castle and drag the knights off in chains. At this, the boys cease their arguing; they barricade themselves behind the castle wall, catapult stones at the approaching Huns, shower them with pitch and overpower them as they try to break down the castle gate. They throw the Huns into the dungeon and laugh at them for looking so ugly, smeared with pitch; they give them stinking, mouldy bread to eat. Meanwhile, the knights hold a roaring victory celebration. For the feast, the leaders must change roles again and as servants, marvel at the brave knights while serving them gigantic portions of game and barrels full of wine.

If the therapists already have roles in the scenario in which they are playing the children's antagonists, they can—from within these roles—express their pleasure that discord has broken out among their enemies. The enemies' argument will come in handy: now they will have an easy time overpowering and defeating their enemies without any great resistance. This act of 'describing the dispute' usually results in the children putting up a fight against this challenge and spoiling their adversaries' fun by joining together out of spite and attacking the enemies as a group. Another possibility for alleviating conflict between the children in the beginning phase of the group consists of identifying the dispute among the animals, knights or whichever roles the children are currently playing as a serious danger for the opposite side (the therapists), which they urgently need to fight against.

Example

A group of eleven-year-olds want to play aliens; the leaders are assigned to play American space researchers. While constructing their spaceship, the children begin to argue and destroy each other's partially-built spaceship capsules. In their roles as American astronauts, the therapists observe these arguments on their monitors and wonder anxiously whether something akin to rabies has broken out among the aliens. They call down to ground control and are given the important assignment of quickly vaccinating the aliens with a serum in order that the disease does not spread to the American scientists and put their important mission in danger. When they repeat these instructions from ground control out loud, the children cease their arguing. Then, when the American astronauts try to dock on to the aliens' spaceship in order to vaccinate them, they are led into a trap. The aliens take the serum away from them and inject them with the rabies virus, causing the Americans to go into fits of rage. The children give the therapists the direction to attack each other, beat each other up and only calm down after the aliens have injected them with a sedative. The children are then amused as the two astronauts begin to argue and attack each other rabidly. They give them alternating injections of sedatives and stimulants. The leaders have to repeat this sequence of fighting and calming down several times. Then the aliens explain to the astronauts that they had not really been fighting in earnest; they were only playing in order to test their strength. The Americans ask the aliens how it is possible to tell whether the aliens are fighting in earnest or simply playing. The aliens answer that their fights only become serious if they really hurt one another. For them, smashing up spaceships is not so bad, since they can always rebuild them very quickly. The astronauts pass this explanation on to ground control so that the Research Station for Alien Studies can record these findings.

If cohesion is stable in a later phase of the group's development, the children will need help in confronting their partners in a conflict and finding solutions. The therapists can offer this support through verbal interventions, especially when the children are more mature. They can describe the group dynamics—for example, how out of rivalry, the children dismiss each other's ideas in the opening round; each one wants to prevail with his or her idea and no one is willing to compromise. Or they can participate identificationally in an attempt to resolve the conflict and address the subject of the protective mechanism and the feeling of safety contained in the approach to the problem—for example: 'I can certainly understand that nobody wants to make a suggestion anymore. I would also have reservations about expressing myself openly if the others immediately attacked me and called my ideas crappy or stupid.' They can also hold a mirror up to the children's interactions for them. In this later phase of group development, it is important not to give into the children's urge to quickly move into the play phase without dealing with the conflict. The leaders must be able to tolerate the fact that the children find it 'stupid' to talk about a conflict and may even threaten to stop coming to the group. Without an agreement on a subject, without consulting with one another and seeing themselves in their roles in relation to the group, every play scenario will fail. If the leaders give in too quickly to 'lazy' compromises, the conflict will simply be shifted into the play phase. The leaders must not allow themselves to be troubled by these threats; rather, they must be able to tolerate the tension, even if no play takes place at all in a given session because the children are not willing to make any kind of compromise or come to any agreement. For the children, tolerating this dissent is an important learning experience. Especially in our pluralistic society, children need to have this ability.

The leaders' interventions are also necessary during the play phase. They can interrupt the play briefly—'freeze the action'—in order to help the children confront their partners in a conflict and to work out appropriate coping strategies. Above all, they need help in finding solutions that allow them to be alternatively strong and weak, powerful and vulnerable.

Example

In the role of a cowboy, an aggressive boy attacks two inhibited girls who are gathering medicinal herbs in their roles as Indian girls. He overpowers them with his superior physical strength and wants to tie them up. The two girls protest and refuse to play the roles of the underdogs. While the other children continue playing, the female leader stays with this subgroup to clarify how the shared play scenario might continue. She reinterprets the boy's action positively and says: 'Franz, I can see that you want to play with the two girls. How could that work so that you could be a strong cowboy but the two girls can also be strong Indians?' To this, Franz responds: 'I only want to tie them up for a little while. During the night they can free themselves and sneak away as far as I'm concerned.' The female leader answers: 'I don't know whether the girls will agree to this. Maybe they also want to show what brave Indians they are?' Here the girls state their conditions: 'We will only let you tie us up if then, at night, we can overpower you and drag you away to our camp.' However, Franz refuses to accept this suggestion. In order to help him find a compromise and also to include the other children in this scenario, the leader asks: 'Could it be that the other cowboys come to help you—that they sneak into the camp at night and untie you from the stake?' Both Franz and the other children are able to agree to this alternative. Because both parties are prepared to alternate the roles of the dominant character and the underdog, they are able to reach an agreement and can continue with the play scenario.

The fact that the children's capacity for self-control is sometimes very poorly developed means that the leaders must contribute actively to the children's orientation and to structuring the sequence of the sessions. In order to prevent group dynamics from spinning out of control, they must repeatedly open up possibilities for negotiations and offer suggestions as to how an agreement can be reached or how individual needs can be satisfied in such a way that the integrity of the other children is not damaged.

Example

A group of ten-year-old boys has agreed on the theme of 'Battle of the Ninjas versus the Marines'. The two armies entrench themselves in the jungle and shoot at one another. Since no one wants to be hit, anger quickly arises. The boys exchange insults and the game is in danger of dissolving into chaos. The male leader briefly interrupts the play and makes the suggestion that characters can act out being dead by lying down and counting to 50 or 100. The children agree that everyone who is shot dead must first count to 50 before he can reappear as a new fighter and join in the battle. After the boys have solved the conflict between being powerful versus being powerless by agreeing on this rule, they are able to continue playing. Soon, however, a new argument arises. The group of ninjas want the marines to fall into a bamboo trap from which they are unable to escape. The marine group, on the other hand, persist in their suggestion that they should ambush and shoot down the ninjas. In response to the leader's intervention that neither group is prepared to play the underdog for the other, they reach a compromise through a process of negotiation: The marines agree to first be ambushed and taken prisoner. In return, however, they demand to be able to dig an underground escape route, break free and lead the pursuing ninjas into a trap. The latter must then surrender and allow themselves to be taken prisoner. The ninja group agrees only on the condition that they can free themselves during the night and get away. Only through this reciprocal negotiation is it possible to continue the play scenario constructively and overcome the congealed, 'canned' pattern of always wanting to maintain the powerful role in conflict situations.

In order to enforce the rule against hurting one another physically or emotionally, the leaders must also step in and stop the fighting or disparaging insults and if necessary, separate the enraged adversaries or even hold onto them until they have calmed down. This form of setting boundaries protects the children and provides them with security.

Since we cannot assume that most children have the capacity to make personal encounters or form relationships, the leaders can also contribute to the development and differentiation of these abilities in their transferred or chosen roles. These interventions at the action level have the advantage that they can address the children on the symbolic level without interrupting the play scenario. Furthermore, in these interventions, children are less likely to offer opposition to the adults' instructions.

In particular, the methods of supportive doubling and the permanent double allow the therapists to reinforce the children's ego functions and set in motion a learning and growing process with regard to finding compromises and resolving conflicts without violence. If, in the initial phase of the session, the children disparage each other's contributions, insult and threaten one another, the therapists could identify them as rival Mafioso families and announce that the boss of all the Mafiosi, Al Capone, is sending out an emissary to pacify the feuding families. In the auxiliary role of the emissary, one of the therapists can go from one Mafioso to the other and inquire about their peace terms and proposals. He or she can then communicate this information back and forth between the enemy Mafiosi for as long as it takes to establish a cease-fire or a peace agreement.

If the children have agreed upon a play subject, but arguments then break out during the construction phase—if they fight over cushions or tear the cloths away from each other—then the leaders can intervene in a supportive or exploring permanent double role. For example, if the children are playing the roles of astronauts and while constructing their rockets, they yank the cushion elements away from each other and accuse one another, the therapist can intervene in the role of a security police officer at Cape Canaveral and as an exploring permanent double, initiate an investigation into purported acts of sabotage. If, on the other hand, the children are playing animals in a zoo, a therapist in the role of the zookeeper can verbalise his or her worries about the animals who are fighting over building materials for their lairs and nests.

In the case of fighting that occurs during the play scenario, the therapists also have the possibility, in an appropriate role—for example, as the king's messenger, if the knights (the children) are fighting amongst themselves—to act as an intermediary and help them work out solutions to their conflicts at the symbolic level.

Example

A group of twelve-year-olds are playing researchers who develop a miracle weapon underneath the North Pole. When an intense argument arises, because no one is abiding by the agreements, the female therapist visits the research station in the role of a doctor from the security agency. There is reason to suspect that a dangerous form of 'polar rabies' has broken out among the researchers. In a process of exploring, she investigates how this fighting came about. Only in this way, she says, can she determine whether the problem is the dangerous polar rabies or simply a normal argument among the researchers. At the same time she attempts, from the standpoint of her role, to help the children find solutions to their different needs. Since the U.S. government wants to avoid the failure of this important research project at all costs, she has been assigned to ensure that the researchers can live together peacefully and to help them resolve their conflicts non-violently in this difficult, closed-off environment.

The therapists can serve as empathetic doubles in the children's confrontations by participating identificationally in their roles and verbalising the thoughts and feelings that they perceive in the children in the conflict situation. For example, as gamekeepers, they could speak about how frightening it must be for the wild animals when suddenly every creature is fighting against every other creature; how strenuous it must be for the powerful lion to constantly threaten the other animals simply because he is afraid they will attack him otherwise; how difficult it must be for the panther to stop fighting with the tiger and retreat into her lair without losing face in front of the other wild animals.

Using role reversal, the therapists can hold the children's conflict up to them as if in a mirror and suspend their defences and denial in this 'immanent mirror'.

Example

A fierce argument has broken out between ten-year-old boys who are playing the roles of astronauts. Two boys who are physically weaker than the other four stave off their fears through aggressive, boastful behaviour. The leaders, who are playing the roles of a dinosaur couple on an undiscovered planet, retreat into their cave and speak aloud to each other. The male dinosaur recounts what happened to him recently when he got into a fight with a much larger dinosaur. He was actually terribly afraid of the other dinosaur and would have liked to avoid the fight. But he was afraid that if he let his fear show and retreated, the other dinosaur might laugh at him or make him feel ashamed in front of the other prehistoric animals. Therefore, he covered up his fear and attacked the other dinosaur pre-emptively. He must have managed a surprise initial victory in this way, but in the end things went badly for him. The female dinosaur recalls how he came home with severe injuries. It would have been better if he had admitted to his fear. He lay wounded in the cave for months afterward. During this dialogue, the children move closer to the dinosaurs' cave and say that the dinosaurs should not notice them. When the male dinosaur speaks about his fear, one of the boastful boys says that he should repeat what he said about his fear again.

The mirror technique is especially suitable for reflecting specific patterns of conflict-ridden interpersonal relationships, roles, positions in the group structure, group constellations, group-specific processes and conflict resolutions. Furthermore, in a soliloquy or dialogue, the therapists can verbalise the children's thoughts and feelings on their behalf.

Example

A group of eleven-year-old boys have become locked in a rigid pattern of rivalry interactions. The two dominant boys, Manfred and Peter, do not play out their rivalry openly. Peter initially submits to Manfred's creative play suggestions; however, during the play scenario he attempts to secretly win the other three more inhibited boys over to his side in order to sabotage Manfred's ideas. In this session, the boys agree to play the roles of robber barons. The therapists are assigned to play wealthy aristocrats who are attacked and robbed. Manfred, a boy with strong verbal skills, immediately lays claim to being the leader of the robber barons. When the leaders ask whether the other boys consent to have Manfred as their leader, they agree. In the course of the game, when Manfred wants to decide exactly how the attack on the wealthy count and countess should take place, the other boys do not contradict him. However, Peter secretly whispers to the other boys. When Manfred gives the signal to attack, they do not obey his command; instead, they steal his horse and ride away laughing. Manfred becomes extremely angry and accuses Peter of ruining the game. He doesn't want to play anymore. The therapists remain in their roles; they flee to their castle, and mirror this pattern of interaction out loud: 'How did it happen that the robber barons, who have made our lives so difficult up to now, are so divided? Do robber barons always behave this way—initially obeying the leader but stabbing him in the back at the first opportunity?' At this, Peter shouts: 'Manfred always decides everything!' In the roles of the count and countess, the therapists continue their discussion; in an act of explorative doubling, they ask each other: 'Are the robber barons afraid of getting into an open confrontation? Are they afraid that if they fought for power everything would fall apart?' The countess remarks: 'I don't believe that. They are so strong and brave otherwise.' Through supportive doubling, the male therapist then suggests an alternative way of behaving: 'At our court, the noble knights announce their claims to leadership openly and keep looking for solutions until everyone is content with the situation.' However, the countess objects with empathetic doubling: 'You have forgotten that during the last military campaign, you also made the decisions for the other knights. And they were good and angry at you for it.' The count admits: 'Yes, I didn't even realise it. I simply had the best ideas. I was certainly disappointed and angry when the other knights complained about it afterwards. But I was glad that they didn't simply defect from my army; they spoke openly about their dissatisfaction. And luckily we found a solution: that we could take turns leading the army each day.' At this, Manfred says to Peter: 'You can be the leader in the next attack.' Franz, one of the inhibited boys, protests, saying that every boy should have a turn. The group then agrees that in this session each boy will have a chance to be the leader.

If the fear of rivalry and conflicts becomes too great, the children have a tendency to stave this fear off and shift the confrontations onto the therapists. They attempt to make the leaders into external enemies upon whom they then divert all of their aggression.

In a further evasive manoeuvre, each child may try to direct his or her individual play toward one of the leaders and to play out her fantasies of omnipotence with that leader rather than having to deal with the other children. This kind of acting out toward the therapists serves the purpose of avoiding and suppressing conflicts and rivalries among the members of the group. The leaders must not follow along with this resistance—they should not play along with the children's game—rather, they should refer the children to each other by means of an active interpretation.

Example

In a group of nine-year-old children, each boy wants to be the greatest. However, since they shy away from a confrontation with each other and avert any rivalry-related conflicts, each child attempts to play his own individual game with one of the therapists. The result is a group of unconnected scenarios in which each child fights with and destroys the monsters (played by the therapists) as an omnipotent, invincible lone warrior possessed with superior skills. During a break in the fighting, the monsters wonder aloud why, in the world of humans, every hero fights for himself alone instead of joining together with other heroes. If they did, it would be easier for them to defeat the monsters. In an act of interpretation, they wonder whether the heroes are afraid that this might lead to a fight over who is the greatest hero or who has contributed the most to the victory. However, since the children continue maintaining their stereotypical play pattern, the therapists switch their roles. They tell the children that more powerful monsters are arriving now, who are too powerful to be defeated by a single fighter. The heroes will only have a chance against these monsters if they join together and complement one another with their different strengths. Furthermore, they would need to coordinate with one another about how they can attack the monsters at the same time and from all sides. The therapists refuse to let themselves be defeated until the children confer with each other and go after the monsters together.

7.3.3 Relationship-Building Interventions

In group therapy sessions, we experience situations like this one again and again.

Example

Six boys want to play the roles of Pokémons; we are assigned to be Pokémon researchers. First they demonstrate their attack moves as combat animals: Bulbasaur shoots off a solar ray; Mewtwo raises a storm; Venusaur chops everything up with his razor leaves and Blastoise smashes boulders. But since all of this takes place in their fantasies, they simply gesture wildly and comment on their movements. Then they begin to threaten one another. However, since none of them responds to the special strengths and attacks of the others—on the contrary: each one wants to triumph over the others—the play quickly becomes chaotic. Each boy shouts that he has anticipated the other and defeated him. In order to be stronger than their opponents, they transform themselves to a higher power level. From our hiding place, lying behind some boulders, we (in the roles of Pokémon researchers) express our fear that a huge war may have broken out among the Pokémons. It would probably be better to run away quickly before they discover us. At this, the Pokémons stop fighting with each other and attack us. However, each one uses one of the therapists as the target for his own attack technique—without any relationship to the others. Thus, for example, the male therapist is frozen by Articuno's blast of cold; in the next moment he is burned up by Charizard's jet of fire; and at more or less the same time, he is hurled through the air by Mewtwo's storm.

In these two play scenarios, each boy plays an entirely self-sufficient, grandiose hero who has no relationship to anyone else and who only requires a victim in order to show his superiority.

If we allow such children to persist in their actions, only following along with mirroring and commentaries, the children will remain stuck in their rigid 'canned' roles—in a dead-end relationship pattern—since they have not developed any alternative, dialogical strategies for action. This was something we had to learn the hard way at the beginning of our work in group therapy. Only when we changed our way of playing along in such a way that through interventions, we stimulated the children to abandon their conservative scenarios and reshape their role behaviour in a more progressive manner, were we able to help them further.

By exchanging roles with strong hero characters and acting out the heroes' stories in the group therapy sessions, the children create counter-images to their feelings of worthlessness, helplessness and abandonment (cf. Heinemann 1992). This 'as if' play allows them to gain control over their environment and thereby develop a feeling of self-effectiveness. Furthermore, these supermen and super-women embody the progressive side of childhood development: the urge to become independent. Armed with every possible ability, these heroes do not need to run away from any danger and can approach any unfamiliar situations or people without any fears or reservations (cf. von Hänisch 1982).

Media research approaches that are grounded in developmental psychology have shown that—from the starting point of their own identity issues—children use the media in order to appropriately deal with their developmental tasks and day-to-day experiences. Here, modern research in socialisation (e.g., Hurrelmann 1983) sees the child as the active recipient who processes these media templates productively and reshapes the action series individually for his or her own purposes. The images offered by television serve as a 'stone quarry' or 'building site' for the child [to borrow the terminology of media educator Paus-Haase (1998, p. 13)]. Children endow the television heroes with their own psychosocial significance, reshape them and develop them further, as we can see in the following example.

Example

Ralf, a nine-year-old boy who has a great longing for a father figure but has been disappointed by the changing series of men in his single mother's life, chooses the role of the powerful Pokémon Blastoise in a children's group therapy session. In the opening round, he convinces the other children that the female therapist should play a Pokémon catcher and the male therapist a Pokémon trainer. While the female therapist, in the role of the Pokémon catcher, is attacked by the Pokémons and wounded by their special moves, Ralf locks up the male therapist in his cave. In the role of the trainer, he marvels out loud in a soliloquy that Blastoise has cooped him up and is not even using him for himself. Apparently, Blastoise cannot imagine that the trainer would stay with him willingly; but in fact, he would even be proud to have the opportunity to train such a powerful and magnificent Pokémon. Maybe Blastoise had bad experiences with trainers in the past. At the end of the monologue, Ralf approaches and says that the trainer should bring over some one-metre-thick steel plates so that he can practice. Then, with the trainer as an admiring mirror, Ralf shatters the thickest plate and savours the 'sparkle in the trainer's eyes'.

However, children do not only attribute meanings to media templates actively. The media also contributes to constructing their reality and thereby influences their perception of the world. In addition to their parental home, nurseries and schools, it contributes in large degree to children's socialisation.

Therefore, the question arises as to what patterns of interpretation these media offerings carry with them, how these patterns for interpreting the social world are reflected in the child's internal psychological life and how they influence children's patterns of thought, perception and experience (cf. Zaepfel and Metzmacher 1999).

These modern heroes often differ significantly from the heroes in fairy tales, sagas and myths. These very differences demonstrate specific changes which can be attributed to our times. Thus, the 'old heroes' could still admit to their weaknesses and require help—and thereby became capable of forming relationships. Or they helped other characters and later received help from them in times of need.

It is precisely this which is missing for the modern heroes—these 'powerful lone warriors'. They are set pieces that represent combat, grandiosity and omnipotence. Thus, for example, the Terminator—the most famous character in the media for children all over the world—is an insensitive, invulnerable and invincible killing machine who is not affected by emotions. With these modern heroes, technology and physical strength take the place of human relationships. Their invulnerability and their lack of needs and feelings are the embodiment of the perfect fantasy of omnipotence.

The hero can deny every danger, since he is invulnerable, needs nothing and has everything under control. Therefore, he is dependent on nothing and no one (cf. Reifschneider 1998).

This lack of ability to form relationships seen in today's action heroes speaks particularly to children who have difficulty with relationships and an insecure, avoidance-based pattern of attachment—children who have had bad experiences with relationships in their families, in nurseries or in school. In fact, the identification with these heroes reinforces their lack of relationships. In group therapy, then, they play the roles of self-sufficient, grandiose heroes who require nothing and no one—or at most, an inferior character that they can overpower. Therefore, it is an important task within group therapy to not only be a participant in the children's play scenario, but also a director—one who attempts to influence the children's play and relationship scenarios in such a way that automatically-running, rigid patterns are interrupted and the children can find new possibilities for relationships. Therapeutic interventions should open up possibilities for the children to enter into relationships with one another, develop solidarity and helpful relationships among themselves and thereby establish an important protection factor. The more burdensome children's family and life situations are, the more essential are the abilities to develop and maintain friendships with their peers. In the context of groups of children, the development of solidarity has so far received little attention, as Rahm and Kirsch (2000) point out.

In our 34 years of working in group therapy, we have had the experience that group therapy holds great potential in this regard. For most of the children in our groups, it is a new experience to become important to the other children over the course of the group process—to give something to each other and to be able to help one another. Up to now, they have more often had the experience of being marginalised and excluded as troublemakers in their nurseries or schools.

Moreno in particular stressed early on in his writing that this experience of being able to help one another—co-operative mutual help—is an essential factor in group therapy.

In order to relate children to one another—to communicate to them the feeling of being reliant on one another and to facilitate helpful relationship experiences, we repeatedly create conditions in the psychodramatic group therapy setting which require interaction and co-operative behaviour.

Using a few sample cases, we would now like to elaborate on the interventions we employ to help children learn to regulate and control relationships without taking away their self-protective identification with the powerful heroes:

1. Through interventions, we repeatedly try to create conditions which require interaction and co-operative behaviour and allow children to have the experience that 'together we are strong'.

Example

The children want to play the roles of Power Rangers; they assign us to be aliens who are attempting to take over the world. Without discussing anything between them or interacting with one another, each child tries to defeat us (the aliens) by him or herself. Each one blows us away with his laser gun; then we have to enter the battle again as new aliens, without any chance against the Power Rangers. After the children have repeated this scene several times and become somewhat battle weary, the male therapist—playing the alien commander—calls an imaginary scout and asks whether there is any chance of defeating the mighty Power Rangers. He repeats the radio message out loud to his co-commander (the female therapist): 'The scout has observed that each of the Power Rangers is fighting all by himself; they never appear all together. This is our chance. We have to just capture one of them, and the others will not even notice. Then we can eliminate them one after another.' Naturally, the children hear this radio message. They retreat; and one child approaches our spacecraft. We jump out and capture him, but the other Power Rangers jump out of their hiding place and overpower us gleefully.

In the following session, we try out another way of opening up possibilities for cooperation. During the course of the play scenario, the male therapist radios the female commander, telling her he has lost four special keys which can be used to open the entrance to the spacecraft (prior to this, he has scattered four Baufix pieces around the room). The female commander is furious: now we are done for. The male commander reassures her, saying that if the Power Rangers find the keys, they will not know that it is only possible to open the lock if all of them insert their keys into it at the same time. Surely they will never come up with this idea. Of course, the radio communication is so loud that the children can hear it. The Power Rangers immediately start to search for the keys. Even though only Tobias and Ergun find keys, they give some to the other children. Beaming with happiness, they all stick the keys into the lock together, open the door and overpower us.

For individual children who want to play out their fantasies of omnipotence without any connection to the other children in the group, such interventions can also help them enter into a positive interaction.

Example

Six-year-old Paul has been enrolled in a therapy group with children of his own age due to his severe aggression and difficulty with relationships. The children suggest a scenario in which a giant and dangerous troll (played by the male therapist) has entered Hogwarts Castle and surprised Hermione in the girls' bathroom. Harry and Ron will rescue her and the headmaster Dumbledore (played by the female therapist) will give them a reward. Once again, Paul wants to defeat the troll by himself in the role of Harry. In order to facilitate cooperation, the male therapist replies that the ten-metre-high troll can only be overpowered if Ron and Harry touch him with their wands at the same time and repeat a spell. If only one wand touches the troll, he will become even more dangerous. During the play scenario, the therapist notices how Maria tenses up when he approaches in the role of the troll. Just in time, he remembers that Maria has witnessed her father behaving violently toward her mother. Therefore, he briefly interrupts the play and suggests to Maria that before the troll can capture her, she can use her good magical knowledge to temporarily shrink him down to the size of an ant so that Harry and Ron can bring her to safety before the troll grows large again. Maria is visibly relieved; she takes pleasure in placing the shrinking spell on the troll before Harry and Ron rescue her from the bathroom. Then Harry re-enters the room alone to attack the troll, who has regained his enormous size. As the therapist warned, the troll only becomes more powerful. Briefly interrupting the play again, the therapist asks if it could now happen that the troll knocks Harry out with his giant club and that Hermione and Ron quickly bring the unconscious boy to the hospital wing run by Madam Pomfrey (the female therapist) where she can cast a spell to revive him. All of the children agree to this change. They drag the unconscious Harry to the hospital wing, and Harry enjoys being cared for by the motherly female therapist. Once he is recovered, the children take off again—despite Madam Pomfrey's worries—to catch the troll together. This time the three of them succeed in touching the troll with their wands simultaneously at Ron's

command, tying him up with a shackling spell and dragging him together to
Dumbledore (the female therapist), who admires their heroism and presents all
of them with awards.

2. A further intervention lets children have the experience that they need to
   combine their different abilities and work together in order to successfully
   master a challenge.

Example

After several sessions in a group of nine-year-olds in which the Pokémons have
repeatedly defeated us (we are playing the roles of Pokémon catchers) with their
martial arts, we change the game. We tell the children that the Pokémon
catchers from another area have captured Pokémons, flown them to an island
surrounded by swamps and locked them in a cage made of steel one metre thick.
We change the scenery, building the island with the cage out of cushions and
laying a black cloth down as the swamp surrounding the island. We place soft
toy animals in the prison. Then we triumphantly telephone the zoo: we say that
we have captured rare Pokémons and demand an amount in the millions. We are
holding the monsters prisoner in a safe place where they cannot escape or be
freed. The cage is made of one-metre-thick steel that only Blastoise might
possibly be able to break through. But of course he wouldn't be able to get
across the swamp; as heavy as he is—weighing several tonnes—he would sink
immediately. It would only work if Articuno were to freeze the swamp with his
cold blast. But we know that Pokémons are lone wolves; they would never do
anything together, so we don't need to worry about anything. They would also
need Venusaur, who would have to cut through the thick chains with his
swords, and Mewtwo, who would have to transport the captured animals back
in a storm. Following this loud dialogue, to which two Pokémons have been
listening, the Pokémons retreat and whisper with one another; then, grinning,
they attack. Articuno freezes the swamp with his cold blast. Then Blastoise
slides forward and, to our horror, destroys the prison. Venusaur cuts through the
chains, and Mewtwo and Bulbasaur carry the captured and weakened Pokémons back to their homeland with a storm. Full of anguish, we describe this
joint action. We had never thought it was possible that the Pokémons would be
so clever and band together using their different abilities. Now we are done for.
The Pokémons pounce on us triumphantly, using their fighting techniques to
punish us.

3. Vitally important interventions are those that promote mutual help and empathy. All observations in infant and early childhood research have shown that empathetically successful interactions must form the starting point for therapeutic action, since they are crucial to a good interpersonal atmosphere. In healing, interpersonal therapy relationships, possibilities for 'reciprocal empathy' (Petzold 1995, p. 14) must be made available. If this does not happen, the result can be risks to development and impairment of the therapeutic process. According to Petzold, therapy works, ultimately, 'because people have inherent capacities for offering mutual help—for healing relationships and sensitive caregiving' (1995, p. 21).

Here is an example from a group of nine-year-olds.

Example

Once again, we are Pokémon catchers and are being chased away by the Pokémons. We wail and cry when Charizard singes us with his fire; when Articuno freezes us and when Alakazam blows us away. Gravely injured, we use our last remaining strength to flee. In a dialogue, we admit to each other that we have no chance of catching these Pokémons. They are simply too powerful and clever. It doesn't make any sense to go back and fight with them again. Just now, we were barely able to escape with our lives. Upon hearing this, the children demand that we try one more time. However, we resist the children's wish and change our roles instead. In our dialogue, we say that we no longer want to place ourselves in such danger. Besides, the Pokémons are such magnificent creatures that it would be a shame if they were to lose their vitality and beauty by being placed in captivity. After all, human beings don't want to live in captivity either. We would actually prefer to make them our friends. That would be great: then we would not have to be afraid anymore. But they are sure to be mistrustful, and they won't believe us. Maybe we should leave out a few chickens for them from our food supply. Maybe they will see that as a sign that we don't have any evil intentions. At this, Blastoise cautiously approaches and takes a chicken. We admire this beautiful and powerful creature. Male therapist: 'I would be so proud and happy to have him as a friend.' He leans up against him. The therapist wonders out loud whether one can also stroke the Pokémons. Blastoise nods, and the therapist strokes his back and admires his muscles. Then the other Pokémons come closer and allow us to admire and stroke them. Jonathan, who lives with his depressed single mother, suddenly falls to the floor and says that he is very ill. He wants us to examine him and determine that he has been poisoned by a giant bee sting. Concerned, we examine him and discover the stinger, which is buried deep under his skin. We wonder how we will be able to save this beautiful Pokémon without any surgical instruments. We would need some very sharp blades—something like what Venusaur has. Might he come and help us? Christof looks at us in bewilderment and then approaches in the role of Venusaur and carefully uses his knife blades to cut the skin open so that we can remove the giant spine. We comment admiringly on the care and skill with which he operates—and how good it is that he has such fine blades that can be used to save lives. We then dress the wound, making a compress out of healing herbs that Charizard fetches from a volcano; and we pour a healing serum into Articuno's mouth. Then the other Pokémons also become ill and compete to see who has been stung by the longest stinger—they are up to 100 metres long! Venusaur lends us his knife blades, and we have to operate on and care for all of the creatures. They lie beside each other peacefully, savouring our care, and only want to recover after being tended to for a long time.

Here is another example, in which we directed the need for help onto ourselves.

Example

Six nine-year-olds, all of whom have severe difficulties in socialisation with their peer group, run into the group space and attack one another, gesturing wildly. In response to our usual opening question of what we would like to play together today, they answer in chorus: 'Dragon Ball, Dragon Ball!' When we ask who they want to be and who we, the two therapists, should be, they choose the roles of heroes in the television series: SonGoku, Master Roshi, Kuririn and other characters. They assign us the roles of normal human beings who should marvel at their fighting skills and be afraid of them. They scarcely take any time to construct the scenery: they throw a few cushions around and say that they are boulders on a strange planet. Then they storm at each other and demonstrate their fighting techniques like shadow boxers, running around the room and making karate-like gestures. One child fires a Kamehameha and says that the gigantic shockwaves are triggering earthquakes and tornadoes. Another demonstrates what he calls Super Ghost Kamikaze Attack. Others show off such techniques as the Kiai, the Special Beam Cannon, a Double Kaio-ken, etc. Immersed in their fantasies of omnipotence, each child demonstrates his techniques with wild arm and leg movements, but none of them take any notice whatsoever of the others' fighting techniques. They only notice our admiring mirroring—reacting with even more grandiose attacks and relishing the sight of us trembling and shivering with fear. Only when they have worn themselves out somewhat do they realise that their adversaries have not reacted to their attacks; then they become angry. Each child claims that he is the victor. An argument ensues as to who first knocked whom to the floor with his attack. They start insulting and pushing each other, and would have come to blows if we had not intervened. In the preceding sessions, the children have repeatedly reproduced the same old relationship structures and the same old methods of resolving conflicts. Therefore we attempt, through the use of a play intervention, to awaken their sense of possibility, bring movement into their rigid viewpoints and relationship patterns and develop solidarity and helpful relationships between them. The male therapist runs toward the children and cries out: 'Help, help! The villains C19 and C20 have kidnapped my wife, and they want to destroy our planet. Help me! You are the only ones who are strong and brave enough to fight against these terrible enemies and rescue my wife!' When the boys leap into action and want immediately rush into the corner where the female therapist has built a prison around herself using cushions, the male therapist gives them a warning. The villains will kill his wife immediately if they attack so openly. Couldn't they use some kind of trick to free his wife first before they chase the enemies away? The boys pause for a moment and come up with the idea that at the count of three, they will join together to set off such a violent shockwave that C19 and C20 will simply be blown away. Then, together, they can break down the one-metre-thick concrete walls using their fighting techniques and rescue the therapist's wife. The therapist marvels that the heroes are not only strong and brave, but clever as well. In order to reinforce the mutual action, the male therapist offers to play the roles of C19 and C20. Confident of his victory, he then entrenches himself in front of the prison. He is sure, he says, that when the Dragon Ball fighters hear about the kidnapping, they will storm ahead without taking any precautions. Then it will be easy for him to shoot them down from his hiding place. When the boys hear the villain's boastful soliloquy, they giggle to themselves. They quietly count to three and shoot forward with their right arms. This shockwave tears the villain away from the prison and sends him tumbling across the room. The heroes then quickly fly to the prison; together they break down the walls and free the prisoner. When she collapses, they bring her to safety. She whispers to the heroes that the villains have implanted a chip in her body with which she can be controlled from afar. She asks the heroes to perform an operation to remove it. The boys immediately accept this play suggestion. Carefully, they surgically remove the chip from her body and care for her attentively. Admiringly, she comments that these heroes are not only strong and brave; they are also empathetic and caring.

Once the female therapist has recovered, the fighters overpower the villain and show off their fighting skills. The male therapist then changes his role: he appears as the President and presents the heroes with the world's highest Order of Merit, since they have saved the planet and humankind from destruction. Their chests swelled with pride, the heroes allow him to pin the medals (clothes pegs) onto them and turn to face the flashing cameras of the international media (the female therapist).

With these and other similar interventions we attempt—in a painstaking process and in small steps—to redirect the children's attention onto each other in order that they can play together increasingly well and their ability to form relationships is strengthened.

7.4   Subgroup Formation

Again and again, subgroups are formed who have opposing ideas for play and do not want to play with each other. Particularly in mixed groups of prepubescent children, a division can arise between the group of boys and the group of girls. The boys frequently dismiss the girls as stupid and say that it is impossible to play with them. In this situation, trying to induce the children to play together would not do justice to the group process and would only provoke resistance from the group. Therefore, the leaders must first accept the separation; then, during the play phase, they can consider what possibilities there might be for creating a connection between the groups.

During the beginning phase of group development, it is sometimes useful for the therapists to divide up and allocate themselves to the two subgroups. From within their roles, they can create a connection within the play scenario. Another possibility for preventing the group from breaking apart consists of combining the opposing suggestions in the context of a shared theme and bringing the different subgroup scenarios into contact with each other through the combined actions of the therapists.

Example

A mixed group of seven-year-olds becomes split into a group of boys and a group of girls, with the boys striving for autonomy and the girls representing a regression to the oral phase. In this session, the three girls want to play the roles of babies, with the leaders as their parents. The boys think this idea is stupid; they want to fight in the roles of robber barons. When asked what roles they would like to assign to the leaders, they say that it is fine for them to be the parents of the babies if they like. Even when we ask them again—saying that then they would not have either of the leaders on their side—they stand by their decision. In order to create a connection between the opposing play ideas, the leaders ask whether they should play a king and queen whose babies are princesses. The children are pleased with this idea. The theme of a royal court makes it possible to accommodate the children's differing wishes—the regressive wish of the girls (all of whom come from families of divorce) to be cared for by both of their parents as part of the royal family and the progressive wish of the boys (both of whose mothers are overprotective) to be autonomous in the roles of robber barons. As the king and queen, the leaders take care of the babies and shower them with admiration and attention. In addition, the boys can measure their strengths in battle against the king, whom they attack and rob. Alongside these two separately-running play scenarios, the therapists repeatedly try to include the boys in the girls' scenario by continually bringing up the subject of the robber barons in conversation. Thus, for example, when the king returns to the palace after a fight with the robber barons and the family celebrates his happy homecoming, he says (under the envious gaze of the boys): 'Those robber barons are brave and daring fighters. If they were my sons, I would be proud.' At this statement, smiles flash across the faces of the boys. They puff out their chests and raise their arms in triumph. The male therapist also includes the girls into the boys' subgroup scenario when, during his heated battle with the robber barons, he speaks aloud to himself about what a good life the little princesses have: they are being cared for and do not have to fight for everything the way the robber barons do. On the other hand, of course, the robber barons can do whatever they want: they no longer have to obey their parents' rules and they have much more freedom than the princesses do.

In later phases of the group's development, the leaders can specifically address the division into subgroups. For example, they might identify the subgroups as two rival gangs, two warring kingdoms or different nations of people. For themselves, they can assume a third position which differs from both of the subgroups. They settle down in between the enemy groups—in no-man's land—and describe what is happening in the rival kingdoms. They express their fears, or their assurance that the parties will certainly find solutions to their differences. If the subgroups persist in their rigid patterns of conflict, the leaders can wonder out loud how it might be possible to overcome this dispute. They introduce new possibilities for behaviour and thereby inspire the children to new, creative solutions.

Subgroups can also develop if, in confrontations with the leaders, some of the children take the leaders' side, are then attacked by the other children, and the leaders run the danger of placing themselves in the position of protecting 'their protectors'. Children who represent the adults' position are often those who have taken over the parent or partner function for one of their parents at home—or they may be children who are very adult-oriented and have trouble getting along with other children. Only when the leaders understand the reason behind this attempt to ally themselves with the adults can they intervene appropriately and help steer the children more toward the side of their peers. Through explorative doubling, they can ask themselves why a child is behaving in this way and address the costs and benefits of this behaviour. If this insight-fostering intervention does not bring about a change, the leaders must turn to other types of intervention in order to prevent children from falling away from the group, being attacked by the others as outsiders and therefore associating themselves all the more with the leaders. In order to interrupt this vicious circle and smooth a path for the children to their peers, it can be beneficial for the therapists to change their roles in such a way that they become frustrated parental figures and attribute the problematic behaviour to the child.

Example

A mixed group of ten-year-olds want to play the roles of children who have run away from home to have adventures. They assign the male therapist the role of a dangerous criminal upon whom the children eavesdrop in secret and from whom they steal a map that leads to a hidden treasure. The female therapist is assigned to play a kind woman who lives alone in the forest. At the very beginning of the play scenario, the children encounter the forest woman. While the boys press ahead and want to venture further into the woods, the two girls— both of whom are very attached to their mothers—remain with the forest woman and allow her to care for them. The boys become angry; they scold the girls, calling them killjoys with whom it is impossible to really play anything anyway; and they continue on alone. While the boys have adventures— sneaking into the criminal's lair, listening to him with fear and excitement and almost letting themselves be caught stealing the treasure map—the girls watch them with glowing eyes, but do not dare to leave the forest woman. When the female therapist notices that the girls are following the boys' play scenario with their eyes, she wonders aloud why these girls continue to endure this boring life in the forest instead of having adventures like the boys. She wonders if perhaps the girls think that she cannot manage living by herself in the forest, and that they don't want to leave her alone. When the girls do not react to this soliloquy, the female therapist turns to a different intervention. She indicates that her telephone is ringing, and she receives a call from the police saying that five children are missing. Even though the girls signal to her not to give them away, she pretends not to notice and tells the police that five children came by her house a few days ago; the girls even stayed with her. She describes the girls and asks whether these are the ones the police are looking for. She asks the police to fly to her house in a helicopter and bring the girls back to their parents. In response to this intervention, the girls immediately disappear from the forest cabin. The female therapist then changes her role and flies low over the forest as the police helicopter pilot. The boys follow this action closely and wave to the girls to join them in their hiding place in the cave. While the helicopter pilot repeatedly circles over the forest, the girls sneak over to the boys and hide with them. The helicopter flies lower and lower, so that the children are lying on the ground, pressed close together, and enjoy the thrill when the pilot flies away directly above them. When she turns away unsuccessfully, the girls remain with the boys and set off to dig for the treasure—still in constant danger of being discovered by the criminal.

Demands on the Therapists

8

Walter Holl

Abstract

In this chapter, we want to deal further with the complex transference processes between the children and the therapists. In doing so, we will refrain from addressing the reciprocal transferences that take place between the children. Although these are important for understanding the dynamics in any given group, such an examination would exceed the limitations of this book. In addition, we will describe some other problems associated with cotherapy.

8.1 Aspects of Transference

In the following descriptions and interpretations, we have followed the definition from Bauriedl's dialectic concept of relationships. This definition states that on the one hand, the dual-therapist team and the group therapy situation have a subjective significance for each child and lead to acts of transference which provoke corresponding countertransference in the individual therapists. On the other hand, each child, as well as the group, also has a subjective significance for each of the therapists which give rise acts of transference from them onto the children. 'I consider it reasonable to speak of transference as well as countertransference on both sides, since each partner in the relationship brings with him or her the transference pattern which is specific to her on the one hand—and on the other hand, reacts in a specific way to the other partner's transference pattern' (Bauriedl 1984, p. 211).

In our setting, the dynamics become even more multi-layered due to the relationship between the male and the female therapist—since the children's

© Springer Fachmedien Wiesbaden GmbH 2017
A. Aichinger and W. Holl, *Group Therapy with Children*,
DOI 10.1007/978-3-658-15813-2_8

transferences onto the female therapist are naturally different than their transferences onto the male therapist, which inevitably influences the dynamics between the 'therapist couple'. If we look at the different phases of a session, we can observe different transferences.

During the warm-up and concluding phases, transferences usually consist of positively or negatively imbued aspects of parental images or other authority figures. During the play phase, on the other hand, the children not only transfer parental images onto the therapists, but also aspects of their own self-images.

It is a major advantage of this form of group therapy that during the play phase—through the mechanism of unconscious role reversal—the transference of symbolic self-images and parental images takes place in a very vivid and comprehensible manner. Thus, for example, a girl playing the role of a 'powerful princess' symbolises an aspect of her ideal self; and the female therapist, in the role of a 'cook who always burns everything', has had a negative maternal aspect transferred onto her.

Or, for example, a boy assumes the role of a teacher and assigns the male therapist the role of a 'scared, stupid pupil', using this transference to externalise an inferior aspect of his self-image.

The children's transferences onto the therapists occur both as individual transferences and as group transferences, which take place either simultaneously or separately during the play scenario. Here, an individual transference can function in accordance with the group transference or complement and enhance it.

Example

A group of five nine-year-old children—three of them girls—wanted to play the roles of a 'Pride of Lions'; the two therapists were assigned to play big game hunters. The children agreed that they would flee from the hunters at first, but would later attack them at their camp. After a short period of play, one boy declared that he would now be a baby lion whom the hunters would find and raise by hand. The group was temporarily irritated and concerned, but then assured themselves that the boy was not a 'traitor'. Despite the feelings of jealousy which were most likely present, they were able to agree to this arrangement by stabilising themselves against further regressions in the roles of the 'pride of lions'. As positively as the differentiation in the group transference can be seen in this example—since it demonstrated to the other children what is possible—it is usually very difficult to deal with such situations methodologically. Strong regression on the part of one child can cause the group to belittle and distance themselves from that child. In this way, the other children stave off their own tendencies toward regression. The situation may also reawaken the negative transference of a sibling rivalry. In the further course of the play scenario, it became increasingly clear that this boy was particularly focused on his relationship with the male therapist, which ultimately altered the entire transference situation between the children and the therapists: in this case, a temporary instance of splitting took place.

In addition to the multi-layered nature of the transference process, which it is rarely possible to comprehend completely, the vehemence of the transferences can occasionally pose a substantial burden for the therapists. This is true for cases of individual transference as well as for group transference. Individual children may express their emotions within the safe context of the group, or supported by it—sometimes with extraordinary intensity and even after just a few group sessions.

Occasionally, a blending and potentiation of fantasies and affects may take place in a group—for example, oral greed or sadistic fantasies—which are not easy to endure even at the symbolic level: for example, when a group of ten-year-olds plays 'School' with their anger at injustices and lack of validation as the theme, and in a role reversal make the therapists into the humiliated and victimised characters. Likewise, narcissistic desires in a circus scenario, in which the children constantly want to be admired in the roles of acrobats and animals, can provoke increasing resistance on the part of the therapists to meet the children's expectations.

Given that the concentration and intensity of the images and affects in the group process corresponds much more intensively with the therapists' unconscious than it does in individual therapy, it is not always easy to be aware of one's own transferences and defensive reactions to the children, the group and one's colleague during the group session.

However, we can only make therapeutic use of the transference process—and especially the process of countertransference—if our viewpoints and actions are not determined by our own unconscious minds.

We would therefore like to outline some of the most frequently-occurring transferences that therapists make onto the children in their groups.

8.2 Transferences by the Therapists

A therapist may act out his or her own unfulfilled wishes through projective identification with a child—for example, oral greed—and therefore be incapable of providing this child with limiting support.

Therapists may be tempted, if they identify with an inhibited child, to support him or her with a great deal of attention, without realising what this means at the level of group dynamics. At the same time, they can then be the good parents that they would like to have had themselves.

A therapist may project his or her suppressed 'rebellious child' onto a corresponding child in the group and then attempt to control him or her from the superego position. The therapist is then no longer able to see the fear that exists behind the child's aggression.

An aggressive child sometimes functions like yeast in the group process, accelerating its dynamics. But if, for example, the child dominates the group with his or her subject matter and evolves into an informal group leader, we may fall into a position of rivalry toward him.

Example

Here is an example of this: In a cleverly funny but nevertheless malicious manner, a nine-year-old boy played out his rivalry with another boy during the opening round. The male therapist was fascinated by his ability and was therefore unable to intervene appropriately. The female therapist, on the other hand, was so annoyed by this that she was paralysed for some time until she finally exploded and released all of her anger toward her colleague onto the boys.

Therapists who, as 'good parents', make the group into a place where unfulfilled wishes are compensated, may sometimes be unconsciously competing with the real parents and be afraid of negative transference. They wish to receive acceptance and approval from the children. This prevents them from maintaining limits because they are afraid that they might face rejection from the children.

Identification with the group can have the result, for example, the therapists' own enjoyment of aggressive play leads them to rationalise the children's actions as cathartic and not to take sufficient notice of it—or that the 'pillow fights' that take place over a period of several sessions no longer constitute any kind of scenario at the symbolic level. It is then difficult to determine what desires or fears lie behind the aggression in the case of individual children.

If one of the therapists identifies with the group's theme, this can lead to a difficult situation for his or her colleague. Thus, for example, in a school scenario in which the male therapist was assigned to play the caretaker, the female therapist identified with the group of children and their anger at authority figures. As a result, the therapeutic cooperation between the two leaders was temporarily stifled completely.

In another group, unconscious desires for dominance led the male therapist to assume a leader position in a subgroup—playing an Indian chief. He no longer noticed how strongly his play was impinging on that of the children.

8.3 Transference Processes in Different Group Phases

During the discussion phase, we are generally still more removed from the children's emotions and themes and can therefore register the transference process more easily. Nevertheless, we have had the experience even in the first session with a group, that the children insulted and blocked one another in the opening round by disparaging and rejecting each other's suggestions for play scenarios. If we then feel ourselves to be disparaged or rejected by such situations, one result may be that we minimise the importance of these insults or deny them altogether—rather than calmly and firmly setting limits for the child in question. It can also happen that due to our personal feelings of being offended, we identify with the child who is being belittled and react in an excessively sharp manner—with the result that the aggressive child, who had initially attempted to overcome his or her fear by disparaging the others, now becomes even more anxious.

Strong emotional reactions and conflicts have a more unsettling effect on us if we are already confronted with them in the beginning phase. For example, we are more likely to be upset by a bitterly crying child in the second group session than we would be in the twentieth session. By this time, we understand his or her behaviour better—we know whether the crying is a 'ploy' or is due to anger or sadness. In the case of verbal injuries, in a later phase, it is not always necessary to defend the boundaries and protect the affected children to any great extent. By then, we will be familiar with the other children's tolerance levels, and we will no longer be as irritated ourselves. Therefore, we will be in a better position to react appropriately to the relationship desires of the 'perpetrator'. We are more successful in being 'good parents' for the perpetrators as well as the victims.

If a strong aversion develops between the girls and the boys in a group, accompanied by mutual insults, this is more likely to worry us in the beginning phase than it does later on. This is especially true if the subgroups do everything they can to ensure that each of them 'acquires' one of the therapists. If the male and female therapists are unconsciously participating in the division at the relationship level, they will naturally have great methodological difficulties in bridging the split within the group. This danger will become less and less the better the therapists know the group and the better they can openly clarify their relationship.

If the goal of the beginning phase has been achieved, and the group has grown together as a unit, we are usually more self-assured. Then, for example, after the children have assigned us our roles, each of us can reflect on what this particular role might trigger with regard to our personal biographies. On the whole, within the dynamics of the play scenario, it is much more difficult to have an awareness of ourselves—and frequently enough, we only recognise everything that happened in the transference during the discussion following the session. Here we present a few examples of this:

Example

The group consisted of four eight-year-old children: two reserved girls and two lively boys. The girls wanted to play the roles of a deer and a rabbit. One of the boys chose the role of a badger; the more aggressive of the two chose to be a puma. The therapists were assigned to play animal caretakers. Almost immediately, the scenario became dominated by the 'puma'. He repeatedly wanted the male therapist to capture him with a rope. Once this happened, he attacked the therapist in order to escape—and then he would be captured again. The female therapist and the other children became peripheral characters. Throughout the entire session, the male therapist literally remained bound to this boy with his rope lasso.

Since, as a child, the male therapist had been unable to live out his own aggression at this age, he now identified with the 'puma'; at the same time, he was preoccupied with trapping this aggression and bringing it under control again.

Example

A group of twelve-year-olds were playing 'Journey on a Luxury Cruise Ship'. The female therapist was assigned to play the tour guide and the male therapist the steward. One of the girls, Angela, was focused on the female therapist in a very clingy fashion. Angela's constant desire for physical contact, in particular, was very repugnant to the female therapist. As a result, the therapist came up with a wide variety of activities at the symbolic level in order to avoid physical contact with the girl. She rationalised her actions with the idea that Angela should learn to get along better with the other children. However, the female therapist could not help but notice Angela's depressed and truculent reaction (she felt pushed away as if by her own mother). As a result, the therapist repeatedly turned her attention back toward the girl, which in turn increased her aversion to her. Therefore, Angela received highly contradictory signals from the therapist and reacted all the more with the behaviour described above. Only during supervision did the therapist realise that as an eight-year-old girl, she had a similar relationship to her own mother.

Example

A group of nine-year-old boys, three of them lively and one inhibited, decided to play a lion hunt scenario. They wanted to play the roles of hunters; they assigned the male therapist the role of the lion and the female therapist that of a cook at their camp. The three lively boys urged the inhibited boy to stay at the camp and protect the cook. Meanwhile, they built traps, and a combative scenario soon developed with the 'lion'—who, in his increasing lust for battle, did not notice how threatening he was becoming to the boys. Only after they repeatedly said 'You shouldn't be so wild!' was he able to restrain himself somewhat. The male therapist had completely forgotten about the 'cook' and her protector.

In supervision, the male therapist remembered that when he was a child, he had to care for his sickly mother, and wild games with boys his own age were not possible for him. The female therapist experienced being 'pushed out' of the play scenario very intensely and could therefore draw attention to this problem. The three lively boys would surely have played along with the male therapist's game for several more sessions because it corresponded to their interest in a 'father' and to a splitting-off from their small children's attachment to their mothers.

Example

In a group of ten-year-olds—two girls and three boys—all of the children had suffered for years in their families of origin because their parents did not have the time or energy to care for them in much more than a very superficial way.

This group staged a scenario about Indians. All of the children played the roles of Indians in the same tribe. The therapists were assigned to play traders who secretly planned to steal a sacred statue belonging to the tribe. The children had spent a long time constructing the scene and playing without including the therapists.

This was not easy for the therapists to tolerate, and they repeatedly attempted to enter into the play scenario. After a few incidental scenes which they staged themselves, the Indians tied them to a stake: once again, they were helpless and excluded, since the Indians did not spend a long time dealing with their prisoners. Again, it was the therapists themselves who could not tolerate their situation: they escaped from their bonds, fought and ran away. They were unable to use their intensely-felt experience of helplessness and exclusion as a countertransference to assist in understanding the children because their own powerlessness made them too uncomfortable.

Example

A group of nine-year-olds—two girls and two very strong and lively boys— were staging an outer space scenario. The girls came from Sirius, the boys from Mercury, and together they seized control of a research spacecraft from Earth. They tied up the researchers (the therapists) and locked them in a cell. The initial cooperation between the children was increasingly undermined by the boys, who ignored the rules of symbolic play and used their physical advantage against the girls more and more often.

The therapists should have intervened much sooner—whether from their roles or as leaders—but they were not able to do so. The male therapist identified with the dominant boys and therefore did not notice what was happening to the girls. As a child, the female therapist had had the experience that her brothers were valued and that she, as a girl, was unimportant. Therefore, she did not have the energy to draw her colleague's attention to the dynamics of the game or to interrupt the play.

From the examples we have outlined here, it is clear that the therapeutic requirements of this method call for thorough self-examination and constant reflection on one's own acts of transference. If this does not take place, it is difficult to understand the psychodramatic role reversal and the experiences of countertransference and to develop therapeutic interventions.

8.4   Problems of Cotherapy

The examples presented in the previous section are an indication of the possibilities and dangers involved with cotherapy. Let us begin by assuming an ideal situation— that the therapist team consists of one woman and one man—and examine the advantages that this has for the children. First of all, we can recognise that together, the therapists and the children form a system which parallels that of a family. This facilitates corresponding transferences, such as, for example, insufficient triangulation and/or oedipal problems.

If the group is led only by a single male or a single female therapist—or by two therapists of the same gender—the possibilities for transference are limited.

Let us also keep in mind, that the number of children being raised by a single parent—or who come from separated, divorced or blended families—is very large and continues to increase (in our groups, four out of six children frequently fit this description). For children from these families, a 'therapist couple' consisting of one woman and one man, allows them to best process their own experiences.

Nevertheless, we know that due to personnel situations at counselling centres and other facilities, it is often not possible to achieve this ideal team combination. Then, it is still better if two therapists of the same gender lead the group, rather than one therapist alone. Once again, let us point out some of the significant advantages for the therapists here:

The dynamics of the group and the position of each child can be registered in a more differentiated manner. The therapists are better able to identify, symbolise and verbalise ambivalences and splitting.

Feelings of belittlement or powerlessness are not only easier to tolerate together as a pair, but they can also be better understood and employed as transference phenomena.

The therapists' own transferences onto the children are recognised earlier. Difficulties may arise in cotherapy if the two therapists' methodological approaches do not complement one another, or if their levels of training are too unequal. Here is an example of this from supervision.

Example

A female therapist who was trained as a group psychodrama therapist was able to recruit an enthusiastic male colleague to lead a children's therapy group with her. However, the male therapist's enjoyment of play became an increasing problem, since he played along with the children without self-reflection, and the female therapist increasingly took on the position of a strict mother figure—for her colleague as well as for the children. This led to the following scenario: In one session the five children, all eight years old, were acting out a hospital scenario. The children wanted to play the roles of paramedics, nurses and doctors; the male therapist was assigned to be the chief physician. The female therapist was to be a patient who was brought to the hospital and operated on following a 'traffic accident'. The operation scene had scarcely begun when the male therapist began to 'play over' the children to an increasing degree, with the result that the children were simply watching wide-eyed as a 'film scene' was played out in front of them. The chief physician (the male therapist) operated on and treated the patient (the female therapist) in an almost sadistic manner. The children simply became helpless extras in the scene.

For the children, these were highly problematic images of the relationship between the 'group parents'.

A problem can also arise from the fact that for many children in the group, it is the first time they have had the opportunity to play together with a man. It can then be the case that the children idealise and court the male therapist, while the female therapist becomes the object of negative transference. Enjoyment and frustration are then distributed very unequally, and it is necessary to process them in a differentiated manner after the group session in order to bring about change over the long term. Ultimately, the goal is to work through the children's disappointment and sadness with regard to their missing fathers and not to remain stuck in a superficial state of compensatory satisfaction.

If one of the therapists—for example, due to his or her individual makeup—pays particular attention to boundaries, the children usually place additional transferences on her, which then push this therapist further into the superego position. The other therapist can then take a relaxed place in the discussion round and react to the children with a great deal of understanding.

We are all familiar with these constellations in families, and we know what a negative effect they can have on the children.

Although we believe that it is better to have two therapists of the same gender leading the group if a female-male team is not possible, this nevertheless changes the transference process. If the group is led by two men, particularly in a group consisting only of boys, this can increasingly lead to the staging of rivalries and aggression-related problems. In addition, it is scarcely possible to deal with oedipal themes in this constellation. We can expect different types of shifts if the group is led by two women. For example, female colleagues have reported on working with families affected by addiction, in which all of the fathers were weak and the mothers dominant: for the boys in the group, this therapist constellation had an unfavourable effect. The family structures were repeated in the group, and confrontations with 'the man' were not possible. Naturally, this was true for the girls in the group as well; however, their reactions to the situation were not as striking.

The question then arises as to what the methodological ramifications are if a therapist works alone. In this regard, we can only pass on the most significant experiences from some of our colleagues: The most important of these is that as a therapist, one can no longer offer to take on central roles. The therapist must work more at the 'peer group level' with the children—in varying roles which he or she usually chooses herself—to stimulate, structure and support the play. She helps the children develop their story and find their roles and then initiates the scenario from the standpoint of a supporting role. As soon as the scenario is underway, she can withdraw or drop the role completely so as to be able to intervene at a later point in time in the same role or in another one. Here is an example of this.

Example

In the story of an 'Emergency Aircraft Landing in the Arctic' the therapist first decides to play the role of an air traffic controller who gives the plane permission to start, controls the flight, etc. She then picks up white cloths and assumes the role of the ice storm which blocks the tail unit, shakes the aircraft and forces an emergency landing. Depending upon the way the group dynamics develop and how well the group maintains the arc of tension, she can then retreat into a corner and wait. Later, she could appear as an Eskimo, for example—admiring the abilities of the stranded passengers and then retreating again. Alternatively, in the role of a dangerous polar bear, she could bring an exciting moment of aggression into the game, which would foster the cohesiveness of the group. As soon as the polar bear is defeated, she can withdraw again. Later, she can once again assume the role of the air traffic controller, who initiates a search for the lost passengers.

In these situations, of course, the therapist must always ensure that the children welcome the intervention—or that it is necessary for therapeutic reasons. With older children, it can also be possible for them to assume various roles themselves, and the therapist can withdraw even more. In this way, the social interaction and social learning as a whole become the focal point.

From the example outlined here, it is clear that the demands on the therapist are not negligible and that work with transferences does not become easier.

Operating in Networks

Alfons Aichinger

9

Abstract

Every subsystem in a child's social atom—child, parents, family, nursery and school—needs to be considered as a cause or sustaining force in his or her problems as well as a potential contributor to the solution. Therefore, the most recent approaches dictate that group therapy must also be context-oriented and multi-systemically oriented. Very early on, Moreno (1946) developed a systemic approach to psychological disorders with his theory of social network analysis and his anthropological concept of the social atom, and he called for therapists to take into account the relevant context in each case and for the restoration of the damaged social atom (cf. Petzold in Integr Ther 8:161–165, 1982a; *Rollenentwicklung und Identität*. Junfermann, Paderborn, pp. 55–127, 1982b). In Moreno's view, the work with the real social atom must extend beyond the family and include children's living environments, such as nurseries and schools. This type of wider systemic view helps avoid the danger of pathologising the family and also takes into account more recent findings about the strong influence of children's networks. Thus, in the case of a child who has fallen into an outsider position in school, it may be necessary—in addition to strengthening the child's social competence in group therapy—to support his or her integration into the class through relationship-building games with the other pupils such as those we have described in our work with school classes (cf. Aichinger in Psychodrama 8, 1995; *Hilfen für Kinder*. Juventa, Weinheim, 131–148, 1999; Aichinger and Holl in *Kinder-Psychodrama in der Familien- und Einzeltherapie, im Kindergarten und in der Schule*. Matthias-Grünewald-Verlag, Mainz, 2002).

© Springer Fachmedien Wiesbaden GmbH 2017
A. Aichinger and W. Holl, *Group Therapy with Children*,
DOI 10.1007/978-3-658-15813-2_9

With the help of a detailed example, we would like to demonstrate what work in the network can look like when it operates in parallel to a child's participation in group therapy.

Upon the advice of her child's classroom teacher, a 29-year-old single mother requested an urgent appointment for her ten-year-old daughter Judith, who was causing major problems both at school and at home. According to the mother, the girl did not accept any boundaries or rules, she was very aggressive and immediately lashed out physically when conflicts arose at school. At home, she was very jealous and aggressive toward her younger siblings. Sometimes, however, she would break down, cry incessantly and threaten to commit suicide.

Biographical history:

Judith's mother lived in a children's home until the age of 18, in order to escape from her violent, alcoholic father. There, she became pregnant for the first time at age 17 and gave birth to a daughter. One year later, she married a man who was also an alcoholic. Soon afterward, her husband began entering into intimate relationships with other women; the couple frequently separated for short periods of time and then reconciled again. In the course of this difficult situation, the mother became pregnant with Judith. From the time of her birth onward, the mother failed to develop an attachment to the child. When Judith was five months old, her parents separated definitively. Soon afterward, the mother became pregnant by her brother-in-law, whose marriage was also breaking apart at the time and who lived in the same building. She moved in with him and gave her flat to her first husband, who returned several months later, homeless and with another woman. The second husband then became violent: he frequently beat her, as well as the first son from this marriage, because he cried often. Four years later, after two miscarriages, Judith's mother gave birth to a second son, who was soon diagnosed with cystic fibrosis. When Judith was six years old, her biological father moved to another city. Her mother's separation from her second husband was also a back-and-forth process of separations and reconciliations. Two months after their final separation, the mother met her current partner and moved in with his parents. By chance, Judith's father came for a visit during this time and took Judith, now eight years old, to stay with him during the school holidays. Since Judith's mother had only a small flat and believed that Judith could receive more attention from her father, she did not fight to keep Judith when she did not want to return to her mother. After Judith told her sister on the telephone that she wanted nothing more to do with her mother, there was no contact between the two of them for one-and-a-half years. Only when Judith's mother received a phone call from the classroom teacher, saying that Judith was completely neglected and uncared-for did she immediately drive to the teacher's home and secretly take Judith with her. She then successfully pushed through a court order for sole custody of the child. Only then did she learn that the father had been drunk most of the time and had provided for Judith very poorly. The girl often had to beg her neighbours for food; and when her father was drunk, he frequently beat her or subjected her to threats—for example, that he would jump off the balcony with her. When Judith returned to the family, she reacted jealously because her mother had given away all of her clothing and toys, and she had no more possessions of her own. Her mother's new partner quickly saw Judith as a threat, who would bring discord into the family, and he reacted to her with increasing hostility.

In the first family conferences, which were conducted by a female colleague, it became clear how much anger Judith had stored up and how threatened she felt by the prospect of once again being rejected by her family, the school and the after-school care centre. In our team, therefore, we decided to take a multi-level approach. First of all, we would support the family, the school and the after-school care centre through counselling. Secondly, we offered the girl help with processing and enrolled her in a psychodrama therapy group. The group consisted of four girls, all of whom came either from families of divorce or families in which there were severe conflicts in the marriage. Here, Judith would have a good environment for acting out her injuries and longings at the symbolic level and working through her bottled-up anger in transference relationships.

With this account of the tenth group therapy session, we would like to demonstrate how Judith processed her conflicts within the group theme.

Example

The girls agree to play a royal court scenario. Judith, Heike and Barbara want to be princesses who will be crowned as part of a huge celebration and will assume their reigns over great estates. Isabel, a mutistic girl who scarcely speaks, is a royal Siamese cat. The two therapists are assigned to play the king and queen, and a female intern plays a servant to the princesses. After constructing the scenery with a throne, a banquet table, the princesses' chambers and a little house for the cat, all the actors adorn themselves with beautiful cloths. We begin the scenario with the herald (the male therapist in a change of roles) announcing the arrival of (imaginary) kings and queens from neighbouring kingdoms. The royal couple sit down at the banquet table and admire the beautiful princesses and the elegant cat as they enter the banquet hall. We invite them to take their places beside us at the table. Only Judith, in the role of a princess, lingers in her chamber. We send the servant to Princess Annabelle (Judith's name in the play scenario) to ask her to join the banquet, since all the guests are expecting her. Threatening to strike her, Annabelle orders the servant to announce to the queen in front of the assembled guests that she is a stupid cow who neglects her children: her children should be taken away from her and brought to live with a kind aunt. When the servant hesitantly repeats this message to the royal couple, we react with horror to these shameful accusations and try to defend ourselves. At this, Judith bursts in, leaps onto the table and dances around on it. The other princesses and the cat join in with her play. They provoke the king and queen and scold us at the tops of their voices. The cat spills wine on the royal robes; the princesses rip the queen's jewellery off her body, and Judith gives the king the finger. When he reacts in shock, she becomes so carried away with her emotions that she departs from the 'as if' level and strikes at him for real. As the leader, he asks her not to really strike blows; as the king, he is appalled at how the princesses are humiliating us in front of our noble guests and reminds them of their good upbringing. After this, the princesses throw us into jail. Frightened, we ask them what crimes we have committed—after all, we have always been good parents. Maybe we didn't always have so much time and energy to devote to the princesses because there was so much turmoil in our kingdom and we were always occupied with that. At this, Judith screams into our faces that we only stuffed her full of sweets instead of giving her good food and fruit to eat. Together with the other princesses, she begins to cry out: 'We're hungry, we're hungry, we're hungry!' Their cries become more and more intense and insistent. The cat scratches and bites us and tears our clothing. Then the princesses fetch our horses out of the stable and ride away together with the cat. They leave us behind, crying and lamenting—if only we had paid more attention to our daughters in the past.

Similar scenes to this one followed in the subsequent sessions. In the opening round, the girls would initially agree on pleasant story scenarios in which we were to play good parents. However, in the course of the play, the family harmony was shattered, and the children released a great deal of anger and annoyance onto the bad 'parents'. In these scenarios, Judith in particular displayed behaviour like that of children with disorganised attachments who are not truly able to make use of their parents' offers to serve as a secure basis for their children because they are wavering ambivalently between anger and protest and the desire for help and closeness.

Over the course of the group therapy, Judith's aggressive outbursts at home, in school, and in the after-school care centre decreased, so that the situation became significantly more relaxed and Judith appeared to be gradually gaining a foothold. Therefore, the mother wished to continue with the counselling more infrequently.

Suddenly Judith's play behaviour changed and became very confusing. She switched her roles—first playing our daughter; she then became a friend of our daughter and then a stranger. We, as the parents, were told not to recognise her—our daughter—anymore, causing us to become very uncertain in our role relationship. Since we assumed that we—in a case of concordant transference—were experiencing the insecurity that Judith had felt in a confusing relationship situation, we decided to schedule a parental conference.

A phone call we received the following day from an employee of the social welfare office helped us to understand what Judith was expressing in her play. He informed us that Judith's mother had approached him with the request that Judith be placed in a children's home for a period of time because she was maligning the mother's partner and telling the neighbours that she was being beaten and receiving nothing to eat. Since the mother's partner was afraid Judith might accuse him of other things—for example, sexual abuse—she needed to move into a home until she began behaving better. In response to this, the female therapist called for a helper conference with everyone involved in the case. However, once the mother had heard from the therapist, the teacher and a care provider from the after-school centre about the progress that Judith had been making, she decided not to send Judith away after all. In this meeting, it once again became clear how uncertain Judith's mother felt toward her. We therefore offered to first work together with her and Judith to process their past separation and strengthen their relationship through family play therapy. The mother readily accepted this offer.

Example

Judith has scarcely entered the counselling room with her mother when she begins to cry. She is still afraid that the aim is to place her in an institution. We assure her that her mother has decided to keep her and that we want to help the two of them to make their relationship closer and more secure. We already know from the mother that the events of the last two years have made both of them very insecure. In order that they can better understand how this break in their relationship came about, we would like to re-examine this period of time with them together.

The therapist asks Judith to choose animals from his collection of wooden figures to represent herself, her mother and her father. For her father she chooses a wild boar, smiling at her mother as she does so; the mother nods in agreement. (Now that I, A. Aichinger, have since developed this method further, today I would let Judith choose an animal to represent the father with whom she had had positive experiences and another animal for the part of the father with whom she had had bad experiences. With this dissociation, Judith could make a better separation between her longing for the good father and her anger at the abusive and neglectful father. If, for example, she had chosen a bear to represent the good father, then the animal standing behind the dog would not be the little wild boar but a little bear, who could express her longing for the good bear-father. And if she had chosen the wild boar to represent the 'bad' part of her father, then the horse could express the anger and disappointment that the wild boar had kept the good bear-father from fulfilling his fatherly duties.) For the mother, Judith chooses a horse; for herself, a dog. In order to offer her a possibility for dissociation in this parts work (not me, but one side of me), I also pick out a little wild boar and a little horse and place them behind the dog with the explanation: 'You know, of course, that when you first began inside your mother's belly, each of your parents gave you some of his or her genes—so you have part of the genes from Mama's side and part of the genes from Papa's side in you. That means that the dog also has a horse part and a wild boar part. I know from other children what it is like for them when their parents are separated and they can't have Mama and Papa at the same time. I am going to let these animals that stand for you, Mama and Papa talk. The two of you— Judith and Ms. Maier—should correct me if I make them say something that is not right for one of you. Of course, you can also make the animals talk yourselves.'

Since it is often difficult for children initially to talk about their feelings, this externalisation through the animal figures provides a good possibility for distance. At first, I am also more active, until the children have warmed up to the process. Since it is often difficult for them to agree with what I say, I ask them to correct me if I say something wrong. Then I begin with the parts work:

A: 'At first the horse and the wild boar lived in the same house, even though they were separated. The little horse and the little wild boar could go back and forth and get whatever they needed. But after a few years the wild boar moved away.' I pick up the big wild boar and place it apart from the other animals. Judith takes the figure and places it even further away. With this, she is already beginning to engage with the animals. A: 'Yes, it moved very far away and you didn't have any contact anymore.' Then I touch the little wild boar and double it: 'I am very sad that Papa wild boar has left me behind. What will happen to me? I wonder whether he still loves me.' Judith nods. Then I touch the little horse and double it: 'I am certainly happy that my Mama is not going away and I can stay with her.' Judith places the little horse very close to the big horse. A: 'After two years, the Papa wild boar finally comes to visit.' I bring the big wild boar closer and double the little one. 'Thank goodness my Papa wild boar is finally coming to check up on me. I am starving.' Judith nods and says: 'And then Papa asked me if I want to come with him.' A: 'Then the little wild boar says: "Yes, please"'. Then I turn toward the big horse and ask: 'And what does the Mama horse say about that?' Since the mother has not been very involved so far, I attempt to draw her in with this question. Ms. Maier: 'I agreed—in fact, I was glad that he took Judith with him for the holidays because I had a lot of problems at that time and I couldn't give her very much attention. And I thought that it would do her good not to have to share with her siblings and to have her father all to herself. (Today, I would ask Judith to also choose an animal to represent this part of her mother that is overwhelmed and does not have any energy or time for her, so that the overburdened mother part is also represented). A (touching the little wild boar): 'Could it be that the little wild boar runs off now and doesn't think any more about the dog and the little horse, but only thinks: "Now it is my turn: you, little horse, have had your Mama horse to take care of you for a long time and you have been well fed; now you have to step into the background."' I pick up the dog: 'And the dog comforts the little horse and says: "We're only going for a visit; you will see the Mama horse again soon."' I move the big wild boar away; the little wild boar follows close behind him, trailed by the dog and the little horse, who turns around to look at the big horse. Judith nods and says: 'And then when we were there, Papa didn't want me to call or write to Mama. And he said I should stay with him forever. And since I was afraid he would be angry otherwise, I did.' I double the Papa wild boar, who does not want to see the little horse: 'The little wild boar is mine; she doesn't need a Mama horse.' A (touching the dog): 'And could it be that then the dog thought: I have to hide the little horse. Papa wild boar doesn't like it that the little horse looks for the Mama horse and calls to her.' Judith nods. A (to the little horse): 'And could it be that you, little horse, resign yourself and think: "I have to be very quiet and I can't show that I miss my Mama horse."' Judith: 'Only at night—then I cried and talked with Mama.' A (addressing the Mama horse): 'What is it like for you, Mama horse? Do you feel the little horse's longing and worry—or do you only see the little wild boar that is turning her back on you?' Ms. Maier: 'No, I only saw the wild boar turning away. And then I got the call saying that she doesn't want to come back. Then I was very hurt and felt rejected. And I was also unsure whether it wasn't really better for Judith to be with her father.' A (to the Mama horse): 'Mama horse, can you show the little horse that you miss her and would like to have her back with you?' Ms. Maier: 'Yes, I sent letters and parcels, but just recently I learned from my sister-in-law that he intercepted everything and didn't give it to her.' A (to the little horse): 'How does that feel for you, little horse, that you aren't getting any messages from your Mama horse?' Judith: 'When I didn't even get a letter or a parcel at Christmas, I thought she didn't want anything more to do with me; and Papa also said, see, they don't want you anymore. They are happy you are gone.' I double the little horse: 'I am so disappointed that my Mama is not checking up on me. Maybe she doesn't love me at all anymore? It makes me very sad that I haven't heard anything from her.' And I'm getting really angry, too. I don't want anything more to do with her.' Now I make the Mama horse and the little horse child turn their backs on each other. And even though Judith is talking about herself, I remain in the distant position via the animals. Ms. Maier: 'Yes, each of us thought the other one didn't want any contact, so we were insulted and pulled back.' Judith: 'Papa also threatened to hit me if I call in secret.' Then she talked about how terrible it was for her—how often she had to search for her father in pubs; how he would come home drunk and be aggressive; how she had to beg the neighbours for food, etc.

(Today I would let Judith choose an animal to represent the alcoholic side of her father which had completely pushed the good father part—the bear-father—into the background, so that he could no longer care for the dog and the little animals).

In order to reinforce Judith's power to survive, I speak to the dog: 'Dog, you have to be very strong now. The little horse is lonely and homesick, but she is not allowed to show it. She is also very angry that the Mama horse is not coming to help her. And the little wild boar has been disappointed by her Papa wild boar—and she also has to hide her disappointment and anger. And you, dog, have to manage everything without any help from outside. How do you do it? You are very strong!' Judith beams at this emphasis on her strength and capability. Ms. Maier responds: 'I didn't know anything about all of this. It was only when the teacher called me and told me some of it that I saw how bad things were for Judith. Then I drove there right away and took her with me, and I pushed through a court order.' I make the big horse come over and take the dog with her, along with the little horse and the little wild boar, and I double the dog and the little horse: 'Finally Mama has come and rescued us. We are so happy.' Then I double the little wild boar: 'But I am also sad that my longing was not satisfied, and now I have to live without my Papa wild boar again.' Judith places all the figures far away from the Papa wild boar and close to the Mama horse and says: 'I don't want anything more to do with him.' I double the animals: 'We are so disappointed and angry. The Papa wild boar should feel how angry we are. He has earned his punishment.' I ask Judith: 'How long should he be punished?' Judith: 'One hundred years!' In order not to portray the father in such a negative light, I pick up the Papa wild boar and double him: 'I am also sad, and I feel guilty about how badly I took care of my little one. If I could only leave this stupid alcohol alone. That is how I ruined everything. The little wild boar is punishing me now with her rejection; I have earned it. I have a lot of things to make up for.' Judith nods vigorously.

This intervention of placing the mother and father parts behind the animal that represents the child has proven to be very useful for separation and divorce counselling and the arrangement of visiting rights. By allowing the individual parts to speak, we can represent longings for the absent parent, annoyance, anger, disappointment, ambivalence, conflict and divided loyalties very well without placing the child in conflict with the parent who is present.

Since the relationship between Judith and her mother was burdened by deep insecurity, we suggested that in the next sessions, the two of them could engage in a shared game to strengthen their relationship and foster the security of their attachment. For this, we chose a resource-oriented mother-child game.

Particularly with parents who have been unable to form a positive relationship toward their child—for whom acceptance and respect for the child are the focal point of the counselling—it has proven helpful to motivate them to engage in shared play therapy in order to strengthen the concept of '*serving* as a secure foundation' for the parents and '*receiving help* from a secure foundation' for the child, and thereby to foster secure attachments. Through the play, we hope to achieve a modification in the quality of the relationship and to open up room for movement and change in a gridlocked situation.

This form of family therapy is also useful for people who have problems with verbal expression or language comprehension.

Example

The mother brings her youngest son along to the next session; she says she had no one who could look after him. Furthermore, she thought it might be good, because Judith's rivalry with him is the strongest.

First, Judith reports that the caregiver at her after-school centre told her that her mother wants to get rid of her. The mother indignantly denies this. In order to allow Judith to play out her ideas for solving this conflict, we suggest that she make up a story and assign each person a role. In this way, we also want to make the introduction to the play easier for the mother, since Judith is already familiar with this method.

Judith wants to play a rain forest story. She assigns the two therapists the roles of animal catchers (intuitively, she senses how she can use this inter-vention of an external enemy to bond the family together). She assigns her mother the role of a gamekeeper; Judith herself wants to play a monkey; her little brother Kai should play the role of a little wild rabbit.

After choosing their roles, the children construct their lairs; the mother sets up her animal care station and we build a lorry for transporting animals and a hiding place in the jungle. Then we begin with the play scenario: Following Judith's directions, the animal catchers build a trap into which they lure the animals. However, almost as soon as we have captured an animal and want to drag it to our lorry, the gamekeeper appears, frees the animal and turns against us angrily. By griping and complaining about the gamekeeper's vigilance while we are together in our hiding place—she must have a sixth sense, the way she always appears just when we have caught an animal in our trap—we indirectly reinforce the positive relationship between the mother and the children and praise her for her good instincts At this 'supportive doubling', the children smile happily at their mother and share their pleasure at the animal catchers' annoyance. In order to likewise provide the children with an opportunity to stand up for their mother, we come up with a plan in our roles as the animal catchers: somehow, we have to get rid of this vigilant gamekeeper once and for all. We could invite her to tea and secretly slip her a drink that knocks her out. Then, when she is sleeping soundly, we can finally capture the animals undisturbed and sell them to the zoo. However, the animals have been listening to us, and they warn the gamekeeper, who then quickly empties out her teacup when we are not paying attention and pretends to fall asleep. We are pleased with the success of our plan: now we can capture the animals without any danger, now that this alert and caring gamekeeper is out of the way. During the night, while we sneak over to the animals' lairs, the gamekeeper hides. We drag the animals out of their lairs, lock them in our lorry and rejoice over our valuable catch. Then the gamekeeper suddenly jumps out of her hiding place, threatens us with a pistol, frees the animals and vehemently scolds us: how could we be so evil as to capture such beautiful animals? This is strictly pro-hibited and punishable by a severe prison sentence. Judith visibly enjoys being defended by her mother in this way; and together with her brother, they attack us fiercely. They bite and scratch us until we run away crying and swear that we will never again try to kidnap the gamekeeper's animals.

Ten minutes before the end of the session, we stop the play scenario. We allow all of the players to step out of their roles and dismantle the scenery together. Then we sit down together for a brief closing round. We do not undertake any interpretation of the scenario; we simply reinforce the positive approaches toward building relationships—the commitment with which the gamekeeper protected the animals and fought for them; how well the animals are cared for and protected by her, and how well the animals watched out for the gamekeeper and kept her from being drugged. Finally, we ask the participants what they liked about the game. The mother says that initially it was very strange for her; she 'hasn't played like this for ages'; however, she began to enjoy it more and more. The children express their enthusiasm about the game—especially the fact that their Mama played along so well. The mother is pleased at this praise.

Given that both the mother and the children have overcome many major crises, the expressions of appreciation both during the play scenario and in the closing round—the emphasis on their successful interactions—were very important. They supported the process of positive relationship formation. From the point of view of attachment theory, this focus on positive sequences of interaction—this resource-oriented process—is extremely important during the beginning phase of the counselling process. 'Particularly for clients who have an attachment background characterised by insecurity or avoidance, it is important to have the experience of tracing their own weaknesses and insecurities in a (largely) anxiety-free context, without experiencing rejection' (Suess and Roehl 1999, p. 175).

It became clear in this session how Judith incorporated her fear of being placed in a home into the image of the animal catchers, processed it, and reshaped it into a longed-for scenario—namely, that of being defended and kept safe by her mother.

The next session began with the mother complaining about how 'impossible' the children were—what a 'pigstye' they made at home and how they did not obey any rules. In no time at all, a 'problem trance' emerged, and the mother slipped back into the role of the helpless, powerless mother. We interrupted this pattern and pointed out that while many things were certainly difficult, we had also witnessed in the last session that some things were working well. Therefore, we wanted to suggest continuing the play scenario.

Example

Judith picks up on the image of a pigstye and suggests acting out a farm scenario. She wants her mother to play a mother dog and Kai a puppy. For herself, she chooses the role of a rabbit and assigns us the roles of the farmers.

After constructing the scenery—the kennel, the rabbit hutch, the farmhouse with a vegetable garden and a larder—and putting on costumes, we begin the play scenario.

In the role of the rabbit, Judith immediately attacks the puppy. The mother dog quickly steps in and defends her baby. In order to break a stereotypical relationship pattern which occurs over and over again in the same way at home, in the roles of the farmers, we wonder out loud whether the rabbit wishes she could be closer to the dog. She must feel very lonely in her hutch. But of course, rabbits don't really know how to play with little puppies without the mother dog smelling danger for her baby and chasing the rabbit away. By offering the mother a possible explanation for Judith's behaviour through our interpretive intervention, we attempt to foster her capacity for empathy. The conflict is immediately alleviated in response to this act of explorative doubling.

The Mama dog and the rabbit begin scuffling playfully. Gradually, the wrangling evolves into purring, until the Mama dog and the rabbit are licking each other's faces (not only 'as if'—they do it for real!). Using the technique of mirroring, we farmers describe the scene out loud and praise our mother dog for realising so quickly that the rabbit did not have any bad intentions and for knowing how to deal with her so well. We admire the rabbit for her efforts to make friends with the Mama dog. During this dialogue between the farmers, the mother dog takes the rabbit with her into her kennel, and all three animals snuggle in together. When we bring the animals their food—bones for the dog and carrots for the rabbit—the rabbit throws the vegetables down on the ground and lets the mother dog feed her bones. We express our astonishment that the mother dog knows what the rabbit really needs even better than the farmers do. Maybe the rabbit is really more of a dog than a rabbit.

Then, together with the puppy, the rabbit sneaks into our vegetable garden, and the two of them dig up the whole garden. When we try to chase them away, they do not react. When we start to scold, asking what the animals think they are doing, they attack and bite us. We complain that the animals do not listen to us, and we do not know how to set boundaries for them (with this, we assume the position that the mother had at the beginning of the session). We wonder whether the Mama dog could teach the little animals how to behave on the farm. At this, the mother dog comes out of her kennel and grabs first the rabbit and then the puppy by the backs of their necks and pulls them out of the garden (in doing so, the mother actually bites into the children's t-shirts and pulls them out with her mouth). With her, the animals obey immediately and trot docilely back into the kennel. In an act of supportive doubling, we express our amazement at how well the little animals listen to the Mama dog and how well she teaches them the rules—in contrast to us. Judith then gives the direction that night should come and the farmers should go to sleep. During the night, the puppy and the rabbit raid the larder and carry all the sausages into the kennel. The next morning, when I discover what has happened and find the sausages in the kennel, I scold the little animals, according to Judith's instruction. At this, the Mama dog growls at me, and I quickly run away. I recount to the female farmer how vehemently the Mama dog protects her little ones. She does not allow me to say one bad word. The female farmer interjects that perhaps we haven't taken good care of the animals; maybe they need more to eat. I argue that we cannot allow the animals to simply take whatever they want out of our larder. Once again—by pushing the puppy and the rabbit with her paws and her head and pulling them with her teeth—the mother dog manages to make them bring the sausages back. We praise our mother dog and admire her ability to teach these little animals the rules of the farm. Then the three animals tussle playfully in the farmyard, enjoying themselves immensely. After they have worn themselves out, the rabbit leads the mother dog into her hutch, where they snuggle together and rest. The puppy comes and joins them.

We end the play scenario, stressing that the participants are no longer animals; we take apart the scenery and sit down together for a closing discussion. All three of them are sweaty and tired. The mother says she could not have imagined that she could have so much fun playing again. She has not had that much fun playing since she was a child herself. Judith and Kai are once again very enthusiastic and look forward to the next session.

It was impressive to see how much more lively and self-confident the mother was when she left the room at the end of the session than when she presented herself as helpless and powerless at the beginning of the hour. The shared play experience made all of the participants proud.

In this play session, we were once again able to strengthen the mother's sense of security and self-confidence; this is 'an important prerequisite for taking the perspective of one's own child into consideration and being able to deal sensitively with him or her' (Ziegenhain 1999, p. 226). Along with her negative childhood experiences, insecurities, excessive demands and a lack of self-esteem had limited the mother's ability to adopt other perspectives. Through play, we were able to bring her into contact with the world of her own childhood, making it easier for her to enter her own daughter and son's childish realm and develop more empathy for them.

In the play scenario, where Judith initially demonstrated through the image of the rabbit how little she felt she belonged together with the dogs, she was able to win over and enjoy her mother's attention and to use her mother as a safe foundation. She expressed this in play by becoming increasingly like a dog.

The multi-systemic approach of group therapy accompanied by family play therapy and consultation with the classroom teacher and the after-school caregiver made positive progress possible for the entire family.

Final Note

The method of group therapy which we have described here is practised by many of our colleagues who have completed their training in this method. They have applied it in a wide variety of professional fields—for example:

- in day nurseries (Aichinger and Holl 2002) and in after-school care centres
- in primary and secondary schools, schools for remedial education (Feinauer 1990), schools for children with learning disabilities and schools for the mentally handicapped (Pflüger 2000)
- in children's homes (Flegelskamp 2004)
- in paediatric practices
- in psychosomatic hospitals
- in practices for child and adolescent psychiatry and in children's psychiatric hospitals
- in combination with riding therapy (Schörle 2000) and experiential education
- with children of addicts in psychosocial counselling centres (Heger 2002; Diözesan-Caritasverband 2004; Weiss 2008)
- in psychosocial counselling centres for parents, children and adolescents (Hinger 1989; Kaup 1991)
- in clinical psychology practices.

We ourselves continue to apply this method in our work in primary and secondary schools (Aichinger 1995; Aichinger and Holl 2002):

- with socially problematic classes in order to improve children's ability to form relationships and deal with conflicts
- for crisis intervention in the case of violent conflicts
- in special projects for social learning.

© Springer Fachmedien Wiesbaden GmbH 2017
A. Aichinger and W. Holl, *Group Therapy with Children,*
DOI 10.1007/978-3-658-15813-2

Due to its clear, graphic nature and experiential quality, this method also offers many possibilities for working with families. It is very well suited to helping children understand the system of their family and the place they occupy in it in an age-appropriate manner, and to initiating changes (Holl 1994; Aichinger and Holl 2002).

Furthermore, through the psychodramatic staging of intrapsychic and interpsychic conflicts, this method can supplement our therapeutic work with children in a very specific way (Holl 1993, 1995; Aichinger and Holl 2002).

Afterword to the English-Language Edition

We are very pleased that this ground-breaking text on the highly effective psychodrama work with children that was developed by Alfons Aichinger and Walter Holl is finally available in an English-language edition. As a result, it is now accessible to an international audience. Stefan Flegelskamp, a pupil of Alfons Aichinger who has extensive experience in working with traumatised children, has introduced this special form of symbolic play at conferences of the Federation of European Psychodrama Training Organizations (FEPTO) on numerous occasions. Thanks to the great interest that was generated, international symposia on psychodrama with children and adolescents have been held every two years since 2012.

In 2013, Stefan Flegelskamp and I conducted two trial training sessions in the Palestinian territory of Gaza. The evaluation showed that this process can indeed be applied even in a very different cultural context, with only slight modifications. In 2014, we initiated a three-year-long group training programme. The motivation for this translation project stems primarily from the intensive experience with our highly committed colleagues in Gaza. Twenty-seven individuals who work with traumatised children in therapeutic and pedagogical contexts are taking part in this group. The project is sponsored by Medico International Switzerland in cooperation with the Gaza Community Mental Health Project (GCMHP). Additional financial support is provided by the Deutscher Fachverband für Psychodrama (German Professional Association for Psychodrama—DFP) and by private donors.

'The psychodrama group is my safe place.', 'Gaza is a prison; in psychodrama we are free', 'This will help 100 × 100 children', 'The children asked us when we will come again'—these are just a few examples of the especially moving and gratifying feedback we have received. For us, it has been a meaningful task to help our colleagues—who themselves are victims of trauma—to achieve their goal of

© Springer Fachmedien Wiesbaden GmbH 2017
A. Aichinger and W. Holl, *Group Therapy with Children*,
DOI 10.1007/978-3-658-15813-2

providing themselves and their families with a life of dignity; to be able to reach their patients and clients; to avoid losing hope and to stave off depression and violence.

There is a worldwide community of psychodrama practitioners who are committed to working against collective trauma. We wish them and everyone who works in these fields every possible success. Even if we do not have the power to change major policies, the people and multipliers whom we are able to reach in this way will be able to pass along some of the healing effects that are activated through this type of psychodramatic work.

Agnes Dudler, Dipl.-Psych.
Qualified psychologist and psychotherapist in Bonn, Germany
Founder of the Szenen Psychodrama Institute, Cologne, Germany
Member of the FEPTO Task Force for Peace and Conflict Transformation

Literature

Ahnert, L. (2005). Entwicklungspsychologische Erfordernisse bei der Gestaltung von Betreuungs- und Bildungsangeboten im Kleinkind- und Vorschulalter. In *Sachverständigenkommission Zwölfter Kinder- und Jugendbericht* (Vol. 1, pp. 9–54). Munich

Aichinger, A. (1987). Psychodrama-Gruppentherapie mit Kindern. In H. Petzold & G. Ramin (Eds.), *Schulen der Kinderpsychotherapie* (pp. 271–293). Paderborn: Junfermann.

Aichinger, A. (1992). Psychodrama — Gruppentherapie mit Kindern. In Biermann, G. (Ed.), *Handbuch der Kinderpsychotherapie* (Vol. 5, pp. 392–404). Munich: Reinhard

Aichinger, A. (1993a). Psychodramagruppentherapie mit Kindern. In K. Hahn &F. W. Müller (Eds.), *Systemische Erziehungs- und Familienberatung* (pp. 202–215). Mainz: Matthias-Grünewald.

Aichinger, A. (1993b). Zurück zum Ursprung. Abweichungen von der klassischen Psychodramamethode in der therapeutischen Arbeit mit Kindergruppen. In R. Bosselmann, E. Lüffe-Leonhardt & M. Gellert (Eds.), *Variationen des Psychodramas* (pp. 220–239). Limmer: Meezen.

Aichinger, A. (1995). Der Gewalt begegnen — Psychodrama mit Schulklassen. Psychodrama 8, 189–208.

Aichinger, A. (1999a). Präventive psychodramatische Arbeit mit Kindern in der Schule. In G. Romeike & H. Imelmann (Eds.), *Hilfen für Kinder* (pp. 131–148). Weinheim: Juventa.

Aichinger, A. (1999b). Abwandlungen des Psychodramas in der Gruppentherapie mit Kindern. In H. Viquerat (Hg.), *Klinische Kinder-und Jugendlichen-Psychotherapie* (pp. 247–273). Bonn: Deutscher Psychologen Verlag.

Aichinger, A. (2003a). Auf der Suche nach einer Wildkatzenmutter. Mit Kindern Kreativität wagen. *Psychodrama und Soziometrie, 2*, 253–267.

Aichinger, A. (2003b). Pokémon, Powerrangers, Spiderman und Terminator in der Gruppentherapie. *Informationen für Erziehungsberatungsstellen, 2*, 14–22.

Aichinger, A. (2004a). Psychodrama in der Psychotherapie mit Kindern. In F. von Ameln, R. Gerstmann & J. Kramer (Eds.), *Psychodrama* (pp. 413–424). Berlin, Heidelberg: Springer.

Aichinger, A. (2004b). Verkleiden und Zeigen. In *Spielraum für Kinder aus suchtbelasteten Familien* (pp. 14–37). Köln: Diözesan-Caritasverband für das Erzbistum Köln e.V.

© Springer Fachmedien Wiesbaden GmbH 2017
A. Aichinger and W. Holl, *Group Therapy with Children,*
DOI 10.1007/978-3-658-15813-2

Aichinger, A. (2006). Die Sehnsucht des kleinen Bären – ein psychodramatischer Interventionsansatz mit Tierfiguren bei Kindern im Scheidungskonflikt. *Informationen für Erziehungsberatungsstellen, 1,* 16–25.

Aichinger, A. (2007). Warum der kleine Löwe immer bissiger wird – frühe Intervention bei einem aggressiven Kind. *Zeitschrift für Psychodrama und Soziometrie, 1,* 67–82.

Aichinger, A. (2008). Sie beißen und zerfetzen, sie wollen gefüttert und gestreichelt werden – der Einsatz des Körpers im Psychodrama mit Kindern. *Zeitschrift für Psychodrama und Soziometrie, 1,* 1–17.

Aichinger, A., & Holl, W. (2002). *Kinder-Psychodrama in der Familien- und Einzeltherapie, im Kindergarten und in der Schule.* Mainz: Matthias-Grünewald-Verlag.

Anzieu, D. (1984). *Analytisches Psychodrama mit Kindern und Jugendlichen.* Paderborn: Junfermann.

Basquin, M., Dubuisson, P., Samuel-Lajeunesse, B., & Testemale Monod, G. (1981). Das Psychodrama als Methode in der Psychoanalyse. Paderborn: Junfermann.

Bauriedl, T. (1984). *Beziehungsanalyse.* Frankfurt: Suhrkamp.

Bettschart, W. (1984). Psychodrama mit Kindern und Jugendlichen. In H. Remschmidt (Ed.), *Psychotherapie mit Kindern, Jugendlichen u. Familien* (Vol. 1). Stuttgart: Enke.

Bettschart, W. (1988). Das analytische Psychodrama bei Kindern und Jugendlichen als Untersuchungs- und Therapieinstrument. In G. Klosinski (Ed.), *Psychotherapeutische Zugänge zum Kind und zum Jugendlichen* (pp. 133–142). Bern: Huber.

Betz, B. (2006). 'Wir sind doch Kinder und wollen spielen': Psychodrama-Kindertherapie als Methode für eine Gruppe von Kindern, deren Eltern sich getrennt haben. *Final dissertation No. 390.* Stuttgart: Moreno Institut Stuttgart.

Biegler-Vitek, G., Piepl, R., & Sageder, T. (2004). Psychodrama mit Kindern und Jugendlichen. In J. Fürst, K. Ottomeyer, & H. Pruckner (Eds.), *Psychodrama-Therapie* (pp. 306–325). Vienna: Facultas.

Bleckwedel, J. (2008). *Systemische Therapie in Aktion.* Göttingen: Vandenhoeck & Ruprecht.

Bosselmann, R., Kindschuh-van Roje, E., & Martin, M. (1993). Einige Einsatzmöglichkeiten des Psychodramas im therapeutischen Heim. In R. Bosselmann et al. (Eds.), *Variationen des Psychodramas* (pp. 240–246). Meezen: Limmer.

Bosselmann, R., & Martin, M. (1979). Psychodrama mit Kindern und Jugendlichen im Heim. *Praxis der Kinderpsychologie und Kinderpsychiatrie, 28,* 272–276.

Brandes, H. (2008). *Selbstbildung in Kindergruppen.* Munich: E. Reinhardt.

Brem, H. (2008). Ein Vergleich von homogenen und heterogenen Kinder-Psychodrama-Therapie-Gruppen. *Final dissertation.* Stuttgart: Moreno Institut Stuttgart.

Diözesan-Caritasverband für das Erzbistum Köln e.V. (Ed.). (2004). *Spielraum ... für Kinder aus suchtbelasteten Familien.* Neureichenau: Edition Zweihorn.

Drabkova, H. (1966). Experiences resulting from clinical use of psychodrama with children. *Group Psychotherapy and Psychodrama, 19,* 32–36.

Ende, M. (1979). *Die unendliche Geschichte.* Stuttgart: Thienemann.

Erikson, E. H. (1974). *Identität und Lebenszyklus.* Frankfurt: Suhrkamp.

Feinauer, E. (1990). Das Psychodrama-Gruppenspiel in der Schule für Erziehungshilfe. *Final dissertation No. 83.* Stuttgart: Moreno Institut Stuttgart.

Flegelskamp, S. (2004). Einmal mutig sein – einmal verletzt. In Diözesan-Caritasverband für das Erzbistum Köln e.V (Ed.), *Spielraum ... für Kinder aus suchtbelasteten Familien* (pp. 61–64). Neureichenau: Edition Zweihorn.

Fried, L. (2004). Kindergartenkinder ko-konstruieren ihr Wissen über die soziale Welt. In L. Fried, G. Büttner (Eds.), *Weltwissen von Kinder* (pp. 55–77). Weinheim: Juventa.

Freud, S. (1907). *Der Dichter und das Phantasieren*. GW 7 (pp. 221–223). Frankfurt: Fischer 1966.

Fryszer, A. (1993). Psychodrama in der Arbeit mit Familien. In R. Bosselmann et al. (Eds.), Variationen des Psychodramas (pp. 196–219). Meezen: Limmer.

Fürst, J., Ottomeyer, K., & Pruckner, H. (2004). *Psychodrama-therapy*. Vienna: Facultas.

Gäbler, N. (2006). Zurück zu den körpernahen Sinnen – somatische Psychotherapie mit Kindern. In G. Marlock & H. Weiss (Eds.), *Handbuch der Körperpsychotherapie* (pp. 796–802). Stuttgart: Schattauer.

Gerstenberg, W. (1979). Psychodrama in der ambulanten psychotherapeutischen Arbeit mit Eltern und Kindern. *Praxis der Kinderpsychologie und Kinderpsychiatrie, 28*, 293–302.

Gottwald, C. (2006). Neurobiologische Perspektiven zur Körperpsychotherapie. In G. Marlock & H. Weiss (Eds.), *Handbuch der Körperpsychotherapie* (pp. 119–137). Stuttgart: Schattauer.

Grawe, K. (2004). *Neuropsychotherapie*. Göttingen: Hogrefe.

Grunebaum, H., & Solomon, L. (1980). Toward a peer theory of group psychotherapy I. *International Journal of Group Psychotherapy, 30*, 23–49.

Grunebaum, H., & Solomon, L. (1982). Toward a theory of peer relationships II. *International Journal of Group Psychotherapy, 32*, 283–307.

Guldner, C. (1991a). Introduction. *Journal of Group Psychotherapy, Psychodrama & Sociometry, 43*, 155.

Guldner, C. (1991b). Creating training contexts for interns in group psychotherapy and psychodrama with children. *Journal of Group Psychotherapy, Psychodrama & Sociometry, 43*, 146–161.

Guldner, C., & O'Connor, T. (1991). The ALF group: A model of group therapy with children. *Journal of Group Psychotherapy, Psychodrama & Sociometry, 43*, 184–190.

Hänisch, I., von (1982). *Reich stark mächtig: Die Phantasiehelden unserer Kinder*. Fellbach: Bonz.

Heger, U. (2002). Kinderpsychodrama mit Kindern aus Familien mit Suchtkranken. *Final dissertation No. 299*. Stuttgart: Moreno Institut Stuttgart

Heidegger, K.-E., & Lintner, A. (2001). Posterpräsentation: Kinderbühne – für Kinder, die im Trennungsprozess ihrer Eltern stehen. 19. Symposion der Fachsektion Psychodrama im ÖAGG. Vienna.

Heigl-Evers, A., & Heigl, F. (1972). Rolle and Interventionsstil des Gruppenpsychotherapeuten, Gruppenpsychotherap. *Gruppendynamik, 5*, 152–171.

Heinemann, E., Rauchfleich, U., & Grüttner, T. (1992). *Gewalttätige Kinder*. Frankfurt: Fischer.

Hinger, O. (1989). Die Entwicklung eines frühgstörten Jungen in der Kinderpsychodramagruppe. *Final dissertation No. 73*. Stuttgart: Moreno Institut Stuttgart.

Holl, W. (1981). Erfahrungen mit einer Psychodrama-Jungengruppe. In E. Engelke (Ed.), *Psychodrama in der Praxis* (pp. 101–119). Munich: Pfeiffer.

Holl, W. (1985). Psychodrama mit Kindern. In A. Leber, H. G. Trescher & C. Büttner (Eds.). *Die Bedeutung der Gruppe für die Sozialisation* (pp. 93–104). Göttingen: Vandenhoeck u. Ruprecht.

Holl, W. (1993). Psychodrama-Einzeltherapie zur Verarbeitung traumatischer Operationserlebnisse. *Jugendwohl, 74*, 32–41.

Holl, W. (1994). Psychodramatische Familienrekonstruktion mit Handpuppen. *Jugendwohl,* *75*, 256–262.

Holl, W. (1995). Der Gorilla, der Bär, der Rabe und Ralf. Psychodrama in der Einzeltherapie mit Kindern. Psychodrama 8, 239–251.

Hurrelmann, K. (1983). Das Modell des produktiv realitätsverarbeitenden Subjekts in der Sozialisationsforschung. *Zeitschrift für Sozialisationsforschung und Entwicklungspsy-chologie, 1*, 91–103.

Hüther, G. (2005). Mein Körper – das bin ich. *Psychoanalyse und Körper, 4*, 7–23.

Hutter, C. (2000). *Psychodrama als experimentelle Theologie*. Münster: Lit.

Hutter, C. (2004). Konzepte in der Persönlichkeitstheorie Morenos. In J. Fürst, K. Ottomeyer & H. Pruckner (Eds.), *Psychodrama-Therapie* (pp. 103–113). Vienna: Facultas.

Hutter, C. (2008). Szenisches Verstehen – Potenziale und Grenzen der Erziehungsberatung, lag nachrichten BW, 1–2, 8–19

Kaup, C. (1992). *Der therapeutische Prozess eines frühgestörten Hyperaggressiven Kindes. Skripten zum Psychodrama Nr. 3*. Stuttgart: Moreno Institut Stuttgart.

Kleiner, T. (2008). *Frühe Bindungserfahrungen und ihre Auswirkungen auf die Gestaltung von Peer-Beziehungen in Gruppentherapien*. Konstanz: Hartung Gorre.

Klosinski, G. (1984). Möglichkeiten und Grenzen der Gruppenpsychodramatherapie im Rahmen stationärer Behandlung von Adoleszenten. In H. Remschmidt (Ed.), *Psychotherapie mit Kindern, Jugendlichen u. Familien* (Vol. 1, pp. 172–177). Stuttgart: Enke.

König, C. (1981). Psychodrama mit schwer gestörten Jugendlichen. In G. Biermann (Ed.), *Handbuch der Kinderpsychotherapie* (Vol. IV, pp. 226–235). Munich: Reinhardt.

Kranz, P. L. (1991). A demonstration of warm-up techniques with young children. *Journal of Group Psychotherapy, Psychodrama & Sociometry, 43*, 162–166.

Kranz, P. L., Lund, N. L., Pruett, T., & Stanley, F. (1982). The use of psychodrama with gifted children. *Journal of Group Psychotherapy, Psychodrama & Sociometry, 35*, 88–98.

Krappmann, L. (1982). Sozialisation in der Gruppe der Gleichaltrigen. In K. Hurrelmann & D. Ulrich (Eds.), *Handbuch der Sozialisationsforschung* (pp. 443–468). Weinheim: Beltz.

Krüger, R. T. (1982). Analytisch-orientierte Psychodramatherapie mit Kindern, Lecture presented at the 3rd wissensch. Arbeitstagung der Sektion Psychodrama im DAGG. Saarbrücken, October 29–31, 1982

Krüger, R. T. (1989). Der Rollentausch und seine tiefenpsychologischen Funktionen. *Psychodrama, 2*, 45–67.

Krüger, R. T. (1997). Kreative Interaktion. Göttingen: Vandenhoeck & Ruprecht.

Krüger, R. T. (2002). Wie wirkt Psychodrama? *Zeitschrift für Psychodrama und Soziometrie, 2*, 273–317.

Kubina, S. (2009). *Kinderpsychodrama in der Prävention von sexueller Gewalt an Mädchen. Skripten zum Psychodrama* (Vol. 22). Stuttgart: Moreno Institut Stuttgart

Lebovici, S. (1969). Das Psychodrama mit Kindern und Jugendlichen. In G. Biermann (Ed.), *Handbuch der Kinderpsychotherapie* (Vol. II, pp. 771–777). Munich: Reinhardt.

Lebovici, S. (1971). Eine Verbindung von Psychodrama und Gruppenpsychotherapie. In: S. de Schill (Ed.), *Psychoanalytische Therapie in Gruppen* (pp. 312–339). Stuttgart: Klett.

Lebovici, S. (1972). Das psychoanalytische Psychodrama. In H. Petzold (Ed.), *Angewandtes Psychodrama in Therapie, Pädagogik, Theater und Wirtschaft* (pp. 118–127). Paderborn: Junfermann.

Lebovici, S., Diatkine, R., & Kestemberg, E. (1958). Bilan de dix ans de thérapeutique par le psychodrame chez l'enfant et l'adolescent. *Psychiatrie de l'enfant, 1*, 63–179.

Leutz, G. (1974). *Psychodrama: Theorie und Praxis.* Heidelberg: Springer.

Lockwood, J., & Harr, B. J. (1973). Psychodrama: A therapeutic tool with children in group play therapy. *Group Psychotherapy and Psychodrama, 26*, 53–67.

Lorenzer, A. (1983). Sprache, Lebenspraxis und szenisches Verstehen in der psychoanalytischen Theorie. *Psyche, 37*, 97–115.

Lott, F. (1986). Die Bedeutung der Gruppe in der Therapie mit Kindern. In H. Petzold & R. Frühmann (Eds.), Modelle der Gruppe (Vol. 2, pp. 273–287). Paderborn: Junfermann.

Lutz, C. (1976). Praxis der Gruppenpsychotherapie mit Kindern. Stuttgart: Bonz.

Lutz, C. (1981). Gruppenpsychotherapie bei Kindern und Jugendlichen. In G. Biermann (Ed.), *Handbuch der Kinderpsychotherapie* (Vol. 2, pp. 337–347). Munich: Reinhardt.

Mathias, U. (1982). Die Entwicklungstheorie J. L. Morenos. In H. Petzold & U. Mathias (Eds.), *Rollenentwicklung und Identität* (pp. 191–256). Paderborn: Junfermann.

Moreno, J. L. (1922). Psychdramatische Behandlung neurotischen kindlichen Verhaltens. In ibid.: *Gruppenpsychotherapie und Psychodrama* (2nd ed., pp. 201–203). Stuttgart: Thieme 1973,

Moreno, J. L. (1925). *Rede vor dem Richter.* Berlin: Kiepenheuer.

Moreno, J. L. (1934). *Who shall survive?* Beacon: Beacon House.

Moreno, J. L. (1946). *Psychodrama* (Vol. 1). Beacon: Beacon House.

Moreno, J. L. (1959). *Gruppenpsychotherapie und Psychodrama.* Stuttgart: Thieme.

Moreno, J. L. (1967). *Die Grundlagen der Soziometrie.* Opladen: Westdeutscher Verlag.

Moreno, J. L. (1969). *Psychodrama* (Vol. 3). Beacon: Beacon House.

Moreno, J. L. (1981). *Soziometrie als experimentelle Methode.* Paderborn: Junfermann.

Moreno, J. L., & Moreno, F. S. (1944). Spontaneity theory of child development. *Sociometry, 7*, 89–128.

Paus-Haase, I. (1998). *Heldenbilder im Fernsehen.* Opladen: Westdeutscher Verlag.

Petermann, F., & Petermann, U. (1987). Aggressives Verhalten bei Kindern. In A. Hormann (Ed.), *Beurteilen und Fördern in der Erziehung* (pp. 212–229). Salzburg: Otto Müller.

Petzold, H. (1979). *Psychodrama-Therapie* (2nd ed.). Paderborn: Junfermann 1985.

Petzold, H. (1980). Die Rolle des Therapeuten und die therapeutische Beziehung in der Integrativen Therapie. In H. Petzold (Ed.), *Die Rolle des Therapeuten und die therapeutische Beziehung* (pp. 223–285). Paderborn: Junfermann.

Petzold, H. (1982a). Der Mensch ist ein soziales Atom. *Integrative Therapie, 8*, 161–165.

Petzold, H. (1982b). Die Rollentheorie J. L. Morenos. In H. Petzold & U. Mathias (Eds.), *Rollenentwicklung und Identität* (pp. 55–127). Paderborn: Junfermann.

Petzold, H. (1985). *Psychodrama-Therapie.* Paderborn: Junfermann.

Petzold, H. (1995). *Die Kraft liebevoller Blicke.* Paderborn: Junfermann.

Petzold, H., & Ramin, G. (1987). Integrative Therapie mit Kindern. In H. Petzold & G. Ramin (Eds.), *Schulen der Kinderpsychotherapie* (pp. 359–426). Paderborn: Junfermann.

Petzold, H., & Schneewind, U. (1986). Konzepte zur Gruppe und Formen der Gruppenarbeit in der Integrativen Therapie und Gestalttherapie. In H. Petzold & R. Frühmann (Eds.), *Modelle der Gruppe* (Vol. I, pp. 109–255). Paderborn: Junfermann.

Pflüger, C. (2000). Der Findefuchs: ein psychodramatisches Theaterprojekt mit geistigbe-hinderten Kindern. *Final dissertation No. 259*. Stuttgart: Moreno Institut Stuttgart

Pruckner, H. (2001). Das Spiel ist der Königsweg der Kinder. Munich: inScenario.

Pruckner, H. (2002). Psychodrama-Therapie mit traumatisierten Kindern. *Zeitschrift für Psychodrama und Soziometrie, 2*, 147–175.

Pruckner, H. (2003). Brauchen Kinder Rollentausch? *Zeitschrift für Psychodrama und Soziometrie, 1*, 37–42.

Pruckner, H., & Schacht, M. (2003). Zur Begrifflichkeit von Rollenwechsel und Rollentausch. *Zeitschrift für Psychodrama und Soziometrie, 1*, 7–15.

Rahm, D., & Kirsch, C. (2000). Entwicklung von Kindern heute. *Beratung Aktuell, 1*, 17–40.

Reifschneider, B. (1998). Der Terminator und die moderne Apokalypse. http://www.nolovelost.com/boris/u-ter.htm

Retzlaff, R. (2008). *Spiel-Räume*. Stuttgart: Klett-Cotta.

Reuser, B. (1994). Warming-up in der Psychdramatherapie mit Kindergruppen. *Psychodrama, 7*, 55–63.

Rubner, A., & Rubner, E. (1982). Das zurückgebliebene Kind und das analytische Psychodrama. Berlin: Marhold.

Sandner, D. (1978). *Psychodynamik in Kleingruppen*. Munich: Reinhardt.

Schacht, M. (2003). *Spontaneität und Begegnung*. Munich: inScenario.

Schacht, M. (2009). *Das Ziel ist im Weg*. Wiesbaden: VS Verlag für Sozialwissenschaften.

Schmidtchen, S., Acke, H., & Henniess, S. (1995). Heilende Kräfte im kindlichen Spiel. *GwG Zeitschrift, 26*, 15–23.

Schmitt, A. (2009). Settingdesign in der (systemischen) Therapie mit Kindern. *Familiendynamik, 34*(1), 74–91.

Schörle, A. (2000). *Pferde Träume, Heilpädagogische Ansätze im Reitunterricht mit Kindern*. Nagold: Buch & Bild.

Schwinger, T. (1994). Erwärmung aus der Konserve. *Psychodrama, 7*, 5–16.

Seglow, J. (1969). Psychodrama mit emotional gestörten Kindern. In G. Biermann (Ed.), *Handbuch der Kinderpsychotherapie* (Vol. 2, pp. 777–788). Munich: Reinhardt.

Seiffge-Krenke, I. (2004). Psychotherapie und Entwicklungspsychologie. Berlin: Springer.

Shearon, E. M. (1980). Psychodrama mit Kindern. *Acta Paedopsychiatrica, 45*, 253–268.

Slavson, S. R., & Schiffer, M. (1976). *Gruppenpsychotherapie mit Kindern*. Göttingen: Vandenhoeck & Ruprecht.

Stockvis-Warnaar, J., & Stockvis, B. (1962). Psychodrama of enuresis nocturna in boys. *Group Psychotherapy and Psychodrama, 15*, 179–196 and 285–303

Storch, M., Cantieni, B., Hüther, G., & Tschacher, W. (2006). *Embodiment*. Bern: Huber.

Straub, H. (1972). Über die Anfangsphase psychodramatischer Kinderbehandlung mit Puppenfiguren. In H. Petzold (Ed.), *Angewandtes Psychodrama* (pp. 218–231). Paderborn: Junfermann.

Straub, H. (1975). Vom Leiterverhalten abhängige Entwicklungsprozesse in Psychodrama-Gruppen. *Gruppendynamik, 6*, 104–108.

Straub, H. (1980). Die Rolle des Therapeuten und die therapeutische Beziehung im Psychodrama. In H. Petzold (Ed.), *Die Rolle des Therapeuten und die therapeutische Beziehung* (pp. 211–221). Paderborn: Junfermann.

Straub, H. (1987). Psychodramatische Kindertherapie mittels Puppen. In H. Petzold & G. Ramin (Eds.), *Schulen der Kinderpsychotherapie*, (pp. 257–269). Paderborn: Junfermann.

Suess, G. J., & Roehl, J. (1999), Die integrative Funktion der Bindungstheorie in Beratung/Therapie. In G. J Suess & K.-W. Pfeiffer (Hg), *Frühe Hilfen*. *Die Anwendung von Bindungs- und Kleinkindforschung in Erziehung, Beratung und Therapie*. Gießen: Psychosozial- Verlag.

Weinberg, D. (2006). *Traumatherapie mit Kindern*. Stuttgart: Klett-Cotta.

Weiss, J. (2008). Kinderpsychodrama unter dem Aspekt der Reinszenierung von Lebensthemen. *Final dissertation*. Stuttgart: Moreno Institut Stuttgart

Wicher, M. (2006). Psychodramagruppen für traumatisierte Kinder und Jugendliche in stationären Setting. Master's thesis, Krems

Widlöcher, D. (1974). *Das Psychodrama bei Jugendlichen*. Olten: Walter.

Winnicott, D. W. (1974). *Reifungsprozesse und fördernde Umwelt*. Munich: Kindler.

Yalom, I. D. (2001). *Theorie und Praxis der Gruppenpsychotherapie* (6th ed.). Stuttgart: Klett-Cotta.

Zacharias, J. (1965). Psychodrama with teen-agers. *Group Pychotherapy and Psychodrama, 18*, 262–266.

Zaepfel, H., & Metzmacher, B. (1999). Soziales Sinnverstehen in der Beratung und Therapie von Kindern und Jugendlichen. In G. Romeike & H. Imelmann (Eds.), *Hilfen für Kinder* (pp. 61–82). Weinheim: Juventa.

Zauner, J. (1985). Gruppentherapie mit Kindern und Jugendlichen. In A. Leber, H. G.Trescher & C. Büttner (Eds.), *Die Bedeutung der Gruppe für die Sozialisation* (pp. 65–77). Göttingen: Vandenhoeck & Ruprecht.

Ziegenhain, U., Dreisörner, R., Derksen, B. (1999): Intervention bei Jugendlichen Müttern und ihren Säuglingen. In G.J. Suess und W. K. Pfeiffer(Eds.), *Frühe Hilfen*, (pp. 222–245). Gießen: Psychosozial.